ALISTAIR KEE

The Way of Transcendence

CHRISTIAN FAITH
WITHOUT BELIEF IN
GOD

PENGUIN BOOKS

Penguin Books Ltd, Harmondsworth, Middlesex, England
Penguin Books Inc., 7110 Ambassador Road, Baltimore, Maryland 21207, U.S.A.
Penguin Books Australia Ltd, Ringwood, Victoria, Australia

—

First published 1971

—

Copyright © Alistair Kee, 1971

—

Made and printed in Great Britain
by C. Nicholls & Company Ltd
Set in Linotype Juliana

PELICAN BOOKS

THE WAY OF TRANSCENDENCE

Alistair Kee was born in 1937 in Alexandria, Scotland. He was educated at Clydebank High School and the University of Glasgow, where he graduated in arts and in theology. From there he went to Union Theological Seminary, New York, as a Scots Fellow, and between 1961 and 1964 received his Master's and Doctor's degrees.

Dr Kee was appointed from New York to the Department of Theology at the University College of Rhodesia, and taught there for three academic years, during the period of the illegal Unilateral Declaration of Independence.

Since 1967 Dr Kee has been lecturing in the Department of Theology at the University of Hull, and in addition is currently a Montgomery lecturer for the Christian Education Movement. He is a member of the Iona Community, within the Church of Scotland. Dr Kee is married, with two children.

TO THE MEMORY OF GRAEME
AND TO
COLIN AND HILARY

that Christian faith may still
be possible for their generation

Contents

Preface

OURS is an age of faith, but not belief. There is a widespread search for an object worthy of faith, and a healthy mistrust of that blind faith in leaders and causes which has proved so disastrous in this century. The attraction of such faith is not that it brings personal responsibility to an end, but rather that a goal worthy of total commitment brings new dimensions to life. Faith is a characteristic of our age, yet it is an age without religious beliefs. In particular, belief in God has disappeared, at least as an effective element of contemporary living. It is therefore tempting to suggest that Christian faith might be presented today without belief in God. But belief in God has always been regarded as an essential part of Christian faith, and certainly the presupposition of Christian faith. This is what makes Christianity a religion.

It is not generally recognized by religious people that while a man may choose to have faith, he cannot choose belief. What we believe – about ourselves, our society, our world – depends on the culture in which we are raised, and the adequacy of its concepts and categories to interpret and explain our experience. We may admire a man who *decides to have faith* in someone or something, but we are rightly suspicious of a man who *decides to believe* something, since this implies that he is deliberately disregarding evidence which would undermine such belief.

In a religious age men have religious beliefs: in a secular age they have secular beliefs, that is, they interpret and explain the world in its own terms. Ours is a secular age and that is why in our time *all* religious beliefs have become problematic, especially belief in God. And if belief in God is the presupposition, the prior condition of Christianity, then Christian faith will not be possible in our secular age. To demand faith is one thing, to require belief is quite another, since changing our beliefs is not something that can be brought about by an act of will.

What then is my concern in writing this book? It is that there is something of supreme value and worth in Christianity, and yet in this age of faith, Christian faith apparently is not

regarded as an option. I am therefore proposing an understanding
of Christian faith, appropriate to our secular age, which does not
require belief in God as its prior condition. And yet I am not
attempting a salvage operation, to preserve what can be accepted
today. Too much of contemporary theology has taken this easy
way, and it inevitably leads to reductionism and positivism. On
the contrary, I am proposing an escalating understanding of
theology which ensures that a secular faith in Christ includes all
the dimensions previously included in a doctrine of God. If I were
to select one sentence which indicates the purpose and the direction of this book, it would be the following: 'The future of
Christianity is not viable unless we can find a way of presenting
it which includes the old doctrine of God, but does not demand
belief in God as a prior condition of becoming a Christian.'

My primary concern is not to attack belief in God, but to
understand Christianity in such a way that in this age of faith,
faith in Christ may be proclaimed as a real option; as I see it,
the option. Yet in the end this does become a criticism of belief
in God. In religious times Christianity was a religious faith, but
in our time it must be a secular one. We cannot halt any longer
between these two ways. But there is no reason why this development should mean an impoverishment of Christian faith. On the
contrary, I shall argue that it is precisely the *religious* form of
Christianity which does less than justice to Christian faith today.

In many Prefaces it has become fashionable to include what
might be called an intellectual autobiography. If I were tempted to
include this, pretentious though it seems, there would be an
obvious problem. Not that I should have any difficulty in record-
ing my indebtedness to my former teachers, notably Professors
Daniel Day Williams, John Knox and John Macquarrie. It is
rather that the position represented here is so different from their
positions that it might be embarrassing for them to be identified
as those most influential on my development. There is no difficulty, however, in taking this opportunity to record my indebtedness to my wife Anne, not only for the specific and tedious task
of typing this book, but for all the support and encouragement
she has given me in our life together.

Cottingham. April, 1970

God the Stumbling Block

IDENTIFYING THE MYTHOLOGICAL

IT is one of the characteristics of our communicating society that interesting expressions are given instant currency and general circulation. In the process they are often applied in areas beyond the one in which they were originally coined. Thus the phrase 'total believer', which might be taken to refer only to religious belief, was for a time used in other areas. For example, the manager of a successful football club could be described as 'a total believer in his club'. Presumably this meant that he had unbounded confidence in it, faith in the ability of the players to win, and a firm hope for success in the future. But more than that, the club gave meaning, purpose and even quality to his life. Above all, the 'total believer' was a man who could speak about nothing else, who was never embarrassed about his belief, and who was always eager to convince others that his faith in the club was justified.

By such a definition, there are few Christians who can be called 'total believers'. It is not uncommon for two men to work together for years in an office or a factory without one man realizing that the other is also a Christian. Unlike the football manager, we Christians do not bubble over with our belief in Christ, grasping every opportunity to put our case to those we meet, even casual contacts. Unlike the early Christians we are not known to rush out into the streets to proclaim our good news and invite others to share the excitement and wonder of it. There is an ironical reversal here. In a recent article entitled, 'Religion – a

Leisure-time Pursuit?'[1] William Pickering pointed out that churches themselves have very often projected a picture of religion as an activity to be undertaken after working hours. For example, they arrange social and recreational programmes comparable to those of other, quite secular, bodies. The irony would be complete if, at a time when religion was increasingly regarded as a leisure option, a truly leisure option such as football should become the basis of 'total belief'.

It would be a gross exaggeration to say that this is an accurate account of the present position of religion, and yet gross only because it brings out a real aspect of the situation in an unqualified way. It is true that, while others feel able to bring their fundamental beliefs before us at a moment's notice, Christians are more likely to feel some embarrassment about having to speak about God in a bus or a pub. Christians are total believers 'in principle'. Our beliefs are supposed to be relevant to any situation in which we find ourselves. We know that there is something very valuable in Christianity. Why is it then that we are inhibited from communicating these beliefs to others?

I am not at the moment asking why we are unable to convert non-Christians to our faith. The issue raised here is a prior one. We shall not convince them without presenting our case to them, and it is here that we fail. And if we fail, we not only fail ourselves but surely we fail other people too. We should like all men to be Christian, but we are doing nothing to convert them at the moment. It is symptomatic of this dilemma that those who constantly challenge others with their faith are regarded as odd or not quite in the main stream. I live a few hundred yards from the parish church. I do not expect an Anglican to appear

1. A *Sociological Yearbook of Religion in Britain*, ed. David Martin, S.C.M. Press, London, 1968, pp. 77–93.

at my door with a kindly invitation to come to church, but of course I have been visited by several Pentecostalists. Their beliefs seemed odd to me, but clearly they could qualify as total believers. The Salvation Army is regarded by many as a rather quaint hang-over from a previous age, yet only a total believer would make his commitment public to the extent of wearing the uniform and undertaking the work of the Army.

It is not easy to convert people to total belief, whether religious or secular. Even if Christians did communicate with others more readily, there is no guarantee that large numbers would become Christian. But that is a familiar problem for the Church. It is to be found in the witness of the New Testament. Why did thousands of people come into contact with Jesus, and yet fail to believe in him? Why did the Jews in the first century fail to accept the preaching of Paul? Why did the intelligent Greeks who heard Paul fail to be converted to this total belief? Paul did not agree with their reasons, but he knew what these reasons were. 'For Jews demand signs and Greeks seek wisdom, but we preach Christ crucified, a stumbling block to Jews and folly to Gentiles.'[2] The Jews and the Greeks already had beliefs of their own, which prevented them from believing in the gospel preached by the Christians. The gospel was that 'the way, the truth and the life' for men are made clear definitively in the life of Jesus of Nazareth.[3] The beliefs which orthodox Jews held at that time made it difficult for them to accept this, not least because Jesus did not fit the picture they had of what God requires of men. Where was the *victory* in being crucified? For different reasons, intelligent Gentiles were put off. Where is the *sense* in being crucified? Paul rightly identified this as the

2. 1 Corinthians i, 22–3. All quotations from the Bible are taken from the *Revised Standard Version*, Thomas Nelson, London, 1957.

3. cf. John xiv, 6.

stumbling block, the σκάνδαλον, the thing which offended men and prevented them from having faith in Jesus Christ.

It is worth repeating this point, because of what is to follow. In the first century, Christians were able to challenge their contemporaries directly with their faith: 'Jesus Christ is "the way, the truth and the life" for you.' Not all who were thus addressed accepted the gospel, but the important thing was that they were put in the position of actually having to decide for or against Christ. Some accepted the proclamation, and many more rejected it. Not only was it unacceptable to them because of their existing beliefs about themselves and their world, but – and this cannot be stressed too strongly – to some of them it was a real stumbling block. The idea that 'the way, the truth and the life' is revealed in the life of a man who lived without security and died on a cross, is an offensive idea to all of us at some time. If we stumble over this, then we have encountered the heart of the gospel.

The possibility always exists, however, that in other centuries different obstacles will present themselves. When Paul preached to the Jews and the Greeks of his own time, although they finally disagreed about Jesus Christ, they were agreed on many other things. They all shared what has been called the 'ancient world-view'. They all believed in God, in heaven up above the earth and in hell under the earth. Individual beliefs about this structure varied, but it was not these variations which led to the fundamental disagreement. The final dispute was over what to make of Jesus Christ. Our present-day situation is more complicated than this. When we begin to speak about Jesus Christ, we recall men to a world which is in many ways quite alien to them. We ask twentieth-century men to enter a world in which everyone believes in spirits, good and evil, which can enter human lives and control them. It is a world in which many men of different cultural backgrounds share such beliefs as the efficacy of animal sacrifice. Such statements in the creed as 'He descended into hell' and 'He ascended into heaven' would not necessarily be accepted by non-Christians, but would at least be conceivable to them. 'The fact that these two phrases in the Creed were not a stumbling block to anyone in the first century shows that they are no part of that original and genuine σκάνδαλον, which must be retained today.'[4] The real stumbling block, which comes from advocating the way of the cross, must not be eliminated. But how can we clear away the false stumbling blocks which do not allow men to reach the point where they must decide for or against the cross? If in accepting Jesus Christ as the way, the truth and the life, men are required to accept first the ancient world-view with its patently false account of the natural world, then there can be no question of becoming Christian. To state the problem briefly, men today, before they can reach the point where they will be confronted by the real stumbling block of Christianity, are prevented by false stumbling blocks, which may well have nothing to do with Christian faith at all. How can these false stumbling blocks be disposed of, so that the true stumbling block can be confronted? It may be that when faced by the central challenge of the gospel the majority of men will be offended. That would be disappointing. But it would be irresponsible if we allowed the false stumbling blocks to prevent them from ever encountering the central proclamation of the gospel. And yet that is precisely what is happening today.

Those familiar with the history of theology since the Second World War will recognize this as the area of 'de-

4. Ian Henderson, *Myth in the New Testament*, S.C.M. Press, London, 1952, p. 13, n. 1.

mythologizing'. In 1941 Rudolf Bultmann identified the problem of communicating the gospel as essentially a cultural one.[5] The New Testament can now be made available to everyone by translating it from one language to another. Greek was its language and English is ours. Yet today translation is more demanding, since the whole cultural context, the world-view in which the New Testament message was first expressed is 'essentially mythical in character',[6] while our world-view has been shaped by the development of the natural sciences. Of course with training we can to *some* extent re-enter that ancient world, and so understand the Gospel in its original terms. But we cannot choose between that time and our own. We have no option but to be modern Westerners, no matter how critical we are of some aspects of contemporary thought and practice. To attempt to live in first-century terms while in church, and return to twentieth-century terms outside, is an unsatisfactory and unstable attitude, diagnosed by Bultmann as involving 'schizophrenia and insincerity'.[7]

Either the whole of the New Testament must be rejected, along with the now discredited world-view in terms of which it was written, or we must find a radical way of changing the terms in which it might be interpreted. Thus Bultmann asks, 'Does the New Testament embody a truth which is quite independent of its mythical setting?'[8] It is from this important question that the famous project of demythologizing the New Testament springs. As long as the message of the New Testament appears to modern man to deal with spirits and demons, incredible supernatural events, superstition and bad science, then modern man will be put off long before he is faced with the central challenge of the gospel. 'Demythologizing ... will eliminate

5. Rudolf Bultmann, 'New Testament and Mythology', in *Kerygma and Myth*, ed. H. W. Bartsch, Vol. 1, trans. R. H. Fuller, Harper, New York, 1961.   6. ibid. p. 1.   7. ibid. p. 4.   8. ibid. p. 3.

a false stumbling block and bring into sharp focus the real stumbling block, the word of the cross.'[9]

Bultmann appears to be addressing himself to precisely the question we have raised: How can modern man be brought face to face with the real stumbling block of the cross? Not how he can be made to accept the way of the cross, but how he can be put in the position of understanding what is involved in such a choice – not how the gospel can be made acceptable, but how it can be made intelligible. Bultmann says of demythologizing, 'our motive in so doing must not be to make the New Testament relevant to the modern world at all costs.'[10] Two standard criticisms have been made of Bultmann's attempted demythologizing. In the first he is criticized for raising such questions: 'there is no need to demythologize the New Testament, because it does not contain any myth'.[11] In the second he is criticized for failing to demythologize the place of Jesus Christ. This project of dekerygmatizing the New Testament is associated primarily with Fritz Buri.[12] I support Bultmann against both of these criticisms. Although his use of the term 'myth' is not always clear and often pejorative, there can be no doubt that a consistent method must be found by which conceptual and cultural translation of the truth of the New Testament can be made. But against Buri, it must be insisted that a faith which could dispense with Jesus Christ – however compelling it might be in theory

9. Rudolf Bultmann, *Jesus Christ and Mythology*, S.C.M. Press London, 1960, p. 36.

10. *Kerygma and Myth*, p. 10. This desire for relevance all to often eliminates not only elements of the Gospel which make it unacceptable to modern man, but also thereby eliminates any significance from the choice of the cross.

11. H. Sasse, quoted by Bartsch, in the foreword to *Kerygma and Myth*, Vol. 1, p. ix.

12. cf. the discussion of Buri in John Macquarrie, *The Scope of Demythologizing*, S.C.M. Press, London, 1960, Ch. 5.

or in practice – would not qualify as Christian faith. Either Jesus Christ is of the utmost significance, or he is one of a long line of great historical figures who have pointed beyond themselves to something or someone greater.

The two criticisms can be dealt with at length, and indeed, the whole debate on demythologizing dominated theology for a time in the late 1950s. My own criticism of Bultmann, and indeed of the whole debate, is that demythologizing has been concentrated on the wrong issues. We are indebted to Bultmann for pointing out that we must uncover the real stumbling block in order to make sure that men are challenged by the gospel. Unfortunately Bultmann chose certain areas for his project which, in retrospect, have truncated and foreshortened the proper debate. This was inevitable, given that in many respects Bultmann is a rather conservative and even old-fashioned Lutheran.[13] Bultmann, as a good evangelical, believes that if the Word is properly and effectively preached and heard, then God is present. 'Only in the preaching is the cross God's saving act of salvation and revelation.'[14] Demytholo-

13. The extent to which Bultmann must be interpreted within the Lutheran tradition is to be judged by his perceptive re-interpretation of the doctrine of justification by faith. 'Indeed, demythologizing is a task parallel to that performed by Paul and Luther in their doctrine of justification by faith alone without the works of law. More precisely, demythologizing is the radical application of the doctrine of justification by faith to the sphere of knowledge and thought. Like the doctrine of justification, demythologizing destroys every longing for security. There is no difference between security based on good works and security built on objectifying knowledge.' (*Jesus Christ and Mythology*, p. 84.) Cf. Barth's warning that 'those who throw stones at Bultmann should be careful lest they accidentally hit Luther, who is also hovering somewhere in the background'. ('Rudolf Bultmann – an Attempt to Understand Him', *Kerygma and Myth*, Vol. 2, p. 123.)

14. Rudolf Bultmann, 'Paul', in *Existence and Faith*, selected, translated and introduced by Schubert M. Ogden, Meridian Books, Cleveland, Ohio, 1960, p. 139.

gizing is intended to make sure that the content of proclamation is intelligible. To that extent demythologizing
is primarily intended to aid non-Christians. It has failed
precisely on this count. It has certainly been of great interest to Christians, and has enabled them to avoid much of
the 'schizophrenia and insincerity' to which we have already referred.[15] It has enabled present-day Christians to live
more integrated lives as twentieth-century believers. But it
has not made faith in Jesus Christ more possible for non-
Christians. They may now understand more about Christian faith than before, but they are no closer to being
Christians themselves. Many of the former stumbling
blocks, false stumbling blocks, have been removed. It is
clear now that being a Christian does not entail accepting
bad science or superstition. And yet, although armed with
the fresh interpretation of a demythologized gospel, we are
still unable to confront men with the challenge of the cross.
A final stumbling block has been overlooked by Bultmann
and his critics, which prevents modern man from coming to
terms with the gospel of Jesus Christ. Like men of every other
generation modern man, when actually faced with the gospel,
might well reject it, be offended by it. But men today are
still prevented from coming to the point of decision because
of one continuing obstacle, and that stumbling block is God.

Once that point is made, certain things fall into place. The
idea of God (or gods) was part of the common pool of beliefs
of the ancient world. We have already pointed out that the
proclamation of the early Church was not original in every
respect. It presupposed many things which might reasonably
be presupposed at that time, such as the flat earth, spirits
and demons, miraculous occurrences – and a divine being.
The Church did not have first to establish any of these things

15. Note the therapeutic effect of honesty concerning these issues,
underlined in the title of John Robinson's best-selling *Honest to God*.
S.C.M. Press, London, 1963.

before proclaiming the gospel. There was but one issue under debate so far as the early Christians were concerned. It was not whether miraculous events could take place or not. It was not whether there were spirits and demons. It was not even whether or not there was a God. It was Jesus Christ. And the issue was this: Is 'the way, the truth and the life' for men definitively revealed in Jesus Christ? Bultmann is right to say that this is not being put directly to men today, but he does not go far enough in identifying the elements in the New Testament which prevent modern men from being challenged by the gospel. His radical critics, on the other hand, are wrong. The issue concerns what we make of Jesus Christ. That is not a false stumbling block. Of course men may look at his life and his terrible death and be offended by it. They may not have faith in him. But the point is that this issue is at least debatable. It is perfectly *intelligible* to ask men to have faith that in Jesus Christ 'the way, the truth and the life' for them is definitively revealed. As Paul says in the passage already quoted, men may think this idea *foolish*. But at least it is meaningful. They may be offended by this challenge, but at least it has been presented to them and they have been made to choose.

At this point a curious reversal takes place. There is no doubt that the proclamation of Jesus Christ as the 'way' for men, and indeed the only hope for the world, is both meaningful and challenging to modern men. The only qualification is that the stumbling block of *prior* belief in a supernatural being must not be a condition for having faith in the 'way' of Jesus Christ. The possibility that, after a man has come to have faith in Jesus Christ, he may later come to believe in God, cannot be ruled out, but I regard it as unlikely. What now stands between modern man and faith in Jesus Christ, secular faith, that is? Setting aside the stumbling blocks identified by Bultmann, and setting aside this final stumbling block of the God of traditional theism, what is to prevent men today from being addressed and challenged to take up their cross? This is where the curious reversal occurs, for just when the last and major stumbling block has been identified, and modern man sees the possibility of being able to face the challenge, we find that the majority of churchmen object. They insist that belief in God is intrinsic to Christianity, and that to speak of being a Christian without believing in God is absurd. And so the proclamation to modern man is postponed again. He cannot believe in God, and the Church will not allow him to come to Jesus on any other terms.

But what is essential to the belief that Jesus Christ is the definitive revelation of the way for man? We shall be discussing this in Part 2 of the book, but a preliminary answer can be given here. Christians are very reluctant to consider the possibility of a secular faith in Jesus Christ, if only for the good reasons that Jesus believed in God, and that the early Church called him the Son of God. On the basis of these 'good reasons' Christians must also consider whether they are committed to belief in a flat earth or in a three-storey universe. Jesus and the early Church believed in demons and evil spirits which possessed people and made them ill. Are we also committed to such beliefs? Let us say that they are beliefs about the natural world, and in such cases it is possible to argue that the word 'belief' functions in a slightly different way from its use in theological language. The force of such arguments is therefore somewhat reduced (though not eliminated). But the crucial case of eschatology is a different matter. It is now two centuries since H. S. Reimarus first forcefully brought the significance of eschatology for Jesus to the reluctant attention of Christians, and it has not even yet been fully appreciated. In the posthumous Wolfenbüttel Fragment, *Von dem Zwecke Jesu und seiner Jünger*, published by Lessing in 1778, Reimarus pointed to the non-occurrence of the parousia, and to the fact that contemporary theologians skate over this matter, since it does not serve their interest.... How many are there today ... who give a thought to the fact that the openly declared time of Jesus' coming again is long passed and that in consequence one of the principle foundations of Christianity has been found untrustworthy?[16]

Reimarus was wrong in the conclusions he drew, but right in pointing out that both Jesus and the early Church firmly believed – in the theological sense – that world history would not continue in any recognizable form for much longer. 'The course of history has refuted mythology.'[17] Yet the proclamation of Jesus Christ, and the call to faith, are independent of these historically false beliefs held by Jesus and the early Church. We should describe them as beliefs appropriate to that age and world-view, therefore why not admit also that Jesus's belief in God was very much a part of the same age and world-view? To describe him as 'Son of God' was surely in the first instance an evaluation of his significance rather than an account of his origins.

There is no doubt that the early Christians did believe in God, and interpreted their faith in Jesus in the light of this belief. But as we have seen, they had other beliefs which they would then have regarded as *equally* intrinsic to their faith – and such beliefs as eschatology have since been shown to be misguided. The issue is not what they, in their context, reckoned to be intrinsic to faith in Jesus Christ, but what we in our context reckon to be intrinsic. It is clear to me that belief in God, at least in the kind of God the early Christians believed in, cannot be intrinsic to faith in Jesus Christ as the way for men.[18]

16. G. E. Lessing, *Sämtliche Schriften*, ed. K. Lachmann and F. Muncher, G. J. Göschen, Leipzig, 1897, Vol. 13, p. 300.

17. Bultmann, *Jesus Christ and Mythology*, p. 14.

18. I have on several occasions used this phrase, 'the way for men',

A NEW DEFENCE OF THE FOOL

We are told that it was on a charge of atheism that Socrates was sentenced to death. Anyone who did not believe in the gods was considered a threat to society. Even in the last century, to be a declared atheist in England was to invite discrimination in many fields, notably education. Atheism in Europe was long regarded with suspicion and fear – those who did not believe in God were assumed to be in league with the Devil. If they did not believe in God, how could they be expected to live decent moral lives?[19]

This general antipathy towards atheism goes back to a verse from the Psalmist:

> The fool says in his heart,
> 'There is no God.'
> They are corrupt, they do abominable deeds,
> there is none that does good.[20]

The atheist is regarded in the history of the Christian Church as, at best, a fool. Thus Anselm in his *Proslogion* moves towards his famous ontological proof of the existence of God by heading Chapter 2, 'Truly there is a God, although the fool hath said in his heart, There is no God.'[21] Within a few lines Anselm develops his argument, concluding: 'Hence there is no doubt that there exists a being, than which nothing greater can be conceived, and it exists both in the

and of course we should recall that the early name for Christians, before they were called Christians, was those of "the Way". (Acts ix, 2.)

19. Heinrich Heine, in *Memorials of Krähwinkel's Days of Terror*, makes the point that the Prussian police preferred people to believe in God since 'whoever tears himself away from his God will sooner or later break with his earthly superiors too'. (Quoted in S. Körner, *Kant*, Penguin Books, Harmondsworth, 1955, p. 129.)

20. Psalm xiv, 1. Cf. Psalm liii, 1.

21. St Anselm: Basic Writings, trans. S. N. Deane, 2nd edition, Open Court Publishing Co., La Salle, Illinois, 1962, p. 7.

understanding and reality.'[22] Anselm's argument was soon
questioned by Gaunilo, a monk of Marmoutier, in a short
essay entitled 'In behalf of the Fool'. Gaunilo wrote as one
who believed in God, but he did not accept the validity of Anselm's argument. The debate has continued ever since, with
fresh lines of approach representing diverse traditions,[23] but
the point I wish to make here is simply that atheism is identified by Anselm as an essentially foolish position, with the
implication that it is a perverse foolishness. Gaunilo's defence
only amounts to saying that the fool might be perverse to
deny the existence of God, but that he would be stupid to
change his position on the grounds offered by Anselm.

It is clear that contemporary atheism cannot be identified
with foolishness, and certainly not with perverse foolishness.
In any case, there are no grounds for this exegesis of the
Psalm. The writer is not considering the case of atheism. It
might be argued that both the term 'atheism' and its possibility were never envisaged by biblical writers. The Psalmist is dealing with a practical form of atheism, namely living
in disregard of God, even while nominally affirming his existence. The people at that time lived for their own purposes
and ends. They did not deny the existence of God : what made
them foolish was that they adopted a way of life which ignored the requirements and commandments of God.[24]

22. ibid., p. 8.
23. e.g. Dieter Henrich, *Der ontologische Gottesbeweis*, (1960);
Norman Malcolm, 'Anselm's Ontological Arguments', *The Philosophical Review*, January, 1960.
24. Artur Weiser confirms this view in his exegesis of this passage.
'It is characteristic of the biblical view of God that this does not
mean reflection on the existence of God, and so a kind of theoretical
denial of God, but a 'practical atheism' which seeks to evade in living,
the claim of the reality of God.' (*Das Alte Testament Deutsch*: *Die
Psalmen*, 7th (revised) edition, Vandenhoeck & Ruprecht, Göttingen,
1966, p. 111.)

When we turn to consider contemporary atheism, we see that this exegesis suggests that the position is somewhat more complicated than has been assumed in the history of the Church. The line drawn by the Psalmist is not one which divides off atheist from believer, irreligious from religious. The line distinguishes those who live for their own ends, and in accordance with their own purposes, from those who live in accordance with the commandments of God. Not that such a line places a man completely on one side for all time. The line runs through each man, and he lives on one side or the other to varying degrees throughout his lifetime. That is to say, those who affirm the existence of God may sometimes live according to his will, and sometimes according to their own. Conversely, those who do not affirm his existence may still, to some extent, live according to his will. The history of theology has tried to take account of this fact of life by speaking of the natural knowledge of God's law within each man, and even of natural grace whereby a non-believer may still please God.

No one today can seriously associate atheism with immorality or even with an amoral view of life. On the contrary, there are many atheists whose behaviour seems quite puritanical. Perhaps in some cases this is because, unlike Christians, atheists feel they must function by applying moral rules to situations. It is far from clear that religious belief is an advantage in moral matters. Contemplation of the Bible and discussions within the Christian community may make a believer more sensitive than his counterpart non-believer, though whether in practice this is commonly so we cannot discuss at this point.

Just as clearly we cannot equate lack of belief in God with nihilism. It may not be clear on what *grounds* an atheist builds a useful and meaningful life (this question will be raised again in chapter 11, but it would be absurd to say that a life without God is a life without meaning. Many atheists give their lives to serve higher causes than their own self-interest.

A man may be unable to come to belief in God, and may therefore be forced to live his life without the 'meaning' and 'sanction' provided by religious faith. But this does not mean that he automatically becomes immoral, amoral or nihilistic. It does mean that if he wishes to avoid the inconsistency of an eclectic or *ad hoc* series of judgements, he must find some other basis for his life. As long as belief in God is required as the *conditio sine qua non* for approaching Christianity, then he must be alienated from it. But if this stumbling block were removed, why should he not be attracted to the way of the cross? Of course when he understands how demanding it is, and how 'unrealistic' its standards in this evil world, he may well reject it and turn to something else. He will indeed, as Paul would put it, have stumbled over the word of the cross. But it is equally possible that he will believe that the way of the cross is the only way for him, that it offers the only possibility of human fulfilment, and the only hope for the world.

This issue will be taken up again in the course of the book, and especially in Part 2, which will be concerned particularly with the question of transcendence. It is appropriate, however, to introduce the term 'transcendence' now. It will be defined more precisely in Part 2, but in this context I wish to relate it to the line drawn by the Psalmist. Throughout the Bible a decision is required of men, and the options are stated. In Joshua's charge to Israel the people are confronted by the demand, '... choose this day whom you will serve ...'[25] A thousand years later the choice is put before Shadrach, Meshach and Abednego, between a life which destroys their lives, or a death which confirms their lives.[26] In the gospels 'the gate is narrow and the way is hard, that

25. Joshua xxiv, 15.   26. Daniel iii, 15.

leads to life, and those who find it are few',[27] and Paul confesses, 'I see in my members another law at war with the law of my mind and making me captive to the law of sin which dwells in my members.'[28] There is a life which is natural to man, and there is another kind of life for which he must consciously decide, and for which if he decides, he must strive with all his determination. There is a style of life to which we hardly need to be 'drawn'; it seems to be the most natural life for man, and in the Bible how we come to have it is mythologically described in the narrative of the Fall. It is not so much the life we choose, as the life with which we find ourselves when we are old enough to realize that it is not the only possible life. The other life is one by which we transcend our 'nature'. 'Nature' here is put in quotation marks because, paradoxically, we may discover later that the life which transcends our 'nature' may ultimately prove more natural, since in it we find fulfilment. I shall not try to justify this statement for the present.

This is only a brief introduction to the way in which the concept of transcendence will be used in this book, but it will readily be seen how it applies to the issues raised earlier. The way of life definitely revealed in Jesus Christ is the life which consistently transcends the natural life. Till now it has been described in various phrases, such as 'the way, the truth and the life' for men, or 'the way of the cross'. It can now be described as 'the way of transcendence'. By this usage we are not seeking to re-establish the old supernaturalistic metaphysic: it is a purely secular transcendence which refers to a consistent option for human existence.

For convenience we could describe the 'natural' life as the 'way of immanence'. This might be somewhat confusing, since the terms 'transcendence' and 'immanence' have, in traditional theology, referred to two aspects of the being of God. But if we do use this phrase, it will not be to describe

27. Matthew vii, 14.   28. Romans vii, 23.

God, but to describe the alternative option. The biblical phrase 'the world', intended in the pejorative sense of being 'that which is opposed to God', can be used here. In this context we can say that the 'way of immanence' represents the natural 'way of the world'.

There is no difficulty in seeing that an atheist might be challenged by the way of transcendence, and might reject the way of immanence.

Those who believe in God will be quite unmoved by the argument so far. They know the presence of God. Far from finding God a stumbling block to Christian faith, they do not see how it is possible even to conceive of Christian faith without belief in God. If everyone believed in God then we could all choose whether to be Christians or not. It seems today as if fewer and fewer people believe in God, but what is not generally recognized by religious folk is that believing in God is not something a man can choose to do. On the basis of their experience, some people can believe and others cannot. In Part 1 we shall be examining religious experience and the grounds for belief in God. And if men, through no apparent fault of their own, do not find anything in their experience which could be identified with God, does that mean that they are disqualified from choosing to follow Christ? In Part 2 we shall examine in increasing detail the problem of God, the problem of making belief in God the presupposition for faith in Christ, at a time when fewer and fewer people can fulfil that prior qualification. We shall end by offering a re-interpretation of our understanding of God, theology and faith, in purely secular terms, using the concept of transcendence. Far from being a reduction of the meaning or significance of Christianity, this will emerge as an enlargement.[29]

29. It would be as well to underline the fact that transcendence will be discussed as a secular term, because in contemporary theology it is always associated with God – the secular meaning of trans-

cendence is never envisaged. G. F. Woods could only conceive of secular transcendence in terms of human encounter, anticipating the divine transcendence. ('The Idea of the Transcendent', *Soundings*, ed. A. R. Vidler, Cambridge University Press, 1966, pp. 58, 63.) Roger Mehl discusses 'a Christian doctrine of transcendence' only in the context of the Incarnation and the *kenosis* of God in Christ. ('La Crise de la Transcendence', *Revue d'Histoire et de Philosophie Religieuses*, Vol. 49, No. 4 (1969), pp. 351, 353 (cf. *Neue Zeitschrift für Systematische Theologie und Religionsphilosophie*, Vol. 11, No. 3 (1969), pp. 329–46).) Ronald Hepburn assumes that for theology the language of transcendence must mean speaking about a personal God, wholly other to man. (*Christianity and Paradox*, C. A. Watts, London, 1958, pp. 193–4.) For H. D. Lewis, transcendence is the experience of worship, and pertains to the object of that act. (*Our Experience of God*, George Allen & Unwin, London, 1959, p. 69.) Similarly Gregor Smith discusses transcendence only in terms of personal encounter, the I – Thou, whether between people or between God and man. (*The Doctrine of God*, Collins, London, 1970, p. 130.) Gabriel Fackre deplores the positivism of much contemporary theology, but transcendence for him is ultimately the divine transcendence, not a secular experience. ('The Issue of Transcendence in the New Theology, the New Morality, and the New Forms', *New Theology No. 4*, ed. Martin E. Marty and Dean G. Peerman, Macmillan, New York, 1967, pp. 178–94.)

PART ONE

LIVING WITHOUT GOD

CHAPTER 1

Religious Experience

THE SIGNIFICANCE OF RELIGIOUS EXPERIENCE

IT is difficult to offer a definition of religion which is not so wide in its all-inclusiveness as to be quite useless for practical study. In any case, my interest here is in Christianity – whatever the implications might be for other religions. The characteristic of the Christian religion is the extent to which the intellectual side has been stressed. I am not only referring to the Protestant tradition of preaching, but also to the doctrinal controversies which so dominate the history of the first few centuries of the Church. The emphasis has been on right belief, and that is literally what orthodoxy means. It is therefore salutary to remember the words of Archbishop William Temple: 'From all this it follows that there is no such thing as revealed truth. There are truths of revelation, that is to say, propositions which express the results of correct thinking concerning revelation; but they are not themselves directly revealed.'[1] One element of Christian faith is belief in the Incarnation, but 'Incarnation' is the orthodox interpretation of the revelation in Jesus Christ. The interpretation is not itself part of the revelation. As an interpretation it could be true or false. The distinction between orthodoxy and heresy is not that one is true and the other false, but rather that the latter is a minority view. And this is what heterodoxy means.

Of course any religious interpretation at all of the events concerning Jesus of Nazareth might be disputed. The whole construction might be written off as an illusion. But while

1. William Temple, *Nature, Man and God*, Macmillan, London, 1949, p. 317.

a vision appearing to one man might be disputed as 'purely' illusory, the events concerning Jesus of Nazareth were real events. The dispute in this case is not over their having taken place (though of course what precisely happened will always be in some doubt historically speaking) but over their religious interpretation. That, as John MacMurray points out, is quite a different issue.

> The data of science are not themselves scientific, nor are the data of religion themselves religious. An illusory experience must arise from some facts which are not illusory, and to hold that religion is illusory is not to maintain that the data from which religion arises does not exist, but merely that religion distorts and misrepresents the data from which it starts.[2]

A religious interpretation may be true or false; more often it is a question of its degree of appropriateness. Further, the interpretation which might be appropriate in one age may be deemed inappropriate in another. To reject a former interpretation is far from denying its significance or declaring it illusory. Only those who still value its significance would be in a position to re-interpret the original orthodoxy. But what must be stressed, in the midst of ever-changing interpretations, is the central place of experience. 'The core of religion is religious experience.'[3] It has long been noted by observers of religion that religion involves a total human response, a response to the world as we experience it.[4]

But having said all this, we have only stated the problem.

2. John MacMurray, *The Structure of Religious Experience*, Faber & Faber, London, 1936, pp. 17–18.

3. H. D. Lewis, *Our Experience of God*, George Allen & Unwin, London, 1959, p. 65.

4. 'One achievement of modern anthropology we shall not question: the recognition that magic and religion are not merely a doctrine or a philosophy, not merely an intellectual body of opinion, but a special mode of behaviour, a pragmatic attitude built up of reason, feeling, and will alike.' (B. Malinowski, *Magic, Science and Religion*, Doubleday, New York, 1954, p. 24.)

Given that religion is concerned with our experience of our world, and the appropriate response to it, what then makes an experience of the world a religious experience? What makes a way of life a religious one, and what is a religious view of the world? This could involve a complex and tedious discussion extending beyond the Christian religion. I wish to cut through this and propose what might seem a rather crude standard, but one which I believe has been implicit in the whole Judeo-Christian tradition. A religious experience is an experience of God. 'In, with and under' the experience of the world there is an experience of a divine, supernatural being. I do not think Christians would be content to classify the experience of a magnificent vista as religious unless the experience were somehow also reckoned an experience of the creator of the vista. Similarly no gracious action would be regarded as of religious significance unless it was reckoned also to be either enabled by God or a response to a gracious God. It must also be stressed that without the experience of God as a 'personal' (in some recognizably analogous use of the word) being, worship as it has been known throughout the centuries could not be carried on.

I do not believe this definition of religion is arbitrary, in view of the place of God in the tradition. The general views can be found in textbooks on the subject, and I refer in particular to the Gifford Lectures by C. A. Campbell. He offers a definition of religious experience (though he in fact goes on to the interpretation of the experience) as 'a state of mind comprising belief in the reality of a supernatural being or beings endued with transcendent power and worth, together with the complex emotive attitude of worship intrinsically appropriate thereto'.[5] We have already discussed what orthodoxy means within the religious circle. Right belief is based on the true interpretation of religious experience, or

5. C. A. Campbell, *On Selfhood and Godhood*, George Allen & Unwin, London, 1957, p. 248.

at least the appropriate interpretation. But this is the internal logic of religion. Religious belief finally rests on belief in the existence of God (granted that 'existence' is a disputed term in this connection). Campbell goes on to make this point rigorously. If we ask 'Is religion true?' then the affirmative answer is justified only if 'there exists at least one supernatural being of transcendent power and value'.[6] Comte is quoted as exclaiming: 'A religion without God! My God, what a religion.' I think this would also be the general reaction of those who have religious beliefs. Further, to be recognizably Christian belief, it must be possible to address this God in the words, 'Our Father'. We shall be returning to this point in Chapter 2.

Having spoken about religious experience and its significance, it is appropriate to consider some specific examples. The first is what might be called the Schleiermacher–Otto tradition, and the second is mystical experience.

Pius XII judged Karl Barth 'the greatest theologian since St Thomas Aquinas', but Barth himself said: 'The first place in a history of the theology of the most recent times belongs and will always belong to Schleiermacher, and he has no rival.' This estimate is the more ironic, since on balance Barth regarded Schleiermacher's influence on modern theology to have been unfortunate, to put it at its mildest. Friedrich Schleiermacher (1768–1834) began to read theology when Germany was under the influence of the Romantic movement. It was a time when its 'cultured despisers' rejected religion as a phenomenon belonging to a more primitive stage in the development of man. They represented an unprecedented blossoming of human achievement in literature and the arts. It was a period of liberation and discovery, when men sought to explore their as yet undeveloped potentialities and achieve new and exciting levels of human fulfilment. 'One was cultured and full of ideas; one was aes-

6. ibid., p. 253.

thetic, and one was moral. But one was no longer religious.'[7]
Whether Schleiermacher's influence has been, on balance,
for good or ill, he must be congratulated for taking up the
contemporary challenge in a brilliant and effective manner.
In becoming 'the theologian of Romanticism',[8] he sought to
show that religion was a necessary part of human life, and
that those who ignored it did not liberate themselves to
achieve new levels of fulfilment, but foreshortened their
experience and truncated their lives. Since the Romantics
paid particular attention to experience, feeling and imagina-
tion, Schleiermacher presented religion with particular reference to these aspects.

Schleiermacher conceded that some of the historical forms
of religion were unworthy, yet the Romantics should not be
put off by such outward features, but should penetrate to
'the kernel of this shell'.[9] Nor should they be content with
an acceptance of the tradition, which for all its value always
represents a second-hand account of religion, speaking about
religion rather than experiencing it. They should not rest
'with the repeated oft-broken echo of that original sound'.[10]
Religion is not primarily about ethics or metaphysics. 'True
science is complete vision: true practice is culture and art
self-produced; true religion is sense and taste for the Infinite.'[11]

Schleiermacher is arguing *ad hominem*, as the terminology
indicates, but he is also attempting to establish an empirical
basis for religion. In this connection he makes the point we
have already discussed, that religion is to be sought in the

7. Rudolf Otto, Introduction to F. Schleiermacher, *On Religion*:
Speeches to Its Cultured Despisers, trans. John Oman, Harper, New
York, 1958, p. vii.

8. The phrase comes from R. R. Niebuhr, in his introduction to
F. Schleiermacher, *The Christian Faith*, trans. H. R. Mackintosh, and
J. S. Stewart, Harper & Row, New York, 1963, p. xii.

9. Schleiermacher, *On Religion*, p. 15.

10. ibid., p. 18.   11. ibid., p. 39.

ordinary areas of life, the central, essential and common areas, rather than the obscure, extraordinary and even bizarre.[12] For Schleiermacher all feelings are at least potentially religious. But he was not content to show that religion was an interesting and rewarding area of study. He maintained that it was an essential part of human life. 'Man can just as little be thought of without capacity for morality or endeavour after government as without capacity for religion.'[13]

This forms the background to Schleiermacher's famous exposition of religion, *The Christian Faith*, which in turn is characterized by his opening definition of religion.

> The common element in all howsoever diverse expressions of piety by which these are conjointly distinguished from all other feelings, or, in other words the self-identical essence of piety, is this : the consciousness of being absolutely dependent, or, which is the same thing, of being in relation with God.[14]

The characteristic religious experience, according to Schleiermacher, is that of being absolutely dependent. As indicated, it does not come unalloyed, but in the midst of other experiences. The value of Christianity as a religion is its success in evoking this experience. The uniqueness of Jesus is defined in this way.

> The Redeemer, then, is like all men in virtue of the identity of human nature, but distinguished from them all by the constant potency of His God-consciousness, which was a veritable existence of God in Him.[15]

12. The bizarre nature of religious experience is often emphasized in works on religious experience, perhaps because it is more easily identified as religious. William James admitted this tendency in his own work, the concentration on the 'pathology of religion'. 'The sentimentality of many of my documents is a consequence of the fact that I sought them among the extravagances of the subject.' (*The Varieties of Religious Experience*, Doubleday, New York, n.d., p. 436.)   13. Schleiermacher, *On Religion*, p. 25.

14. Schleiermacher, *The Christian Faith*, p. 12.   15. ibid., p. 385.

Whatever the objections to this definition of being in relation with God, it is a more subtle analysis than that of Tillich. Tillich describes God by saying, 'That which is ultimate gives itself only to the attitude of ultimate concern.'[16] While Schleiermacher identifies the human condition which is made clear to man by the presence of God, in Tillich's system the recognition of God is always in some sense a function of human striving.

In the light of the foregoing discussion, we must now conclude that while Schleiermacher may well be right in identifying such a human experience as absolute dependence, the alternative description, 'or, which is the same thing, of being in relation with God', is an interpretation of the experience. The experience of being absolutely dependent, if such an experience were possible, does not of necessity include that of being absolutely dependent on a reality which is 'personal'. This is not a criticism of the work of Schleiermacher in trying to bring men to belief in God. He turned the Romantics away from the idea that religion was superstition or speculation. He pointed to an empirical basis for belief. But at the end of the day the dispute remains. Is it 'the same thing' to describe this experience as the experience of being in relation with God? Clearly the majority of the Romantics did not draw his conclusion.

In 1917 Rudolf Otto published his investigation of the experience of 'the holy'.[17] While the experience of holiness

16. Paul Tillich, *Systematic Theology*, Vol. I, Nisbet, Welwyn, 1953, p. 15.

17. 'So far from keeping the non-rational element in religion alive in the heart of the religious experience, orthodox Christianity manifestly failed to recognize its value, and by this failure gave the idea of God a one-sidedly intellectualistic and rationalistic interpretation.' In view of this intended corrective, it is one of the great ironies of translation that *Das Heilige* should appear in English under the title *The Idea of the Holy*. (The quotation is taken from the Penguin edition, 1959, p. 17.)

carries with it ethical implications, Otto points out that in Hebrew, Greek and Latin, holiness does not derive from ethics. He therefore coins the term 'numinous',[18] to refer to this experience, without the ethical element.[19] 'This mental state is perfectly *sui generis* and irreducible to any other.'[20] Because of this uniqueness, Otto criticizes Schleiermacher's analysis of absolute dependence, which does not safeguard the qualitative difference between the experience of God and other experiences. The experience is illustrated by reference to Abraham who, when confronted by God, felt himself to be as 'but dust and ashes'. It is more than dependence: it is 'creature-consciousness'.[21] He also criticizes Schleiermacher for leaving the gap to which we have referred. God is an inference from the experience of absolute dependence. For Otto, 'The numinous is thus felt as objective and outside the self.'[22]

Although Christianity in its more sophisticated forms has rather successfully eliminated the experience of the numinous, it breaks through at odd times, and in particular circumstances. It is characterized by '*mysterium tremendum*', the experience evoked occasionally by old churches or solemn rites. It involves a mixture of elements of awe. There is shuddering fear in the presence of the 'uncanny', when we stand 'aghast'. The primitive (Old Testament) experience of God may break through, exposing us to a non-rational power which is both 'incalculable and arbitrary'.[23]

Before this 'Wholly Other', different in kind from us, we are filled with dread, yet drawn by wonder. This is the element of fascination. The numinous experience, the encoun-

18. As *omen* gives us *ominous*, so Otto decides *numen* will give us *numinous*.

19. This point is made without prejudice to a discussion of God and the basis of ethical and value judgements. Cf. Reinhard Schinzer, 'Wert und Sein in Rudolf Ottos Gotteslehre', *Kerygma und Dogma*, Vol. 16, No. 1, 1970, pp. 1–31.

20. Rudolf Otto, *The Idea of the Holy*, p. 21.   21. ibid., p. 24.
22. ibid., p. 25.   23. ibid., p. 32.

ter with the Wholly Other involves the complex elements of
mysterium tremendum et fascinans. We should flee from its
awfulness, dread and horror, and yet we are attracted and
invited to surrender. The terror is clearly identified in many
primitive religions, but Christianity combines this with the
invitation: the judgement and grace of God are both recognized.

Otto's analysis of the experience of the holy has rightly
attracted attention beyond the field of theology. It is a very
subtle and careful dissection of a complex experience. The
problem of assessing the analysis is essentially the one presented in the work of Schleiermacher. To what extent must
this experience be viewed as an encounter with God? This is
not to deny the experience. We are all familiar with it in
varying degrees. It is not the fear of the known but of the
unknown. It is the experience evoked in horror films and
remembered from childhood walks through a wood at night;
in another form, the experience is known to those who have
stood on a cliff edge, swaying against the hypnotic invitation of the valley below. The experience is real, and Otto
has dissected it without losing any of the pieces. But has he
presented us with any extra pieces?

Perhaps it makes sense to describe it as *sui generis*, qualitatively different from other experiences. Certainly it takes
place at the limits of our existence, where the will to death
and the struggle for survival meet. The one bridge which
Otto throws across the gap left by Schleiermacher – the gap
between the acknowledged experience and its disputed interpretation – is the element in the numinous experience
identified as 'creature-consciousness'. But is this in fact a
neutral description of the experience, or does the terminology
already prejudice the outcome? Otto does not develop this
point into an argument for the existence of God, but it certainly functions in this way. It is reminiscent of the teleological argument for the existence of God in the form offered

by Archdeacon William Paley in his *Natural Theology*
(1802). If a man should chance upon a watch in some deserted place, even though he knew nothing of watches, from
the intricacies and interconnection of its parts he would be
forced to conclude that some intelligent craftsman had
created it. Are we not to conclude by a careful examination
of the components of our world and their interconnection
that it too was made by a (supremely) intelligent Creator? To this leading question the tradition of David Hume
gives the answer No, and I suspect that on the same grounds
we must reject 'creature-consciousness' in Otto's argument.
The strength of Schleiermacher's position, criticized by Otto,
is that since it is possible to experience a feeling of being
dependent, it is at least conceivable that we might experience
a feeling of being absolutely dependent. It is the weakness of
Otto's argument that while we can describe the *situation* of
a creature – for example, finite and dependent – we cannot
experience *being* a creature. That is to say, while we can
be conscious of our finitude and dependence, i.e. the known
characteristics of a creature, the fact that we are creatures is
a *deduction from* the experience of finitude and dependence,
and does not constitute part of the experience itself.

Once this bridge is dismantled between the numinous experience and the experience of God, we are left only with the
'Wholly Other'.

The truly 'mysterious' object is beyond our apprehension and
comprehension, not only because our knowledge has certain ir-
removable limits, but because in it we come upon something
inherently 'wholly other', whose kind and character are incommensurable with our own, and before which we therefore recoil
in a wonder that strikes us chill and numb.[24]

It is to be noted that the 'wholly other' is described in neutral, even neuter, terms and not in personal terms. The experience is real, but does it have an 'object'? And what is

24. ibid., p. 42.

the difference between a 'mysterious' object 'beyond our apprehension and comprehension ... whose kind and character are incommensurable with our own ...' and no 'object' at all? Clearly the experience can be interpreted as one of encounter with a mysterious object, and just as clearly some may describe the experience without reference to such an object.

Precisely the same situation confronts us when we turn from the Schleiermacher–Otto description of religious experience to the mystical tradition. We shall be dealing with this topic in a very limited way, but even so it is a subject on which few of us feel competent to pass comment, let alone judgement. This was the feeling of W. T. Stace at the outset of his study, *Mysticism and Philosophy*.[25] He calls to mind that Mohammed once compared a philosopher who writes about mysticism – without having had any mystical experience – with a donkey carrying a load of books.[26] But mystics have written a great deal, even about the ineffable, and we can at least begin from this witness.

Before we can inquire into the significance of mystical experience, we must try to form some systematic understanding of its nature. This is not easily done. In particular the difficulty which we have already encountered, namely the distinction of the experience from its interpretation, is increased in the case of mystical experiences. William James records several examples of mystical experiences, and tries to systematize them under four headings:

1. *Ineffability*: only those who have had the experience can understand it.
2. *Noetic quality*: the experience not only concerns emotion, but is claimed to yield insight.
3. *Transiency*: the experience not only lasts for but a short time, it is not subject to accurate recollection or recall.

25. W. T. Stace, *Mysticism and Philosophy*, Macmillan, London, 1961.   26. ibid., p. 18.

4. *Passivity*: although the state can be induced, and may require careful preparation beforehand, the experience itself involves a sense of passivity.[27]

But James, as a pragmatist, was more interested in the effect which mystical experiences have on people, and in particular whether there is any moral advance. His analysis is not very subtle, since his interest is in the outcome rather than the content of mystical experiences.

William James delivered his Gifford Lectures in Edinburgh in 1901, and ten years later Evelyn Underhill published her work *Mysticism*,[28] in which she was critical of James, and undertook to provide a more satisfactory study of the subject. Unfortunately, her presentation[29] errs in the opposite direction. It is clear that she seeks to answer criticisms and counter prejudices, but equally clear that she expounds her analysis of mystical experience so that such criticisms and prejudices are shown to be misguided. The main deficiency in the exposition, apart from this reactive approach, is another methodological one, that she refers the division within mystical experience to the traditional theological division, namely the transcendence and the immanence of God. Nothing in her discussion of the characteristics would lead us to suspect that God was a necessary element in the experience.[30]

27. These characteristics, with examples, appear in William James, *The Varieties of Religious Experience*, lectures XVI and XVII.

28. Evelyn Underhill, *Mysticism*, Methuen, London, 1957.

29. ibid., ch. 4.

30. This is confirmed in the summary which comes at the end of the analysis. 'To sum up. Mysticism is seen to be a highly specialized form of that search for reality, for heightened and completed life, which we have found to be a constant characteristic of human consciousness. It is largely prosecuted by that "spiritual spark", that transcendent faculty which, though the life of our life, remains below the threshold in ordinary men. Emerging from its hiddenness in the mystic, it gradually becomes the dominant factor in his life; subduing to its service, and enhancing by its saving contact with reality, those vital powers of love and will which we attribute to the heart, rather

What is given is an analysis of a very extraordinary human experience, and we should therefore expect the division to refer to characteristics of the experience rather than a division in the mode of God's being.

A more rigorous and systematic study of mysticism is presented by W. T. Stace. The division in mystical experience already referred to is based on the fact that one general type of experience concerns a new way of seeing the external world, while another general type involves a complete and utter withdrawal from the world. Stace, quite properly, attempts to build up the characteristics of the two experiences, without setting them within a theological framework. The experience of Jakob Boehme will serve as an example for the 'extrovertive' form of mysticism. Boehme underwent an experience one day while at home, in which he saw everything completely united, and all divisions removed.

He believed that it was only a fancy, and in order to banish it from his mind he went out upon the green. But there he remarked that he gazed into the very heart of things, the very herbs and grass, and that actual nature harmonized with what he had seen.[31]

In contrast, 'introvertive' experience involves the gradual and then complete exclusion from the mind and consciousness of everything but the self, until even the self is absorbed in the Void.

Stace offers seven characteristics of both forms of mysticism, in which five are identical; blessedness, objectivity, holiness, paradoxicality and ineffability. Only the first two differ. The extrovertive form involves the unifying vision of all

---

than those of mere reason and perception, which we attribute to the head.' (ibid., p. 94.)

31. Stace, *Mysticism and Philosophy*, p. 69. Cf. Meister Eckhart's assertion: 'All that a man has here externally in multiplicity is intrinsically One. Here all blades of grass, wood, and stone, all things are One.' (ibid., p. 63.)

things, while the introvertive finds the unity in the One, Void or pure consciousness. Similarly the extrovertive involves a more concrete apprehension of the inner life of all things, whereas the introvertive is a nonspatial, nontemporal experience.

The two forms of experience are too similar in structure to be considered as finally different. Stace interprets their relationship in the following way. The extrovertive form is actually but the lower level of the introvertive type. It is an incomplete form of that experience, and shows tendencies which are fulfilled in the introvertive.

> In the introvertive type the multiplicity has been wholly obliterated and therefore must be spaceless and timeless, since space and time are themselves principles of multiplicity. But in the extrovertive experience the multiplicity seems to be, as it were, only half absorbed in the unity.[32]

The mystical experience must be a truly remarkable experience, in either form, whether occurring spontaneously or being induced either by spiritual exercises or by the use of drugs.[33] The only question under discussion here, however, is its witness to the being of God. I consider that the analysis given by Stace is a very able and convincing one, as distinct from the speculative use to which he later puts it. God does not seem to appear as an intrinsic part of the experience as described by Underhill. Stace goes further. 'Atheism is not as such, I believe, inconsistent with introvertive mystical experience. For as we have seen, the concept of God is an interpretation of the experience, not part of the experience itself.'[34] It is perhaps significant that Stace says this in connection with a comparison of western and eastern mysticism. The experience seems to be the same, no matter the religious

32. ibid., p. 132.

33. e.g., R. C. Zaehner, *Mysticism: Sacred and Profane*, Appendix B: 'The Author's Experience with Mescalin', Clarendon Press, Oxford, 1957.   34. Stace, op. cit., p. 124.

commitment of the mystic. The Christian mystic gives a theistic interpretation of the experience, but the interpretation very often suggests that the experience is not compatible with belief in the God of Christianity. 'In the essence the Father loses His Fatherhood completely; nor is there Father at all,' claims Eckhart, straining the credibility of his claim to orthodoxy.[35]

We have not reviewed all possible kinds of religious experience, but in this section we have not only given a context for religious experience, but we have also examined two very important and influential traditions. We began by saying that as normally understood, and practised, religion in the Judeo-Christian tradition involves the belief in a personal God, who is worthy of worship. Later we shall be considering two contemporary approaches to the Christian religion which vary from this common understanding, but there is no doubt that this is how religion in our culture has been traditionally understood.

In the Introduction two themes were discussed. The first was that a large number, and an increasing number of people in our society do not believe in God. The second was that there is considerable interest today in the issues which are involved in what was described as 'the way of transcendence'. The challenge of Jesus Christ, if put directly to people today, would be a meaningful challenge, and I am hopeful that many would feel the force of this option. The stumbling block which prevents them coming to terms with Jesus Christ was there identified as belief in God. So long as belief in God is made a condition of their coming to terms with Jesus Christ, then they will be disqualified. They just do not have belief in God. But more than that, there is nothing in their experience which can be automatically identified as God. It is tempting to say there is no such thing as religious experience. If we were to make this point in a polemical way, it would

35. Quoted by Stace, ibid., p. 172.

be to underline the fact that what is normally meant by 'religious experience' is 'experience which is given a religious
interpretation'. This is true both in extrovertive and introvertive forms (to widen the reference of the terminology of
Stace). We have already noted that the numinous experience, described by Otto, is an experience of the world around
us, but does not intrinsically involve the experience of God.
Even in purely subjective conditions the problem remains.
Thomas Hobbes commented in characteristically blunt fashion on the suggestion of direct communication from God to
a man. 'To say he hath spoken to him in a dream, is no more
than to say he dreamed that God spake to him . . .'[36]

All this is far from disproving the existence of God. (In-
cidentally I doubt whether such a disproof could ever be
given, since it would involve demonstrating the impossibility of a being, *a posteriori*.) It is always open to people to
interpret experiences in a religious manner. What is at stake
is the fact that it is not necessary to interpret *any* experience
in a religious manner. If it were claimed that certain very
rare experiences, such as those associated with the mystics,
were direct experiences of God, then this would be of interest. It would mean that religion could not be a popular
phenomenon, being reserved for a select few.[37] But even this
claim cannot be maintained. There is no direct experience of
God, only experiences which are interpreted in a religious
manner. This may in fact be the appropriate manner in

36. Thomas Hobbes, *Leviathan*, J. M. Dent, London, 1914, p. 200.
37. Both Stace and Underhill, whose commitments to mysticism are
quite different, stress that the experience is possible only for a very
few. 'We may take it then that the genesis of mystical consciousness
is explicable in terms of the psychological and physiological make-up
of those who have it.' (Stace, op. cit, pp. 26–7.) Cf. Underhill's claim
that part of the necessary equipment of a mystic must be 'an appropriate psychological make-up, with a nature capable of extraordinary
concentration, an exalted moral emotion, a nervous organization of
the type.' (Underhill, op. cit., p. 91.)

which to interpret them. The only point that is being made here is that no experience is *necessarily* interpreted in a religious manner. It may be justifiable, and perhaps even correct in some sense, to give a religious interpretation to various experiences, but it is always possible for others to say that such an interpretation is not appropriate. In particular, the man who has no prior belief in God may well reckon that an experience interpreted as religious by one person does not bear the weight of such an interpretation for him.

Nor does the Bible throw any light on the problem. The Bible begins with God, before going on to mention anything else. It does not record a period when men had no belief in God. If it did, then we might be given an account of how a man without belief in God came through certain experiences to interpret things in a religious manner. But God is always there already in the Bible. Clearly our interest was not the interest of the writer of the account of Moses at the burning bush (whatever the historical basis for such a story). We are told that God simply made himself known to Moses directly. In contrast to the fashion of scholarship earlier in this century, we must recognize that many of the turning points in the history of the Old Testament must be seen as resulting from experiences in which individuals are said to have been confronted directly – and addressed verbally – by God. In neither case does the Bible help us with our problem. On the one hand it offers no examples of men who came to belief in God when previously they had no supernaturalist view of the world at all. On the other hand, while it is of considerable significance to an individual in the Old Testament to be confronted by the living God, this can hardly give a non-believer today any hope that he will be enabled to come to belief in God. I am neither a Calvinist nor a Barthian, but understand and appreciate the strength of the positions which preserve the divine initiative. The difficulty is, however, that predestination logically implies double predestination. If God reveals himself directly to whomsoever he chooses, this is less than good news to those to whom he denies himself.

The vicious circle is formed in this way. If a man has an experience of God, then he may well interpret many (or all) of his experiences in a religious way. But how does a non-believer get started? If he has no experience of God, no experience he is likely to have *must* be interpreted religiously. Nor do I accept the optimistic view of H. D. Lewis when he assures us, 'If they can be induced to see what we mean when we speak of God, they will at one and the same time be convinced of His existence.'[38] On the contrary, a non-believer may be able to understand why another man interprets an event in a religious manner. He may even wish that he could so interpret it, but to be true to his own experience he must admit that he would not be justified in doing so.

It is one of the traditions of religious education that if a child can be brought up in a religious context, then he will believe in God. It is also traditional that when children reach a certain age, many of them reject belief in God. Yet the important thing is that the cultural context provides a basis for believing in God, for giving a religious interpretation to life. We speak of our time as a 'post-Christian' era. In the light of what was said in the Introduction, I should prefer the phrase 'post-religious' era. By this I am referring to the fact that our culture no longer provides a basis for a religious interpretation of our experience. I believe that our culture, or perhaps just our way of life, is open to many fundamental and serious criticisms, but I believe these criticisms arise from comparison with the other way of life, the 'way of transcendence'. It has yet to be shown that decline of religion bears any direct relationship to man's inhumanity to man. As we have already discussed in the Introduction, mere belief in God does not imply high moral achievement or social sensitivity. In this context I should say that non-belief in

38. Lewis, op. cit., p. 44.

God has no ethical or social significance. By that I mean that the man who has no experience of God may still be committed to the 'way of transcendence'.

THE DENIAL OF ATHEISM

We have already referred to that thin but influential series of theophanies in the Old Testament, where it is said God revealed himself directly to individuals. This line runs on into the history of the Christian Church. There are of course difficulties involved in dealing with this tradition. Some of the accounts may not refer to historical events at all. They may be purely legendary. Others may already incorporate the interpretation of the experience within the account of the experience. This would be characteristic of the mythical style. But when all that is said, I doubt whether those who believe in God would wish to rest their case on such examples. The knowledge of God must surely come from what is common and familiar rather than from that which is bizarre, extraordinary and exceedingly rare. Otherwise most people, the vast majority in fact, would simply be condemned to a second-hand knowledge of God.

In the previous section it was said that although experience is sometimes given a religious interpretation, such an interpretation is never logically necessary. But there is a continuous position represented in the history of the Church, which denies that atheism can be ultimately sustained. Those who hold this view maintain that it is inevitable that experience gets interpreted in a religious way. It is said that atheism finally *must* give way to faith in God. The problem we have been examining is that many people today do not believe in God. Religious experience means the religious interpretation of experience. It is always possible, on this view, that people may genuinely think it inappropriate to give a religious interpretation to their experience. Against this conclusion there is, as I have just indicated, a long tradition maintaining that in the end men are inevitably led to see that the religious interpretation is the appropriate one. A modified version of this view would be that non-believers are at least shown that they are wrong, whether they choose to admit it or not.

Of the writers we have already mentioned, we have noted that Schleiermacher believed man cannot be imagined 'without the capacity for religion'. By this, as we have seen, he implied that if men looked carefully at their experience they would inevitably recognize and acknowledge God. The 'consciousness of being absolutely dependent', if they would come to identify and assess it properly, would be seen to be the same thing as 'being in relation with God'.

A more familiar example, however, comes to us from Augustine, who in his prayer to God declares, 'Thou hast made us for thyself, and our hearts are restless till they rest in thee.'[39] Man actually needs God, not just for peace of mind, but for his whole fulfilment. This reflects Augustine's own experience. Looking back over his life, he could see a series of attempts to live life to the full, yet without God. Each had failed, and he found peace at last when he acknowledged God. His was a life spent fleeing from God and in search of fulfilment. Paradoxically, it was only when he turned to God that he found his searching to be at an end. Augustine recounts his experience and thus justifies his conclusion. But if this is the conclusion for Augustine, must it be the pattern for everyone? In recent times two voices have been raised against this view. The first is that of Dietrich Bonhoeffer, who warns us against thinking of God as a problem solver and need fulfiller. The danger is that as we solve more of our problems, and fulfil more of our own needs, God gets pushed out to the periphery of our concerns. He is no longer found in what is

39. The Confessions of St Augustine, tran. F. J. Sheed, Sheed & Ward, London, 1943, p. 3.

central to our lives. But perhaps a more pointed remark has been made by William Hamilton. His response to these famous words of Augustine is, 'maybe some hearts are, and maybe some are not'.[40] These words of Augustine have been treasured throughout the centuries, because Christians have found in them not simply a history of Augustine's experience, but in some strange way an account of their own paths. Yet today we find men who are unmoved by these words. Their hearts are not restless, or if they are, then they expect to find fulfilment within the secular world. Their restlessness with an immanent way of life may eventually be satisfied with the 'way of transcendence'. In this they may find fulfilment. But they do not entertain the idea that a supernatural being will bring them peace. The attempt to deny atheism may involve saying that they *should* seek God, but the Augustinian thesis is often proved false in practice. Many people do live mature lives today without God. As indicated in the Introduction, the restlessness which some may have, which would be satisfied through faith in Jesus Christ, may continue simply because, through their inability to believe in God, they may feel cut off from the way of Christ.

A more recent example of the final denial of atheism is to be found in the work of John Baillie, former Principal of New College, Edinburgh, who was an outstanding example of the proper relationship of piety and critical scholarship. In discussing the solipsist position, Baillie says:

We should say that though they deny the reality of their neighbours and of the world about them with the top of their minds, they believe in them all the time in the bottom of their hearts. Why then should we be precluded from occupying the same ground with regard to the so-called atheists?[41]

40. Thomas J. J. Altizer, and William Hamilton, *Radical Theology and the Death of God*, Penguin Books, Harmondsworth, 1968, p. 121.

41. John Baillie, *Our Knowledge of God*, Oxford University Press, 1939, p. 52.

Baillie comes very close in this passage to taking a line of argument which is unanswerable. By this I mean the kind of argument found throughout the works of Freud. For example,[42] Freud maintains that we each desire to expose ourselves, sexually. We are inhibited from doing this openly, but the desire takes other forms, such as the telling of jokes about sex. If I were to respond to this analysis and say that I understand and appreciate it, but that personally I do not feel, in all possible honesty, that it is true of my situation, then I should be confronted with the typical Freudian counter. Yes, 'in all possible honesty', but quite apart from what you think, you *really* desire sexual exposure. It is one of the difficulties of discussing the Freudian position, that we cannot continue a rational discussion in face of the 'really'. In a remarkably similar fashion, Baillie comes very close to telling the atheist that while he thinks, in all possible honesty, that there is no God and that he has no experience or knowledge of God, 'really' there is knowledge of God in the depths of his being. When we get ourselves into the position of saying that contrary to all available evidence we know what a man 'really' thinks, better than he himself knows, then there can be no further discussion.

It is this *line* of argument that is unanswerable, however true or false its conclusions may be. However, Baillie's paradigm suggests that the argument may be evaluated on other grounds. The paradigm is that the solipsist may say that he does not believe in the reality of his neighbour, but in stretching out his hand to greet his neighbour, he undermines by his practice what he claims to believe. The way he lives contradicts what he says he believes. On the basis of this paradigm we should have to ask Baillie: What kind of action performed by an atheist would count as evidence of belief in

42. 'Jokes and Their Relation to the Unconscious', *The Complete Psychological Works of Sigmund Freud*, trans. James Strachey, Hogarth Press, London, 1960, Vol. 8, p. 98f.

God? I cannot conceive of such evidence (if we leave aside the 'really' line of interpretation). No act of goodness, kindness, justice or mercy need be interpreted as evidence of belief in God.[43]

More recently the final denial of atheism was presented by J. A. T. Robinson in an esssay entitled 'Can a Truly Contemporary Person Not Be an Atheist?'[44] Robinson states the atheist case in three propositions. God is intellectually superfluous. God is emotionally dispensable. God is morally intolerable. The first two correspond to Bonhoeffer's rejection of God as the problem solver and need fulfiller. The third is the old chestnut about God and the problem of evil. Therein lies the weakness of Robinson's case. It is not an account of atheism at all, but a *religious* view of atheism. It is a tame atheism, allowed out of its cage for a stroll around. It is encouraged to growl at given points, and only those points, before being led back into the cage again. Three cheers for the brave secular theologian, who has faced the terrors of a confrontation with atheism and maintained his faith! Meanwhile the beast slips off its coat to reveal the vicar's son, who is only reacting against his father's profession, and 'really' believes in God after all. Such is the pantomime of the debate between secular theology and tame atheism.

For convenience the term 'atheist' has been used in this

43. There is of course the classic case of the man who claimed to be an atheist, but when he was questioned it transpired that his atheism began on the day when his fiancée ran off with a Sunday School teacher. Such a man might indeed believe in God despite his protests of atheism. But this example does not assist Baillie, for two reasons. The first is that it could not be held to be a general paradigm of atheism. Baillie would not want to argue that there is some such psychological crisis behind every assertion of atheism. The second reason is that even so, it would still be impossible to point to evidence in the man's life which would count for belief in God. Even Voltaire raised his hat as he passed a church.

44. J. A. T. Robinson, *The New Reformation?*, Appendix I, S.C.M. Press Ltd, London, 1965.

section, but we should not be misled by it. It is a short way of referring to those who live without God. Strictly and historically speaking, it represents a position which is arrived at by considerable argumentation. It is the denial of the existence of God. But there are very few people going around these days who qualify for the title 'atheist' in this strict form. Some vicars, with a 2 : 2 in Philosophical Theology, enjoy tackling the difficulties in believing in God. The problem of free will, and problem of evil – these are always good for a start. Now these may be problems for religious people, but they are not problems for atheists, contemporary atheists. For those who do not believe in God, free will and evil are not talking points. Nor has it ever occurred to them that their problems might be solved by a supernatural being, or their needs fulfilled in the same way. We do not speak of 'a-unicornists', to refer to those who do not believe in unicorns. No one qualifies for that title, since no one thinks there is anything to deny in the first place. The contemporary situation is, I believe, similar with respect to belief in God. In the strict sense of the word, there are few a-theists going around today for the simple reason that it does not occur to a large number of people that there is anything to deny. It is in this sense that Robinson's question 'Can a truly contemporary person not be an atheist?' should be put. The majority of people today are atheists not because certain 'difficulties' prevent them from believing in God, but because there is nothing in their experience which might lead them to suspect that there is a God.

Robinson in this essay wishes to indicate that although a contemporary person might fall into an easy atheism because of a superficial view of life, when he looks at life as it 'really' is, he will not be able to maintain his atheism. I wish to quote at some length the experience of the world which Robinson considers makes atheism finally untenable.

The man who finds himself compelled to acknowledge the reality of *God*, whatever he may call him or however he may image him, is the man who, through the mathematical regularities and through the functional values, is met by the same grace and the same claim that he recognizes in the I–Thou relation with another person. It may come to him through nature, through the claims of artistic integrity or scientific truth, through the engagements of social justice or of personal communion. Yet always it comes with an overmastering givenness and demand such as no other thing or person has the power to convey or the right to require. Like the child Samuel in the Temple, confusing the call of God with the voice of Eli, he may think at first that it can simply be identified with or contained within the finite relationship by which it is mediated. He may not be able to tell what to make of it, he may find it profoundly disturbing, but he knows it in the end to be inescapable and unconditional. In this relationship, too, he discovers himself known and judged and accepted for what ultimately he is. He finds in it for himself the way, the truth and the life. And if he is a Christian, he recognizes and acknowledges this grace and claim supremely in the person of Jesus Christ, the definition at one and the same time of a genuinely human existence and of this intangible, ineffable reality of 'God'.[45]

This passage has importance beyond the particular place in which it is here discussed, and has a bearing on the whole of this book; at the risk of tedium I wish to make some detailed comments about it.

One of the basic assumptions of the religious man's denial that atheism can be finally sustained, is the assumption that atheists are fleeing from God – in much the same way that Augustine fled from God. Thus Robinson speaks of the man who is 'compelled' to acknowledge God, and also of the 'inescapable' nature of the reality. I have in mind some very fine individuals who never have believed in God. They do not need to be compelled to look nor prevented from escape.

They are in fact already seeking something. My argument is that they may find this something, if they are encouraged to face the challenge of the way of transcendence, the way which involves faith in Jesus Christ as the definitive revelation of the way, the truth and the life for men. It is interesting therefore to see some of these points paralleled at the end of the above quotation from Robinson, where he speaks about the way, the truth and the life, and also of Jesus Christ as 'the definition ... of a genuinely human existence ...'. The option I am describing is a purely secular one, and the problem in this passage we are considering is in trying to identify in what way Robinson agrees with this and yet tries to say something more.

What more is there to be said? In the final chapters of this book we shall be considering the transcendent nature of the elements of our experience which we call judgement, grace, faith and so forth. But what is there left over apart from the secular understanding of these experiences? It is not clear, when Robinson uses the terminology of I–Thou, whether he is saying that the experience of grace and judgement in our lives, when correctly understood, leads us to see that in these elements we have a relationship with a supernatural, or non-secular, being. The difficulty is that Robinson appears to be encouraging men to identify an experience of what I have been calling transcendence, and then call it the experience of God. Surely we cannot confer on a general experience a name which has had such a specific use in the past. The opening sentence in the above quotation says that a man can give an experience the name 'God', 'whatever he may call him or however he may image him. . .'. But if our language is to bear communication, there must be some consistency in our use of words. God, for Christians, actually refers to a personal being. Unless in and through the transcendent experience there is *also* an experience of personal encounter, then to call the experience an experience of God is a very arbitrary and misleading use of this specialized name.

Are there two realities here, the experience of various transcendent elements and also another reality, called God? Robinson compares the relationship of the two to the legend about the prophet Samuel when a boy. God called Samuel, and at first the child thought the voice was the voice of Eli, the priest. But is this really a helpful analogy? That incident is one of the thin line of theophanies referred to at the outset of this section. The legend about Samuel tells us that God spoke directly to the child, and that Eli had *not* spoken at all. The example is precisely the opposite of the situation Robinson wishes to describe. The analogy should be rather with the prophetic works, in which the prophets often convey God's word to the people in the first person, as if their speech were identical with the word of God. Then, to have an encounter with the word of the prophet would be to encounter the word of God. But only those who believed in God already would interpret the words of the prophet as the word of God. In the words of the prophet, the sensitive non-believer would meet only transcendent elements of human existence, such as judgement and grace.

To move to the conclusion, if there is to be any consistency in our language, then the word 'God' must refer to a supernatural being not identical with any or all of the elements of our experience of the secular world. The experience of God (theophanies apart) must be in connection with our experience of the world, but must involve something more. Above all, the 'more' must carry with it the experience of personal encounter. And this is what divides contemporary atheism off from the tame atheism described by Robinson. The contemporary atheist may well experience transcendent elements in human experience, and may – as I have argued in the Introduction – come to faith in Jesus Christ as the definitive revelation of human existence. He may experience all this, and yet not experience a personal encounter in this new understanding of reality. As religious experience was defined in the previous section, this personal encounter is fundamental. On balance, it seems from the passage quoted that Robinson believes that man experiences a 'relationship' through the elements of experience of the world. This is crucial. There can be unworthy and highly anthropomorphic images of God, and there can be purified and proper images of God. But either way I do not believe that the majority of Christians would understand an experience to be justifiably described as an experience of God, unless part of the experience was that of relationship, personal relationship. The contemporary atheist is not necessarily a man who is oblivious to morals or ideals. He may be sensitive to transcendent values, but above all he is a man who does not find himself involved in any personal relationship with reality. I realize this phrase 'any personal relationship with reality' sounds very odd indeed. It is not the kind of expression that an atheist would use. It is the kind of odd phrase that a theologian is tempted to use when he tries to argue that atheism is untenable, and it simply reflects the fact that there must be something very wrong with the way in which the argument is developed.

Robinson would be right in maintaining the final denial of atheism, if, and only if, sensitive atheists who are aware of and committed to transcendent values and elements in their experience, experienced in and through all this a personal relationship with One who judges and commands, who forgives and loves. But unfortunately for Robinson such atheists do not find themselves 'compelled to acknowledge the reality of God'. The reason is the same reason given in the previous section. The supposed relationship is part of the interpretation of the experience, and also, the terminology is consciously or unconsciously calculated to predispose us to a theistic interpretation of the experience.

Some other statements in the Appendix indicate the persistent tendency to misrepresent atheism. 'God is a reality of life whom one cannot ultimately evade.'[46] But as already stated, atheism is not necessarily a flight from transcendence. The atheist may well be seeking, not evading. It is too easy to *blame* atheism. The final quotation tends to settle the extended discussion of the long quotation. 'The one who is superfluous as a hypothesis becomes all too present as a subject in encounter.'[47] Unfortunately, although the tradition of the final denial of atheism would like to maintain this, it just is not so. The characteristic of contemporary atheism is the absence of anything which could justifiably be interpreted as experience of a subject of personal encounter, a subject with whom a relationship is possible.

46. ibid., p. 119.   47. ibid., p. 119.

CHAPTER 2

New Definitions of God

So far we have been considering two groups of men. The first group are religious, and the second are not. The first group believe in God, and the second do not. But the situation is more complex than our analysis would suggest. We turn now to look at two other positions, not satisfactorily placed within the old framework. Both of these positions are atheist positions, at least by traditional standards. The first position involves looking for a new and credible way of thinking about God. Ultimately I think such attempts have failed, and so we have, paradoxically, men who claim to be religious, but who have no acceptable definition of God. The other position is also paradoxical, exemplified in the phrase 'Christian atheism', which if somehow still Christian is by traditional standards equally atheist. We shall discuss these two modern forms of atheism in turn in this chapter and the next.

In discussing the nature of religious experience, we took a definition from C. A. Campbell, who claims it to be 'a state of mind comprising belief in the reality of a supernatural being or beings endued with transcendent power and worth, together with the complex emotive attitude of worship intrinsically appropriate thereto'. We said that although some might consider this a somewhat arbitrary definition, yet it represents the main stream of thinking of every branch of the Church, throughout its whole history. In the long history of the Church, if we are objective and honest about it, few things would satisfy the definition of catholicity given by Vincent of Lérins: 'that Faith which has been believed everywhere, always and by all . . .'[1] Given the development in Christian thought on every conceivable element of the faith, only one element of Christian faith seems to qualify. Appropriately enough this one element, which has been maintained throughout the history of the Church, and through the spread of the Church geographically, has been the belief in God very much as defined in the statement from C. A. Campbell. The doctrine of God has developed, but it has always been based on the early understanding of God as a supernatural being who is to be worshipped. It is for this reason that in the previous chapter atheism was characterized as the position of those who have no belief in such a being, and cannot worship him. Surely when the day comes that God cannot be addressed as 'Our Father', where the word 'Father' bears some analogous relationship to the ordinary word 'father', then this change will be so central that the Christian religion will be changed into something else.

It will not escape the careful reader of contemporary theology that there are not a few theologians today who do not believe in the traditional God of the Christian religion. Or conversely, the God in whom they believe is essentially different from the traditional understanding of God. I wish to examine in some detail two new definitions of God, and inquire into the relationship between the new and the traditional understandings of God. It will be my contention that they are not compatible with the traditional understanding, and are therefore, by catholic standards, atheistic. A second objective more central to our argument will be to show that neither position is likely to bring contemporary atheism any closer to belief in God. And, ironically, should modern men be

1. Vincent of Lérins, *The Commonitory*, II/6, trans. C. A. Heurtley, *Nicene and Post-Nicene Fathers* (second Series), W. B. Eerdmans, Grand Rapids, Michigan, 1955, Vol. XI, p. 132.

impressed by these new definitions of God, they would only be converted to a new form of atheism.

We are told by sophisticated theologians that two factors in the main are responsible for the present position, in which it is no longer possible to believe in the 'God of traditional theism'. By this phrase I shall mean precisely the God defined by Campbell, that God who has been believed in 'everywhere, always and by all' within the Church. The seriousness of the contention about the impossibility of belief in the God of traditional theism has not been fully realized. It is not comparable to a statement that it is no longer possible to believe in spirit-possession. In so far as the Christian religion is based on belief in the God who is called 'Our Father', then if such belief is said to be impossible today, this would mean for Christianity a μετάβασις εἰς ἄλλο γένος. It may be an interesting social phenomenon, but it cannot be called the Christian religion.

Bearing this in mind, the two factors could be identified as the secularization of our culture and the influence of fundamental ontology. The first factor is a very complex one indeed, but it is related to what Bonhoeffer said about being unable to believe in God as a problem solver and a need fulfiller. The world is understood and controlled in its own terms, and not by reference to a supernatural being. The second factor, though of considerably less importance in our culture, has been very important in modern theology. It involves the influence on theology of the 'fundamental ontology' of the phenomenologist, Martin Heidegger. As is well known, the aim of his *magnum opus* was 'to work out the question of the meaning of *Being* and to do so concretely'.[2] Being, according to Heidegger, is said to be the most universal of concepts, 'but the "universality" of "Being" is not that of a *class* or *genus*'.[3] Being is not the uppermost in

2. Martin Heidegger, *Being and Time*, trans. J. Macquarrie and E. Robinson, S.C.M. Press, London, 1962, p. 18.   3. ibid., p. 22.

a series of entities, and certainly not one entity among others. 'The Being of entities "is" not itself an entity'.[4] Already we see that it is difficult to speak of Being using the grammar which normally serves us well enough in describing the world. But Heidegger has promised that his work will be concrete, phenomenological, and not merely speculative. 'Being is always the Being of an entity.'[5]

The implications of fundamental ontology for theology were seen in the 1920s by Tillich, and his whole system reflects the contribution of Heidegger (though Tillich was too eclectic to be called a follower of Heidegger). One of the many insights of Professor John Knox is that Christology became 'higher' and 'higher', since whenever a new challenge to the significance of Christ appeared, the Church always chose the more exalted option. In a not dissimilar way, the doctrine of God has been raised to higher levels. God is no longer conceived of as one god among many. When the question about location was put, it was inevitable that he would eventually be worshipped as the one God, and the God of the whole world. But what is his relationship to other beings? Anselm confessed God as 'a being than which nothing greater can be conceived'. In our own century this has been reckoned not 'high' enough. The way forward was offered by Heidegger's work on Being. Thus when Heidegger says that Being 'is' not, Tillich applies this to theology. 'God does not exist. He is being-itself beyond essence and existence.'[6] He can also speak of God as 'the ground of our Being' and can refer to 'the God above the God of theism'.[7] Thus theologians came to the conclusion that while it was no longer possible to believe in the God of traditional theism (and Anselm's definition is within the traditional form), it might be possible to speak of God in a higher and

4. ibid., p. 26.   5 ibid., p. 29.
6. Tillich, *Systematic Theology*, Vol. I, p. 227.
7. Paul Tillich, *The Courage to Be*, Collins, London 1962, p. 183.

more 'worthy' way yet. Tillich's own position would qualify as a new definition of God, but I wish to consider two more recent attempts to find new ways to speak about God.

PROCESS THEOLOGY

No single author or work can be taken as representative of the school of Process Theology, and there is no particular justification for concentrating attention on one essay written from this standpoint. Of the many works which could have been examined[8] I have selected one which is manageable in the context of this discussion, and one which has been rightly praised by those who find this approach helpful. Schubert Ogden delivered a lecture entitled 'The Reality of God'[9] in 1965, during the hectic period of the Death of God movement in America. It sometimes appears that even more important than coming to the right answer, is finding an adequate way of formulating the right question. Ogden considers that the way in which the problem of God was approached precluded an adequate solution. In his essay, he sets out to reformulate the question, confident that a new and satisfactory way of speaking about God can be found – indeed has already been found but not yet taken seriously throughout the theological world.

I should like to begin with a quotation from the essay which is important for Ogden, but which also has some relevance to this book and the position outlined so far. In rejecting the analysis of the 'Death of God' theologians, Ogden concludes by saying this:

8. e.g. D D. Williams, *The Spirit and the Forms of Love* (1969); P. Hamilton, *The Living God and the Modern World* (1967); J. B. Cobb, *A Christian Natural Theology* (1966).

9. Published in Schubert M. Ogden, *The Reality of God, and Other Essays*, S.C.M. Press, London, 1967.

However absurd talking about God might be, it could never be so obviously absurd as talking of Christian faith without God. If theology is possible today only on secularistic terms, the more candid way to say this is to admit that theology is not possible today at all.[10]

The first point of course runs counter to what has been said above in the Introduction. I see no objection to having faith in Jesus Christ as the definitive revelation of the way, the truth and the life for men, without belief in God. We have already dealt with secular faith in Jesus Christ at some length. What would be absurd, of course, would be to have faith in Jesus Christ as the *Son of God*, without belief in God. But that is quite a different position. (Ultimately the two kinds of faith might produce the same kind of life, but naturally the content of the two faiths would be different.) The second point to note from the quotation is that God is necessary for the doing of theology. This might seem unobjectionable, but it will be discussed more fully in Part 2. It would certainly be the end of Christian *religion* if the being of God could not be affirmed. So confident is Ogden that he has found a way through the current impasse that he indulges in some bridge-burning. There can be no theology without a viable way of speaking about the being of God. This is his position, and should he finally fail to establish a new and viable way, then we should expect him to stop doing theology.

So far in this book we have not dealt with any criticisms of religion or belief in God. We have simply noted that many people do not and apparently cannot believe in the traditional Christian God. It is interesting to note that the attack upon the God of traditional theism has been mounted most acutely by contemporary theologians. *Why* men cannot believe in such a God, when at least some of their ancestors did, is a very complex cultural problem indeed, as we have

10. ibid., p. 14.

already noted. But *that* they should not believe in such a God, Ogden holds to be completely right.

> We are justified not in rejecting God, as such, but in casting aside the supernaturalistic conception of his reality, which is in fact untenable, given our typical experience and thought as secular men.[11]

It is an interesting exercise to note in the margin of a book each occasion on which the author promises to deal further with a topic at a later stage, or give a justification for a contentious statement at the end of the book. (I hope that the margins of this book have been suitably marked.) We must not be carried along too uncritically by Ogden's phraseology here. When he speaks about not rejecting God 'as such', he is implying that there is another way of speaking about God apart from the (in his view) now untenable way of traditional theism. On the same page, he further insists that 'the major obstacle to real progress in dealing with the problem of God is the supernaturalistic theism of the metaphysical tradition'. This may well be, but the language of 'God as such' will only be justified if Ogden's new way of speaking of God represents to us a God in some recognizable continuity with the God of traditional theism, the God in other words in whom the vast majority of Christians of every age – including the present – have believed. Unless there is a recognizable continuity, then we shall have been led astray by this phrase 'God as such'.

In the previous chapter, we dealt with examples of a tradition within Christian thought which denies that atheism is finally tenable. To those examples we might have added the work of Schubert Ogden, who wishes 'to claim that for the secular man of today, as surely as for any other man, faith in God cannot but be real because it is in the final analysis unavoidable'.[12] He was not included with the others, partly because of this more detailed study to follow, but partly be-

11. ibid., p. 19.   12. ibid., p. 21.

cause his position is in fact in basic disagreement with theirs. He actually denies the existence of the God they affirm to be unavoidable. He applauds those atheists who have refused to affirm belief in such a being.

> The real force of this denial is not to exclude faith in God altogether, but to make fully explicit the incompatibility between our experience as secular men and the supernaturalistic theism of our intellectual tradition.[13]

When Ogden moves on to say, 'By its very character, Christian faith so understands God that everyone must in some sense believe in him and no one can in every sense deny him,'[14] he goes beyond the requirements of dogmatics, and begins to pave the way for his own restatement of belief in God. The only way in which the phrase 'must believe' can be meaningful is by redefining God in such a way that the experience of God becomes part of what it means to be alive-in-the-world. Such a redefinition is not difficult. The real problem is to show that this God is in recognizable continuity with the God of the Christian tradition.

We have already noted Robinson's identification of the elements of 'grace' and 'claim' in our experience, which are in his view the locus of the experience of God in our lives. Ogden, with acknowledgement to the help he has found in the works of Stephen Toulmin, speaks of 'an original confidence in the meaning and worth of life'[15] and of 'our invincible faith'[16] that our moral choices make a difference. As Robinson identifies God with the experience of reality as grace and claim, so Ogden moves to the point of saying, 'I hold that the primary use or function of "God" is to refer to the objective ground in reality itself of our ineradicable confidence in the final worth of our existence.'[17]

13. ibid., p. 25.   14. ibid., p. 21.
15. ibid., p. 34.   16. ibid., p. 36.
17. ibid., p. 37.

It is at this point that Ogden begins to indicate what is involved in his new conception of God. It certainly looks interesting, exciting, intriguing and very creative. But unfortunately with the conclusion reached in the last quotation, all is lost. He is now set on a course of describing how we experience reality, but there is no justification whatsoever for describing this reality as God. We saw that Robinson wavered for a time, but finally opted for what is essentially the position of traditional theism. In the end, although we experience God in our other experiences, he is quite distinct from them. Ogden, with more consistency, maintains that there are not two realities but one. But the cost of consistency is, I believe, that he breaks the necessary continuity between his new use of the word 'God', and the traditional use of the term.

The traditional doctrines of Creation and Providence affirm that we are right to have a basic confidence in reality. But this is far from saying that 'faith' in the trustworthiness of our environment is an experience of God. We may now recall what Ogden said earlier, that 'faith in God cannot but be real because it is in the final analysis unavoidable'. We can see now precisely why it is unavoidable. 'Faith in God' now means that 'original confidence in the meaning and worth of life' without which we could not function as human beings in the world. The crudest possible analogy for what Ogden has done is to say that every man believes in God, where 'believing in God' = 'having a head'. Did you ever know a man who did not have a head? It is not difficult to find some element in reality which is basic to human existence as we know it, and then call that element 'God'. The objection is of course that the result is very confusing, since the word 'God' already has a meaning which is quite different.

The reason why Robinson withdrew from the consistency of a position such as Ogden's is, I believe, because Robinson saw that part of the content of the word 'God' is that the experience of God must be in some sense personal. If Ogden could show that 'the objective ground in reality itself' on which our 'ineradicable confidence' is based was experience as in some sense personal, then he might yet be permitted to use the word 'God' to describe it. And so we proceed with his argument.

Ogden wishes to make sure that this 'secular faith' corresponds to our experience of the world. The experience of God must be 'dipolar'. That is it must reflect two basic characteristics of our experience. God must be actually involved in real relations in the world, involved in all its relativity, but since he also is the basis of our unshakable confidence, he must be in some sense also absolute. God must be conceived of 'as at once supremely relative and supremely absolute'.[18] The traditional theism, now rejected by Ogden, could not fully integrate God with the whole while yet maintaining his absolute nature. But a dipolar conception of God can be developed by the application of neoclassical metaphysics.[19] Unlike classical metaphysics, this contemporary form is not based on static categories of substance and being, but makes use of the concepts of process and creative becoming. It is concerned with the embodied nature of personal existence and social relationships.

If we begin by taking the self as thus experienced as paradigmatic for reality as such, the result is a complete revolution of classical metaphysics.[20]

By *this* 'analogy of being', however, God, too, must be conceived as a genuine temporal and social reality . . .[21]

Whatever this means, it is clear that the word God is now

18. ibid., p. 48.
19. e.g. A. N. Whitehead, *Science and the Modern World*; *Process and Reality*; C. Hartshorne, *The Divine Relativity*; *The Logic of Perfection*; *Creative Synthesis and Philosophic Method*.
20. Ogden, *The Reality of God*, p. 58.   21. ibid.

being applied to 'reality as such', whatever that means. The argument is in danger of becoming circular. Reality as we experience it seems to justify our ineradicable confidence in the worth of our lives. God is the basis of this confidence. And now God is identified with reality as such. It seems to amount to saying that we are justified in having confidence in reality, because it is that kind of reality. Of course we could conceive of other realities which would not justify our confidence. But it does seem rather arbitrary to distinguish between these two kinds of reality by calling one 'God'.

But our main problem has not yet been answered. Does this new conception of God preserve any personal dimension? There are not a few attempts being currently made at redefining the concept of God, and once you have learned the ground rules of the game, it is always intriguing to look out for the first appearance of the personal pronoun. It is not difficult to define reality as we experience it in some unified way. Nor is it difficult to apply to it the term 'God', however arbitrary the application may seem. But the trick is to establish continuity in usage between the normal use of the word 'God' and the new use. This theological sleight of hand is regularly exposed by the sudden appearance of the pronoun 'he' to describe a reality which hitherto has been described as 'it'. On page 59 of *The Reality of God*, the bridging pronoun is thrown across the gap, and 'reality as such,' alias 'God' can now be addressed as 'he'. God is not understood in the old static unchanging categories.

Rather, he, too, is understood to be continually in process of self-creation, synthesizing in each new moment of his experience the whole of achieved actuality with the plenitude of possibility as yet unrealized.[22]

Let us be clear that neoclassical metaphysics is vastly more credible, adequate and meaningful as an expression of our

22. ibid., p. 59.

experience of reality and our present state of knowledge about the individual, society and the natural world than any previous system. Over a century ago, Kierkegaard could not find words adequate to praise the achievement of Hegel as a philosopher. Nor could he find words adequate to describe the absurdity of basing theology upon that philosophy. I have no desire to detract from process philosophy, as one of the most brilliant and creative attempts at a metaphysical system as yet conceived by man. Every element of our experience can, in principle, find a place within it. But why any theologian should try or even want to entitle this cosmic chop-suey, 'God', is beyond my understanding.

No case as yet has been made out for any justifiable use of the personal pronoun 'he', and yet this is a necessary element in the concept of God, if the name is to be used with any continuity with the normal understanding of God. The basis finally rests on the paradigm already quoted, the embodied self.

As the eminent Self, by radical contrast, God's sphere of interaction or body is the whole universe of nondivine beings, with each one of which his relation is unsurpassably immediate and direct.[23]

I can see no justification for this use of the *analogia entis*. In its traditional forms the 'unknown' to be established by analogy may vary:

analogia entis		*analogia gratiae* (Barth)	
$\dfrac{\text{human existence}}{\text{human love}}$	$\div$	$\dfrac{\text{divine existence}}{\text{divine love}}$ $\div$ $\dfrac{\text{divine existence}}{\text{divine love}}$	$\dfrac{\text{human existence}}{\text{human love}}$

In the traditional form of analogy it is the meaning of the divine attribute which is to be established. In the Barthian analogy, of course, it is the proper meaning of human characteristics which is to be established. Quite apart from the

23. ibid., p. 60.

whole question about the logic of analogy, I suggest that Ogden is now in the position of offering something which is in effect quite the opposite of the analogy of being. His proportionality would look like this:

$$\frac{\text{physical/temporal nature of human existence}}{\text{existence of the self}} \div \frac{\text{physical/temporal nature of the world}}{\text{existence of the world self}}$$

But the basis for the analogy of being is the known existence of beings on either side of the proportionality equation. It cannot be used as an analogy of 'physical/temporal nature', because there is no analogy between an individual and the whole world. Or more precisely, the elements of human existence which most resemble the world (of which they are part), are just those elements which have least to do with our understanding of the self. There is no evidence that the world is self-conscious, rational, purposive or capable of exercising moral choice. Contrary to Ogden's claim, he has not given us an analogy of being, and worse than that, there is no basis to the analogy which he has given us. Ogden has not shown us why 'reality as such' should be called God, and has certainly not given grounds for conceiving of God in any personal sense.

At the beginning of his essay we were told that although the God of traditional theism was no longer credible, this did not mean that we were justified in rejecting 'God as such'. But what other God is there than the God of traditional theism, or how else can he be conceived of? Ogden is in the unenviable position of having said that he cannot continue his work as a theologian without a viable way of speaking about God, and yet having dismissed the God of traditional theism, he has failed to establish an alternative way of speaking about God.

ONTO-THEOLOGY

As previously noted, Tillich would serve very well as an example of a theologian consciously relating his work to ontology. But I wish to inquire into the relationship of Heidegger and theology, as a possible way of redefining God. Tillich used Heidegger, but does not represent a 'pure' use of his work. There were many influences present in Tillich's work. He was most open-minded. He not only listened to criticism, but always seemed to be able to absorb it into his system. To this extent it is more difficult to see precisely what did come to him from Heidegger.

Instead of the system of Paul Tillich, we shall consider the 'existential-ontological theism' of John Macquarrie. The first lecture I ever attended as a theological student was in a course offered by Macquarrie at Trinity College, Glasgow. Since that time I have never ceased to be impressed by his work. At that time he had already published *An Existentialist Theology*,[24] the definitive exposition of Bultmann's use of Heidegger. Since then Macquarrie has pursued his own use of Heidegger, and the result is to be seen in his *Principles of Christian Theology*.[25] This last mentioned book provides the best example to date of onto-theology, and in particular the use of Heidegger in the refashioning of the concept of God. It is not simply that Heidegger is more consistently used by Macquarrie than he was by Tillich. It is rather that Macquarrie has understood Heidegger better than Tillich, and has carried the insights of Heidegger, sometimes only enigmatically hinted at, into all aspects of theological thinking. It is with some hesitation that I shall conclude that, for all his sensitivity and sophistication, Macquarrie has not found a new and viable way to speak about God.

24. John Macquarrie, *An Existentialist Theology*, S.C.M. Press, London, 1955.

25. John Macquarrie, *Principles of Christian Theology*, S.C.M. Press, London, 1967.

The old textbooks on theology used to begin with Natural Theology. They sought to establish – *remoto Christo* – the framework within which Christian (Dogmatic) Theology could be presented. Natural Theology attempted to demonstrate the existence of God, the immortality of the soul and so forth, constructing a rational view of the world which would be acceptable to any man of intellect and sense. Once the foundations had been laid without recourse (at least acknowledged recourse) to revelation, the unbeliever seemed to be led unwittingly to the very threshold of faith. Natural Theology has not been fashionable in this century, partly because of the Dialectical Theology of Karl Barth and the rejection of the idea of jumping into the theological circle from a common platform with atheism. But Natural Theology has lately been ignored because it failed to do what it set out to achieve. On logical grounds many of its arguments are now seen to be invalid, but even the parts not subject to this criticism do not constitute an acceptable account of the world for the non-believer today.

It may seem surprising, therefore, that Macquarrie begins with Natural Theology, or at least what he calls a New Style Natural Theology. It is new style, not least because instead of being a supposedly 'neutral' account of reality offered by theologians, the basis of the Natural Theology now is the fundamental ontology of Martin Heidegger. Three points have to be made in this connection. The first is that it is still Philosophical *Theology* because Macquarrie wishes to maintain that the way in which reality is described turns out to be the way in which we should speak about God. Macquarrie does not set out to prove the existence of God, or indeed to re-establish a place at all for the God of traditional theism. But happily (and this is why Heidegger has been chosen) by rejecting the direct approach of focusing attention on the existence of God, it transpires that by the long way round the being of God is established. Having cast his phenomenological bread upon the waters, he finds that it returns – even if by a rather devious path. The second point about Philosophical Theology is that, unlike the old Natural Theology, it actually contributes something to Dogmatics. To pursue a metaphor already used, the old Natural Theology led men to the doorway of faith. But the Dogmatic house was not determined by it. New Style Natural Theology is quite different. The Dogmatic house is actually determined in shape by its Philosophical foundations. Macquarrie is not only looking for a way of speaking which will assist non-believers to understand the being of God. Having rejected the traditional way of speaking about God, Macquarrie himself is looking for a new way. So that Philosophical Theology has a much more important relationship to Dogmatics (or Symbolic Theology as Macquarrie calls it) than the old Natural Theology. It is supposed to assist the non-believer, but it actually provides a new way whereby the believer may speak of God, and it influences the rest of theology. The third point about Philosophical Theology, thus conceived, is that it automatically suffers from a certain weakness. It can only be as useful as the original philosophical position allows. Now, as already noted, Macquarrie develops some of the enigmatic insights of Heidegger, and he also deals with minor objections to Heidegger. But what of the major objections to Heidegger? No matter how well conceived the use to which fundamental ontology is put, any basic criticism of it will be carried into Philosophical Theology. We shall be looking at this later in respect of the predication of the verb 'to be'. The other question raised against Macquarrie's Philosophical Theology is the choice of Heidegger at all in giving a non-religious account of reality. For example, Heidegger's existential analytic is certainly very congenial to theology. But does it give, as it were, *independent* confirmation of the correctness of the biblical doctrine of man? Bultmann is clear on this point.

The question is not whether the nature of man can be discovered apart from the New Testament. As a matter of fact, it has not been discovered without the aid of the New Testament, for modern philosophy is indebted to it and to Luther and Kierkegaard.[26]

Bultmann readily used Heidegger's analytic, but he found it convenient to use mainly because Heidegger did not function as a 'pure' phenomenologist.[27] Heidegger's account of the modern situation is not generally acceptable in non-religious circles, and this is a serious criticism, since at least part of the purpose of Philosophical Theology is to describe reality in a current manner. We shall return to this point also.

Macquarrie wishes to provide a non-religious context in which the terms such as grace, faith and sin can appear naturally. Inevitably he begins with an analysis of human existence. It follows the division into inauthentic and authentic life which characterizes the analytic developed by Heidegger. We cannot fully discuss the point yet, since we have just got started but this is an example of the difficulty of using Heidegger as a basis for Philosophical Theology. Heidegger has taken over from the Christian doctrine of man the Pauline division of man in sin and man in faith. In the light of what God intended for man, the former is inferior to the latter. But Heidegger never gives any justification for *his* judgement that one kind of life is inferior (inauthentic).

The first theological term to be given a philosophical con-

26. Bultmann, *Kerygma and Myth*, Vol. I, p. 26.

27. We should in any case examine the assumption that pure phenomenology is even possible in principle. A phenomenologist might gain some objectivity on his subject by escaping from the cultural assumptions of his time and place, but the idea that there is a standpoint from which he might have a pure vision of his subject seems to me to be pre-Einstein and even pre-Hume. The sole exception to this would be the case of the standpoint of traditional theism, and this is precisely why there is a question raised against Heidegger as phenomenologist.

text and meaning is that of 'sin'. It describes the disparity between inauthentic and authentic living. As the etymology of ἁμαρτία implies, the former life misses the mark. Man is alienated from his authentic self. He is alienated too from society, but there is 'a deeper level where one feels alienated from the whole scheme of things'.[28] This is our first encounter with one of the criticisms of Heidegger already mentioned earlier. Heidegger gave a very fine analysis of human existence in his own time. So apt was the analysis for that period after the First World War, that Tillich throughout his life concentrated attention on alienation – or estrangement as he termed it.[29] The same situation which obtained in Europe after the First World War was recreated after the Second World War. In both periods, Europeans, especially the intellectuals, found that all cultural landmarks had been destroyed, and the fragile framework which gave life a context, significance and meaning, had been roughly dismantled. Both situations were ripe for the heart-searching despair of the French existentialist movement, the leading names of which were Sartre and Camus. With the recreation, after the Second World War, of the situation which had prevailed in the 1920s, it is not surprising that for a time Tillich's work, now produced in America and not Germany, should be read avidly. But this is not a description of Europe today, and certainly not of America or the Third World. I hope to discuss this point more fully in Part 2, but something can be said now. There are problems today, and men are no better than they were. But it is not a time for nursing one's existential despair. It is for this reason that existentialism as a philosophy, a literary standpoint and a theological basis has virtually no influence in Europe today, or anywhere

28. Macquarrie, *Principles of Christian Theology*, p. 62.

29. See especially Tillich, *Systematic Theology*, Vol. II, 1957, Ch. 14, 'The Marks of Man's Estrangement and the Concept of Sin', and Ch. 15, 'Existential Self-destruction and the Doctrine of Evil'.

else in the world. It brilliantly caught the mood of its day, but ours is another day and ours is another experience. I should be very surprised indeed if secular men today experienced 'a deeper level where one feels alienated from the whole scheme of things'.

By reading Heidegger, Sartre and Tillich, we can get a good idea of what the options were for men in a previous generation. Unfortunately, Macquarrie accepts their analyses as the options for today. This comes out clearly in the following passage, which is worth quoting:

> We can say then that the alternatives confronting us have been sharpened. Either we must go along with Sartre and company, and acknowledge that life is indeed a useless passion, so that the best we can hope for is to reduce its oppressiveness at one point or another, to patch up the situation here and there, without any hope or possibility of really overcoming the absurdity and frustration that belong intrinsically to human existence, as thrown possibility; or, if we are still seeking to make sense of life and to bring order into existence so that its potentialities can come to fulfilment, we have frankly to acknowledge that we must look for support beyond humanity itself, pervaded as this is with disorder.[30]

My concern with this line of reasoning is that while Macquarrie attempts to lay a foundation for speaking about God in ways meaningful to modern man, his failure is inevitable simply on cultural grounds. This is not the situation in which we find ourselves today. I personally do not know anyone who thinks life is absurd, or 'a useless passion'. Instead I see a threefold division: those who want to drop out of society (not life) as they find it; those who are relatively content to join society as they find it; and those who are passionately keen to change society for the better. In this context it is possible to call men to a secular faith in the 'way of transcendence', away from the thoughtless way of immanence. These

30. Macquarrie, *Principles of Christian Theology*, p. 63.

options have not as yet been fully described, but clearly this is a totally different analysis from the one offered by Macquarrie. The criticism I offer here is not in the first instance a logical one, but a cultural one. Just as I know no one who thinks of life as absurd, I know no one who feels 'cut off at the deepest level'. I fear Macquarrie may be misled into thinking that he has created a meaningful context for discussing sin, grace and so forth, when in fact the situation he describes is quite foreign to modern secular men. In discussing the failure of Natural Theology, it was pointed out that it is reckoned to have failed for logical and for cultural reasons. In the end it was but a religious man's view of how secular men thought. We should not be misled by the fact that professional atheists (of another generation) are being brought forward to testify. What we are presented with here is yet again a religious man's view of the world, and I have no doubt that it is meaningless to most secular men today (even to intellectuals, if that restriction were called for).

In discussing William Paley's *Natural Theology* [*sic*] we noted the tendency of theologians to drop into the use of terms which already have connotations prejudicial to the process by which we try to find a secular way to speak of the existence of God. We find this tendency exhibited throughout Macquarrie's argument. I am not simply referring to such an expression as 'feeling alienated' at 'a deeper level', which rather suggests that 'behind' reality, as we experience it, there is a depth not identical with the dimensions of the entities we experience in the world: we also hear of 'a depth beyond both man and nature',[31] and having faith in 'the wider being'.[32] But when we hear the following assertion, do the terms not already prejudice the 'philosophical' nature of Philosophical Theology? 'Human existence can make sense if this wider being supports and supplements the meagre heritage of our finite being as we strive to fulfil the

31. ibid., p. 64.   32. ibid., p. 70.

potentialities of our being.'[33] It is not difficult to see how our natural environment might assist human fulfilment, or prevent it. Similarly it is easy to see how society might assist or prevent human fulfilment. But what is the difference between the natural and social environment and 'the wider being'? Is the word 'being' used in some way that suggests it is not identical with things that have being? More to the point, it seems that being is regarded as somehow active. And above all, the suggestion is that being is discriminating: being assists fulfilment. We shall return to this last point later, but there is also another disturbing feature of the analysis, and that is the introduction of the concept of religion. Religious faith means faith in God. Nothing has been said so far about God. He is introduced much later, after the groundwork has been done. Yet quite suddenly we find 'religious faith' being identified with 'faith in being'.[34] This begs the whole question and makes a nonsense of the procedure of establishing a Philosophical Theology before proceeding to Symbolic Theology. If religious faith and faith in being can be identified so early in the argument, then it must already be possible to identify God and being. This is in general the *conclusion* to which Macquarrie wishes to come. Are we then involved in circular reasoning, when the conclusion becomes an assumption? This argument draws a line through the human community. On the one side are those who have faith in being (epitomized by religious faith) and on the other those who do not have such faith (Sartre *et hoc genus omne*). It is my argument throughout this book that this supposed division among men just does not correspond to our modern world.

Having noted the tendency to use terminology which predisposes us to accept a religious view of reality, we are not surprised to find this language becoming even more explicit, as in this statement that 'his *quest* for the sense of existence is met by the *gift* of a sense of existence',[35] and more particu-

33. ibid., p. 70.   34. ibid., p. 71.   35. ibid., p. 75.

larly, in the view that our quest for meaning encounters 'the directionally opposite *quest for man*'.[36] It is a standard criticism of Barth that he begins with Dogmatics, and does not build on a 'neutral' analysis, acceptable to men without faith. When we hear that 'holy being' is out looking for man, we might well conclude that it is more honest simply to begin, as does Barth, with Dogmatics.

Being has not really been discussed yet, but already it is taking on a certain character by the language of personification. Recalling what was said about Ogden's first application of the personal pronoun 'he', to 'reality as such', it is interesting to note that on page 78 of *Principles of Christian Theology*, being not only becomes 'holy being', but also for the first time the word is capitalized to stand out as Being. But what does it stand out from? From nothingness. (Or should it be Nothingness?) Once again we have the existential analysis; Heidegger on the significance of death for a true perspective on life, and of course Sartre on Being and Nothingness. It is, apparently, in the mood of anxiety that we receive revelation. But is this our experience today? It was not our age that W. H. Auden described as 'the age of anxiety'. Personally, I do understand what is meant by anxiety before Nothingness, but I still do not think this such a characteristic experience of this age that it can bear the weight of being the 'capacity for receiving revelation'.[37] How could we possibly know whether as a matter of fact revelation always presupposes the experience of anxiety before Nothingness?

We have been concerned about the way in which being, undefined, has been gradually referred to in ways which make it ripe for some kind of identification with God. Macquarrie says, at last, that being is not the being of any particular thing or the sum of the being of everything (and every person), and that it, being, 'is more truly beingful

36. ibid., p. 78.   37. ibid., p. 78.

than any of the particular beings which *are* in virtue of their participation in being'.[38] It is easy to be carried along by such an argument, especially when it deals with being, while inviting us to assimilate being to God. But we must not lose sight of the danger of this line of reasoning. It is open to the classical Kantian objection. '"Being" is obviously not a real predicate; that is, it is not a concept of something which could be added to the concept of a thing.'[39] Strange though it may seem at first, Kant says that 'a hundred real thalers do not contain the least coin more than a hundred possible thalers'.[40] Nothing is added to a thing to say that it exists. This additional fact is not an additional predicate. This holds true also of a thing which exists with a defect. This can be illustrated by the following example. A vehicle could be described thus: pick-up truck, four-wheel drive, V-8 engine, under-sealed bodywork. To add the word 'is' after the fourth predicate would not in fact add anything to the description. Of course whether or not a truck of that description existed would make a great deal of difference to a supplier or owner. We might say that the truck either exists or it does not, but the description of it remains the same. I suspect that Macquarrie, in introducing the idea of 'more truly beingful', is approaching a theory of degrees of being. In this case we might ask whether 'exists or does not exist' actually exhausts the possibilities. Perhaps the truck is as described, except that someone forgot to under-seal it. Clearly the truck exists, but not completely as described. But this is not a difference in degrees of being. The inferior truck is inferior by production standards, but its *existence* is not inferior. There are no degrees of being. Things either exist or they do not, have being or do not have being. Whether they are as good as they

38. ibid., p. 87.

39. Immanuel Kant, *Critique of Pure Reason*, trans. Norman Kemp Smith, abridged edition, Random House, New York, 1958, p. 282.

40. ibid.

might be, as efficient, as durable, as aesthetically pleasing – these questions refer to other standards of judgement. The bad truck is just as real as the good one. The weakness of paradigm cases is that they are never exactly the same as the case in question. It is one thing to say that the bad truck is just as real as the good truck, but would this be true of a bad man and a good man? Yes. A man might live a life shot through with contradictions, inconsistencies, alienated from himself and his fellows – but it would add nothing to this description to say 'and – is'. But is he not less of a man than he might be? Yes, by any kind of value-judgement he is less than he might be, but the less does not refer to his *existence*. Perhaps the point might be made more convincingly by Heidegger himself. In his terms (which are Macquarrie's terms too), the question is whether inauthentic existence is less real (or less 'beingful') than authentic existence. 'But the inauthenticity of *Dasein* does not signify any "less" Being or any "lower" degree of Being.'[41] Of course Macquarrie is not tied slavishly to what Heidegger says, but I think it is indicative of the fact that he has confused himself by the phrase 'holy being'. While there are clearly degrees of holiness, there are no degrees of being.[42]

41. Heidegger, *Being and Time*, p. 68.

42. For many years Macquarrie has had a special interest in the thought of Athanasius. (e.g. 'Demonology and the Classic Idea of Atonement', *Studies in Christian Existentialism*, S.C.M. Press, London, 1965, especially pp. 221ff.; 'Types of Theological Discourse. Case Study: The Language of St Athanasius', *God-Talk*, S.C.M. Press, London, 1967, pp. 123-46.) In *De Incarnatione*, Athanasius makes a very interesting connection between sin and non-existence. Through sin man loses the knowledge of God and is therefore turned back towards what does not exist (section 4). The salvation of man, who is by nature *logikos*, is achieved by his restoration through the incarnation of the *Logos*. (For a full account of this theology, see J. Roldanus, *Le Christ et l'Homme dans la Théologie d'Athanase d'Alexandrie*, E. J. Brill, Leiden, 1968, pp. 98ff.) We cannot pursue this subject at length, but it could be shown that this terminology

Heidegger's analytic is divided into two parts, inauthentic and authentic existence (though, very significantly, he can in practice say little about authentic existence). Heidegger, especially in the light of the last quotation given from *Being and Time*, does not think of Being playing an active role in man's affairs. This way of speaking does not make sense in the context of *Being and Time*. It is man's authentic self which calls to inauthentic man, calling him to his true existence.[43] As Macquarrie develops his argument, the division between inauthentic and authentic gets extended. It becomes not the authentic self calling its inauthentic, but Being, calling to the self. Being is conceived of as 'holy being', and is therefore to one side of the extended line. And yet evil men exist: they participate in being. But if 'Being is always the Being of an entity', as Heidegger says, is the being of an evil man evil or holy? The fact that this is an impossible question to answer merely indicates that it should never be asked. Being is not a predicate, but neither can it be qualified by adjectives such as 'holy' or 'evil'. Before leaving this point I should like to draw attention to the last phrase in the previous quotation from Macquarrie where he speaks of particular beings existing 'in virtue of their participation in being'. This is another confusing idea. Participating in being[44] implies that being exists apart from the entity which

associates an increase in evil with a diminution of being. It is precisely this tendency towards degrees of being as somehow a measure of value, which constitutes the fundamental weakness of Macquarrie's position.

43. I realize that the 'later' Heidegger says things which are more congenial to Macquarrie's position on the specific point which is to follow. But if Heidegger in *Being and Time* was regarded as being under the influence of Christian theology, the later Heidegger is clearly more so. (Cf. J. B. Cobb, and J. M. Robinson, *The Later Heidegger and Theology*, Harper & Row, New York, 1963; J. Macquarrie, 'Heidegger's Earlier and Later Work Compared', *Anglican Theological Review*, Vol. 49, No. 1, January 1967, pp. 3-16.)

44. Again the ontology exemplified by Athanasius.

is to come into existence. Heidegger has just been quoted again to the effect that this is not so. The phrase 'participating in being' really stems from the confusion about the predication of the verb 'to be'. It is as if 'being' were something bestowed upon an entity in order to make it exist. But as we have seen, being is not a quality which entities possess and *in virtue of which* they exist. Being does not pre-date the appearance of an entity. It is in fact the way we refer to the fact that there is such an entity. The same point is to be made about the following assertion. 'We ourselves *are*, and only through our participation in being can we think of it or name it, and only on the basis of its self-giving and self-disclosing to us can we know it.'[45] There could hardly be a better example of the need for linguistic analysis to prevent us misleading ourselves by our own language. Macquarrie maintains that it is only in virtue of the fact that we exist that we can investigate being. It would certainly make it more difficult if we did not exist, but I think the confusion still persists because basically even yet we have not been given a proper definition of being. After all the truck exists (if it does exist) because it was manufactured, not because the idea of a truck was there, and it was suddenly endowed with being. There is a medical (not to mention ethical) problem about defining life. When should a foetus be defined to be alive, so that to terminate a pregnancy would be to kill? Even if we decide that it is not 'alive' until it takes its first breath after birth, we cannot say that at the moment when it sucks in its first breath it begins to participate in being. Previously a foetus, now a baby. Clearly a great step, but not a step into being, as if being were waiting for it or calling it. Yet this is precisely what Macquarrie wants to say when he speaks of the 'self-giving' of being. When we say that 'the new motorway system will come into being in two years' time', we are using a circumlocution for 'there will be a

45. Macquarrie, *Principles of Christian Theology*, p. 96.

motorway system at the end of two years'. If we cared to speak about the being of the motorway we should be referring to one of two things : either the existence of the motorway, or the nature – character – function, etc. of the motorway. Presumably it would be less expensive if a motorway system suddenly appeared because the idea of a motorway had been actualized by the 'self-giving of being'.

Throughout Macquarrie's argument Being has become increasingly autonomous, inviting, claiming, judging, disclosing and giving of itself. Being somehow seems to control whether entities come into being or not. Thus Macquarrie maintains that the appropriate expression is 'letting-be'. 'Being, strictly speaking, "is" not; but being "lets be". . . . '[46] Hence it is more beingful than any being. The pace is quickening, as Macquarrie moves to relate Being and God. 'The religious man experiences the letting-be of being as being's self-giving, the grace of being which pours itself out and confers being.'[47] Why the religious man? Because at the beginning, not at the end, faith in God and faith in Being were identified.

And so finally the conclusion. Not that God and Being are synonymous. 'We could, however, say that "God" is synonymous with "holy being". . . '[48] It is interesting to note that 'holy being' has the same elements as those by which Otto characterized the numinous, the holy, the Wholly Other. 'Our final analysis of being as the *incomparable* that *lets-be* and is *present-and-manifest*, is strikingly parallel to the analysis of the numinous as *mysterium tremendum et fascinans*.'[49] God, according to this analysis, has an ontological aspect, outlined in the description of being, but there is also an existential aspect, corresponding to our commitment of faith in being. It is for this reason that Macquarrie, redefining the word God, speaks of 'existential–ontological theism'.

46. ibid., p. 103.   47. ibid., p. 104.
48. ibid., p. 105.   49. ibid., p. 105.

Has Macquarrie succeeded, in his New Style Natural Theology, in establishing a viable and meaningful way of speaking about God today? I think not, and apart from the criticisms interspersed with the above presentation of his position, I should like to end with the following points. They concern the three criteria which Macquarrie's position must satisfy, logical, cultural and theological.

1. There are two main areas in which I find the position logically unsatisfactory. Both have already been dealt with. The first is the predication of being, exemplified in talk about degrees of beingfulness. The second is the introduction of prejudiced terminology which, without any basis in analysis, suggests that being is autonomous, active and purposive.

2. The second criterion is the cultural one. Again there are two main objections. Philosophical Theology (in Macquarrie's sense) is supposed to present an analysis or account of reality acceptable and meaningful to men today. Instead of this we have been presented with a description of reality comprehensible to the generation which lived some fifty years ago, the generation of the young Heidegger and the young Tillich (and even that understanding of reality was not shared in Britain or America). The second point is that the analysis presents us with a very artificial view of the options open to men. A line is drawn between those who think life is absurd, and those who commit themselves to it, and discover meaning.[50] It is because I regard this as inadequate that I have spoken about being committed to transcendence. There are many people today who do not think life absurd, who think life rich and meaningful, challenging and heart-breaking, who are willing to commit themselves to values which transcend their own self-interest. But these people, so far as I can see, do not have faith in being. They are not religious. They do not recognize themselves or their experience

50. Note the similarity with Ogden's analysis of 'our ineradicable confidence in the final worth of our existence'.

in the ontological chat about 'the directionally opposite *quest for man*. . .'. In describing Robinson's presentation as 'a religious man's view of atheism', I meant that it was a tame atheism, lined up finally to conform to the theologian's view of man. Macquarrie has given us, not a description of contemporary experience of existence, but a religious man's view of what existence would be like if he had his way. Then all would be simple. The world would be divided along religious grounds. Those on one side would have faith in nothing. Those on the other could have religious faith=faith in being=a life characterized by commitment and humility, receiving judgement and grace . . . . But this is not our world. The religious division is not a major line drawn in our time. Those who have religious faith are a tiny minority. The basic division which will decide the future of the human race is not the one which finds a tiny minority on one side, and the vast majority on the other. Nor do I think Macquarrie would disagree with this. But his analysis does make the false division between those who have 'faith in being=religious faith', and those who do not.

3. The third criterion is the theological. The criticism is not unlike that made against Ogden. Ogden criticized the Death of God school, insisting that there can be no theology without God. Unfortunately, at the end of the day, he himself had not established a legitimate claim to the word. Macquarrie also is moved to criticize the Death of God school, dismissing it as a form of positivism, with a Jesus-centred ethic. It is not really a radical school of theology at all. A really radical theology 'lives in the tension of faith and doubt, whereas here the tension has been resolved by the abolition of God. . . .'.[51] Apart from the Tillichian flavour, faith and doubt, I find this an extraordinary criticism. It implies that theology thrives not only on faith in God, but also on doubt about God (his existence? his mercy?). If the Death of God school

51. ibid., p. 143.

is positivist it is not because it has stopped speaking about God, but because it has no analysis of transcendence.

Macquarrie rightly points out that a-theism depends on the theism which it opposes. By the standard of traditional theism, he would quite happily admit that he is an atheist. Such a God is not ultimate enough. He denies that God is a being. Further, as a corollary to this he rejects the I–Thou language of encounter with God, since the Thou, however exalted, is another being. The question has already been raised about the logical adequacy of the argument which leads to the identification of God and (holy) Being, but there are also theological points to be raised. We have been working with an idea of God in mind, the idea that he is a supernatural being, worthy of worship, and so far as Christians are concerned God may be addressed as 'Our Father'. Now, of course, it is open to anyone to offer a new use of the word God. But Macquarrie would not be content with a licence to start a new religion. He quotes the definition given by Vincent of Lérins and declares that he is not interested in developing a one-man theology (heterodoxy).

We are all familiar with radical changes in the interpretation of the Bible, especially for example in the demythologizing of the accounts of the life of Jesus. Controversy has raged over the question of the messianic consciousness of Jesus, the predictions concerning his own fate, the historicity of the resurrection and so forth. Certain things have never been questioned, and these include the fact that Jesus addressed God in prayer as Father, and encouraged his disciples not only to say Our Father, but to ask God for things, notably bread. The Lord's Prayer, it seems to me, provides something of a test case for Macquarrie. He would not wish to appropriate the word God in a sense which had no essential continuity with the way in which it has been used 'everywhere, always and by all'. One of the most revealing sections in the rest of his book is the one on Prayer.

Macquarrie concentrates on prayer as adoration, confession and thanksgiving. When he can put it off no longer, he turns to intercession and petition. 'Are we perhaps being evasive in our account of prayer?'[52] Then follows an account of how we can pray for the wrong things, in the wrong way. After that our attention is drawn to the fact that we intercede within a community. Finally, the only example of petition is 'Thy Kingdom come'. The answer is: Yes, perhaps we are being evasive. Prayer as described by Macquarrie is meditation. He speaks of opening our lives to judgement and grace – and of course petition about the Kingdom falls within the same category. What we cannot do, and Macquarrie in all honesty and consistency cannot bring himself to say we can do, is pray to Our Father in heaven to give us this day our daily bread, when God is conceived of as Being (even holy Being).

This is only one example, but its importance can hardly be overestimated. The lack of continuity between God and Being is exposed. Two alternatives remain. We can either persist with Being, or return to the God of traditional theism. And this is the dilemma. It was not Being that brought Israel from Egypt, the Philistines from Caphtor and the Syrians from Kir. Being did not command Cyrus to lead or Nehemiah to build. It was not Being that raised Jesus from the dead and brought the Church into existence. But Macquarrie, like Ogden, has rather burned his bridges behind him. He has rejected the idea of the supernatural God (whether of Israel or of Christendom). He will not speak of God in this way, and yet cannot speak of him (or has not shown sufficient justification for speaking of him) in any other way.

I have argued in the Introduction that most people find themselves without the supernatural God, whether conceived in the mythological terms of the Bible, or the terms of traditional theism. To that extent, both Macquarrie and Ogden have done a service in showing that this God is no longer

52. ibid., p. 439.

viable. But they have both failed to establish any other way of speaking about God. They have failed for many reasons, already mentioned, but also for a final reason. They have both thought that the problem is to develop a new conception of God, on the assumption that modern men are turning away from Christianity because of an untenable *conception* of God. I do not think this is altogether realistic. Most Christians still function with a belief in the God of traditional theism. Many know that it is an inadequate way of speaking of God. They realize that it is impossible to bring together their secular view of the world and their 'religious' view of the world. But they do not give up their belief in God because of *conceptual* difficulties. To think this would be completely to fail to recognize the pragmatic nature of ordinary people (and this is one of the penalties of being an academic, that we think people are changed by ideas). They will continue to bump along with this very unsatisfactory concept of God so long as it actually corresponds to their experience. A man might suddenly say he no longer believes in God, but this would not be the result of an intellectual debate. Tolstoy records an incident relevant at this point.

S., a frank and intelligent man, told me as follows how he ceased to believe: – He was twenty-six years old when one day on a hunting expedition, the time for sleep having come, he set himself down to pray according to the custom he had held from childhood. His brother, who was hunting with him, lay upon the hay and looked at him. When S. had finished his prayer and was turning to sleep, the brother said, "Do you still keep up that thing?" Nothing more was said. But since that day, now more than thirty years ago, S. has never prayed again; he never takes communion, and does not go to church.[53]

The problem does not lie in the conception of God, but whether it corresponds to anything in our experience. The

53. Quoted in W. James, *The Varieties of Religious Experience*, pp. 165–6, note 8.

problem which faces us today does not arise from any failure to conceive of the God of traditional theism; rather the crisis stems from the fact that there is an absence of any experience which could be interpreted as experience of God. Ogden and Macquarrie do not come to terms with this new situation, and we must therefore turn to those who take it as their starting point.

CHAPTER 3

The Death of God

SUPERFICIALITY OF REFORMS

IN the mid 1960s the Death of God school, like a true nova, was the brightest and most dramatic object of interest in the theological sky, and like a nova, it burnt itself out until hardly any trace of its influence is now to be seen. This at least was its course in America, but it aroused little interest at all in Britain, and less in Europe at large. The varying levels of concern have their own significance. In this chapter I shall indicate what was the strength of the Death of God theology, and also suggest why it has had so little effect on the Church.

By contrast with the lack of effect of the Death of God theology, the reception of *Honest to God* was without parallel in the history of religious publishing. I do not wish to discuss J. A. T. Robinson's book, or rake over the familiar ground of the debate it provoked: that has been done too often, to no effect. But why did it have such an impact, when the Death of God theology has disappeared almost without trace? Not because the content of the book was more original than the work of the American school – it was not so very original, nor even coherent, judged by theological standards of the day. But the more it was criticized by professional theologians, the more these men found their criticisms turned back on themselves. Robinson did not claim to be saying anything new. In fact he displayed perhaps too much modesty over his achievement.[1] But if more professional theo-

1. 'I am struggling to think other people's thoughts after them. I cannot claim to have understood all I am trying to transmit.' (J. A. T. Robinson, *Honest to God*, Westminster Press, Philadelphia, 1963, p. 21.)

logians had done their job properly, and communicated the insights of modern thinking to the Church in a comprehensible way, then Robinson would not have felt obliged to undertake his 'attempt at communication' and 'mediation'.[2]

The success of *Honest to God*, in spite of the defects which its author would not want to deny, depended on the insights and skill of the bishop, but no less on the fact that it appeared at just the right historical moment of the life of the Church, at least in England. In Germany, theologians contended that the Church there had long since passed this point.[3] We shall consider the American position in a moment. The book became more than a book. It was the name of a new way in theology, a turning point in the thought of laymen, and indeed a therapeutic experience. For a century, Christians had felt the weight of criticisms based on the findings of the natural sciences, and later the claims (whether true or false) of psychology. The result was that Christians found their lives governed for the most part by the modern world-view, and yet their faith in Christ was intrinsically bound up with an ancient world-view that they could not, or should not try to, accept. This was the dilemma which Bultmann described as one requiring 'schizophrenia and insincerity'. And it is for this reason that the call to honesty had a therapeutic effect.

Up till that time laymen had been given a very raw deal. The clergy had been given the opportunity, while studying theology, to find a way out of the dilemma, but they very often communicated a form of Christianity which still embodied the dilemma. With *Honest to God*, laymen too were

2. ibid.

3. While sophisticated Germans said 'Nothing new for us', it was Bultmann himself who challenged the easy assumption that everything said by Robinson had been appropriated. 'And is our situation really so enlightened, and have the relevant problems been so finally solved, that there is no need for them to be constantly thought out afresh?' (*The Honest to God Debate*, ed. D. L. Edwards, S.C.M. Press, London, 1963, p. 134.)

given the opportunity to live integrated lives as believers. Robinson's book was received with interest in America, but not with the same effect, and I believe the reason for this is to be seen by considering a comparable best-seller there, *The Secular City* by Harvey Cox.[4]

As previously indicated, the dilemma for Christians in England did not depend on the validity of nineteenth-century (determinate) physics or biology, or the quasi-scientific Freudian analysis. It was enough that the challenges had some strength. The situation in America was similar in form, though quite different in content. I do not think the dilemma of the change in world-view bore heavily on Americans. Instead, the dilemma was posed by inexorable urbanization. To understand the implications of the growth of the 'three cities',[5] we must remember the associations of Christianity and its rural background in the early settlement of the continent. Not that there is any justification for this myth,[6] but the dilemma remained, that as for ancient Israel the desert was the place of obedience, and the city the place of corruption, so, for Christians in America, their religion was in danger from the continual spread of urbanization. In particular, Christians were faced with the problem of being true to their historic faith, with its rural setting, and yet being forced to make their lives in the cities.

It was in this different cultural setting that *The Secular City* appeared, and brought a similar therapeutic experience. The subtitle, 'Secularization and Urbanization in Theological Perspective', explains the intention of the author. The book has a negative and a positive aim. Cox sets out to show

4. Harvey Cox, *The Secular City*, Macmillan, New York, 1965; Penguin Books, Harmondsworth, 1968.

5. The demographic map of the U.S. now indicates an almost complete joining up of urban centres down both east and west coasts, and down the mid-west.

6. F. H. Littell, *From State Church to Pluralism*, Anchor Books, New York, 1962.

that, negatively, *although* 'technopolitan culture is the wave of the future',[7] Christians need not despair. And positively he asserts that not although, but precisely *because* it is the wave of the future, Christians may actually take courage. On the negative side Cox argues that the city is in the providence of God, and that its secular culture has actually been made possible by the biblical view of man, society and the natural world. On the positive side, Cox goes on to claim that far from being an alien environment, the secular city actually provides circumstances and opportunities which are more congenial to mature and responsible Christian faith, than those provided by the rural environment. What Robinson did for the English dilemma, Cox did for the American one.[8] They both offered their fellow Christians a way in which to integrate their secular and their religious lives.

Notwithstanding the value of these books, and the sensitivity with which they approached the problem, I believe that this whole approach has in fact failed. Not that it should never have been attempted, but that it has failed by falling short. Even in the Preface to *Honest to God*, Robinson may have suspected this. 'The one thing of which I am fairly sure is that, in retrospect, it will be seen to have erred in not being nearly radical enough.'[9] The failure of this reform movement can be summed up in at least two respects.

The first is that the schizophrenia still remains, but now at a deeper level. All the peripheral elements of Christianity are open to question. We may question the miracles, and doubt the ascension. What is not on the agenda of debate is that there is a supernatural being, and that Jesus of Nazareth is his son. But *beside* these items, the question of Jesus

---

7. ibid., p. 20.

8. The parallel extends to the publication of a companion volume, *The Secular City Debate* (Macmillan, New York, 1966), in which the editor, Daniel Callahan, acknowledged that he was 'brazenly imitating' Edwards's collection.   9. *Honest to God*, p. 10.

walking on the water pales. We are now in the illogical situation that the *conclusions* reached by the earliest Christians are still accepted, but the *grounds* on which they came to these conclusions are in question or even rejected. Alternatively, there are some conclusions reached by the early Church that are unacceptable to us on any grounds. For example (and I realize that the present position has not been created entirely by John Robinson), some attention has been paid to the miracles of Jesus. Whereas in the nineteenth century they were ruled out on scientific and historical grounds, today with a new understanding both of physics and historiography, the miracles have some claim to authenticity. This debate continues, and yet the conclusion drawn by the early Church, namely that the miracles of Jesus are very significant witness to his divinity, is quite unacceptable to us. Whether the miracles can be demonstrated to have happened or not, they cannot bear their former conclusion for us. Or again, we may through the highest critical scholarship seek out the historical Abraham, the historical Moses, the historical Gideon or the historical Elijah – yet when all this work is done (and it looks as if it never will be completely done) we have simply got back to a better historical account of events, individuals or tribal legends. We are still no closer to believing that a supernatural being tempted Abraham to child sacrifice, divided an arm of the ocean, appeared with a stick which worked like a gas poker or sent fire from the sky to burn up sacrifice and altar. That kind of belief depends on a world-view which is incompatible with our world-view. Once again, the grounds on which the conclusions are ultimately based are regarded as up for discussion, but even if the ground could be established to the satisfaction of physicists and historians, we should not want to accept the conclusions previously drawn from them. Much more could be said on this score, but the present position is that Christians have been given grounds for manoeuvre. By being allowed to question every secondary issue they feel that they are after all being honest to God and to themselves. But at the end of the day they have not faced up to the changes in the conclusions which must stem from the changes in our assessment of the grounds. This is largely due to the fact that many still regard the conclusions as having been revealed. We have already discussed this point, that the proposition 'Jesus is the Son of God' has not been revealed. It represents the conclusion which faith draws from revelatory events and experiences. Failure to appreciate that our statements about God and Jesus are actually derived from revelatory events and experiences has led to the false assumption that the events and experiences can be questioned without affecting the conclusions.

The second way in which the modern reform movement has failed leads us to our discussion of the Death of God theology. Robinson represents (as does Cox) the very worthy attempt to integrate the secular lives and the Christian faith of modern man. If his way is to be criticized[10] for not going far enough, it is infinitely preferable to the position of those theologians and churchmen, the true heirs of the title 'Flat-Earthers', who neither see the problem nor seriously attempt to deal with it. He has brought a great deal of peace of mind to Christians, worried about maintaining their faith in the present age. And in putting it this way, we see the root of the criticism. We hear a good deal – though not enough – about the Church being an inward-looking institution, mainly concerned with itself. It is concerned with its own financial problems, recruitment and staffing of churches. The only 'outward' view of many churchmen is the ecumenical movement, and that means looking out towards other parts of the Church. The reformist theology of *Honest to God* has en-

10. It is not generally realized for how long the name of John Robinson has been associated with controversy. Cf. *An Answer to John Robinson* (1609), ed. Champlin Burrage, Kraus Reprint Co., New York.

couraged this ecclesiastical navel observation, this time in the
field of belief. Its effect at best has been to make it possible
for Christians to remain Christians in face of various intellectual difficulties. But we may doubt whether it has enabled
one single non-believer to come to faith. I have listed this as
a second criticism of the reformist way, and the fact that it
may be regarded by some as a not very relevant criticism is
simply further evidence of the fact that we think of theology
today exclusively in terms of the reforming of the statements
about belief, a service function for those within the Church.
But the Church has a gospel to proclaim (and why this
should be done only in a building where *Christians* meet is a
very strange reversal of the required practice), and a mission
to fulfil. The reformist theology is regarded as exciting and
successful only by those who preach to the converted and
have no time left for mission to those outside. This theology
has no more effect on those outside the Church than the
traditional theology. The new way of speaking may seem
less crude to non-believers, in so far as they know any changes
have taken place, though somewhat ironically, non-believers
may think the old conservative position more consistent than
the new. That is to say, while they may think religion absurd, they may understand the old conservative position to
be a complete system in its own terms. It will therefore be
absurd, which is one better than being absurd and inconsistent – their judgement on the reformist position. In making
this judgement, non-believers actually know better than the
theological whizz-kids. They see that to tamper with the
world-view is to destroy the grounds for the traditional conclusions. As a result non-believers may see two options only,
the first being the conservative position (the Flat-Earth,
Supernatural-Being syndrome), which is frankly not a real
option at all today, and the second being the rejection of
religion entirely.

I have referred to Robinson's position as 'reformist', and

of course this includes such positions as Ogden's and Macquarrie's. In their own ways – and these three theologians represent *very* different ways – they attempt to make it possible for Christians to maintain their faith today in a way which is integrated with their secular view of the world. But none of these reformist ways in fact has had any effect on those who have no religious belief.

The failure of the reformist theology finally comes to this, that religious belief means belief in God, and this theology has not brought belief in God any nearer to non-believers. It has been influential in the Church. Those who believe in God have been led (and even misled) to think that there is a credible way of integrating belief in God and our contemporary experience. But the significance of this theology for the Church has been purely internal and has not, as a matter of fact, made any difference to those outside.

Before leaving this criticism of reformist theology, we should note that it applies to a much wider field than that of theology. For example, it applies to the whole liturgical renewal movement. Changes in the architecture of places of worship can assist changes in attitudes and understanding in those who worship. This is true also of vernacular services. But when all such changes in building, in language, in content, shape and form of services, have taken place, the conclusion is still the same. Those who can worship, worship better: those who could not previously worship are still unable to do so. The reforms have been internal to the life of the Church, because they presuppose belief in God, and it is precisely lack of experience of God which constitutes the barrier to non-believers.

The same could be said about changes in the administration of the churches, and indeed the whole ecumenical movement of the 1950s. These are for the most part tidying-up operations, necessary to the efficient running of the Church as a community of people. While theological grounds might also be found for undertaking them, David Paton is near the mark in describing them unromantically as 'plumbing'. There is no particular merit to maintaining the household of faith in the worst possible state of repair. But when all *that* has been said, it is an internal matter to the life of the Church, and does not bring men any nearer to belief in God.

The Catholic Church can be relied on at present to provide copy when there is no world crisis to hand. But the whole *aggiornamento* movement is exactly that. It is not the Catholic Church giving a lead to the secular world, but rather an example of a near fatal and disintegrating trauma by which that church has been dragged kicking and fighting into the first (not second) half of the twentieth century. The issues reported tend once again to be purely internal to the life of the Church, and do not make belief any more possible.

Finally, before leaving the reformist approach, I should like to repeat on a wider scale the point made earlier with respect to theology. It does not follow that reforms make Christianity any more attractive to non-believers. For example, on the ecumenical question, this was demonstrated by the publication of the report on *Relations between Anglican and Presbyterian Churches*.[11] There was widespread hostility in Scotland towards the proposals by atheists who were, nonetheless, 'presbyterian atheists'. This may seem quite trivial, and at the time it seemed senseless. The Church of Scotland could not be influenced in such matters by non-believers. But in retrospect, I am not sure that such people were out of place, since they would be to some extent affected by any change in the character of the established Church. Anything making the Church of Scotland less democratic (to take one example) could have cultural repercussions on the life of the nation.

A second example concerns the reforms in the celebration

11. *Relations between Anglican and Prestbyterian Churches: A Joint Report*, Saint Andrew Press, 1957.

of the Mass. There is no doubt that the new Mass is a much more significant and meaningful occasion for many Catholics; the level of understanding and participation gives them a new involvement in the liturgy. But it does not follow that this makes worship any more attractive or meaningful to non-believers. On the contrary, precisely those features of the reforms which make the Mass more valuable for those who participate serve to detract from its significance for those who observe.

These examples may serve to illustrate the point that reforms in liturgy, theology, inter-church relations and organization have an internal significance to the Church which they do not have to non-believers. Further, since the reforms are judged by quite different standards among non-believers, the reforms may in turn make the position and practice of the Church either more or less credible. But at the end of the day the reforms do not have the effect of making belief in God any more possible for non-believers. And worst of all, John Robinson, who has been singled out as a very able leader of theological (and liturgical) reform, earlier provided an example of a theologian who holds the position of denying the final tenability of atheism. This combination of reforms of language and practice together with the denial of atheism disguises the fact that throughout the whole of this century the most creative and exciting work done on renewal has been short-circuited. It has made religious belief and practice quite different, but has not made belief in God possible for non-believers. If renewal means finding a way of converting men to Christianity, then renewal has clearly failed. And if renewal is concerned with something other than converting men to faith in Christ, then renewal is a distraction from the work of the Church to 'make disciples of all nations'.

THE DIAGNOSIS OF THE DEATH OF GOD

In 1963, *Time* magazine carried a report on the expansion planned for the University of Göttingen. Most of the £80,000,000 was to go towards the development of medicine and physics, not towards theology, although the Faculty is a very distinguished one. As one of the architects involved expressed it: 'Theology gets short shrift: they'll never discover anything world-shaking.' And yet just at that time a major discovery took place in American theological circles: that God is dead. As a public relations job it was without parallel in history. God has never been so much in the news as since his sad passing. When he was alive, the mass media contrived to ignore him, but with his tragic death – as so often happens – they have vied with one another for exclusive interviews with those who were there when it happened.

With typical insensitivity, all the morbid details have been spread over the cover of *Time* and serialized in the *New Yorker*. But it is an ill wind, and the death of God has been like a shot in the arm to theology. The publishing trade is confident that it can sell any paperback as long as the blessed phrase is incorporated in the title.

But all that lies in the recent past. The Death of God movement, which in America lasted from 1963–7, was not the first theological debate to generate more heat than light. This is not surprising, since its whole object, at least so it seemed to more orthodox Christians, was to generate darkness rather than light. It has now become fashionable to frown on the journalistic excesses of that period: people are not themselves during a wake. One of 'the morticians in the case' (to use J. W. Montgomery's phrase), Paul van Buren, has given his retrospective assessment of it all.

Now that the hot air has leaked out of the recent 'death of God' balloon, and as we push the flaccid remains to the back of the drawer reserved for mementoes of our more foolish exploits, it may be said that behind all that journalistic nonsense lay an important issue. It is an old issue in a contemporary form: a rediscovery in our time that man's question about God, or the meaning of life, or however it may be put, does not long admit of clear and simple answers.[12]

One of the most unfortunate features of human argumentation, or lack of it, is the tendency to attack anything but the conclusions of debate. A favourite substitute is of course to attack the person instead of his argument. David Jenkins has provided us with such an example of argumentation by character assassination. 'Clearly, none of these writers has ever had joy in worship or prayer, or ever felt in contact with glory through their relations with the Church and the Christian tradition.'[13] I have never had the opportunity of meeting the central figures of the Death of God movement, but I should be surprised if their work was the result of never having had any rich religious experience. To the contrary, and I should guess that this applies particularly to William Hamilton, the poignancy of much of the Death of God theology *presupposes* a richness which has now gone, and presumably gone for ever. This kind of attack on the movement I find particularly distasteful, and it confirms for me the fact that David Jenkins, who has made a good deal of mileage on the topic, has not after all understood it – a serious position for one who is reckoned to be an expert on secular man.

12. Paul van Buren, *Theological Explorations*, S.C.M. Press, London, 1968, p. 6.

13. D. E. Jenkins, *Living with Questions*, S.C.M. Press, London, 1969, p. 59. Apart from this kind of remark, the whole book is an unfortunate example of a specialized publishing house taking a decision on a purely commercial basis, without regard to the long term effect on the movement it is supposed to serve. We are all familiar with books in which all the chapters have previously appeared in print before, on separate occasions, but this is perhaps a unique example of a book in which the sections *within* each chapter have nothing in common, and all derive from separate occasions.

We have dealt at some length with the point that belief is related to experience, but that theological statements are derived from, not revealed in, our experience. This is no less true of the radical theology than of the orthodox. That is to say, the statement that 'God is dead' is a conclusion which some theologians have reached as a result of their experience of the world. The phrase is a very odd one, and in the common understanding of the words 'God' and 'dead' it is of course meaningless. But that is not how theological statements are normally tested. If it were, then it would be impossible (improper) to speak of God as a 'father', who is 'in' heaven, or who has 'become a man'. The statement 'God is dead' is no more paradoxical than the fundamental assertions of the creeds. What we should examine is the experience of the world to which it refers, and the adequacy both of the radical analysis of the experience and the use of the phrase to describe it.

Much of the antipathy towards the Death of God theologians is due to the fact that they are quickly associated in many minds with the death of Christianity. They themselves have become identified as the great enemies of faith. We should do well to separate the various elements of this rather irrational response. In the first place these men did not invent the situation which they described. They drew attention, very effectively it would seem, to a situation which was already in existence but largely ignored by other theologians and church leaders. In the second place the Death of God theologians do not see themselves as prophets of the death of Christianity. On the contrary, as we shall see, they wanted to develop a specifically Christian response to the new situation in which they found themselves.

What is the situation as they see it? Very briefly it is that fewer and fewer people today have any knowledge of God. There does not seem to be any way in which the Church can enable them to come to belief in God (see the comments above on the failure of reformist moves). But most of all, living without God has now become a feature not only of those outside the Church, but of many within it. A significant number of Christians now find themselves without any experience of God. I do not see how it is possible to deny that this is the situation in which we live today. It is either a quite new situation, or it is the first time in history that we have been able to recognize it. We are not dealing with intellectual atheism, a strident or belligerent denial of the possibility of God. It is a much more calm atmosphere, in which many people find nothing in their lives which would enable them honestly to speak of belief in God. Nor has this realization produced any particular wave of panic within society. Robert Adolfs has described the situation in the following way.

Indeed, unbelief seems to be the sign of our time. I do not mean by this primarily the cultural phenomenon of atheistic humanism. Rather, it is a question of disbelief among Christians, and it is not a rebellious disbelief. It is a quiet indifference, which develops in people who discover that they can be complete human beings without religious faith.[14]

Those who oppose the Death of God theologians must first of all show that this is not in fact the situation in which we find ourselves. Of course there are psychological reasons why Christians may not wish to see that this is the situation. It is very difficult for a hard-working parish priest to face the fact that neither he nor his congregation of 200 are making any impact on the parish of 15,000. It is difficult for him to accept that because of something in our cultural situation he is not going to be able to reach the vast majority of his parish. Most difficult of all to recognize is that a significant number of his own congregation, even those who are 'active' around the church buildings (perhaps especially those) have lost their early knowledge of God. Similarly, there are psycholo-

14. Robert Adolfs, 'Is God Dead?', in *The Meaning of the Death of God*, ed. B. Murchland, Vintage Books, New York, 1967, p. 83.

gical reasons why theologians and bishops are not always ready to face the situation which actually exists. Indeed if there is any panic it is more likely to be in the hearts of those who fear that if the radical analysis of the situation is correct, then all is lost. Thus they turn on the Death of God theologians, as if these men were somehow responsible for the situation. The reaction bears comparison with a letter sent out, in November 1969, from the Vatican to all bishops, dealing among other things with the sort of people allowed to instruct priests. 'Suitable persons for these functions are those who can solve the problems that are laid before them, and not those who raise and increase doubts.'[15] The problem lies not with those who raise the difficulties, but with the difficulties themselves. The Death of God theologians are not responsible for the situation to which they point. But those who ignore the situation are surely guilty of irresponsibility.

Another typical response to the Death of God theologians is a full acceptance of the situation. Yes, the situation is very bad indeed; in some respects it is even worse than these theologians say. At the end of the day this second group ends by advocating purely reformist solutions – but anyone who returns to *that* position has not after all understood the present situation. The Death of God theologians are not responsible for the situation, nor are they responsible for the fact that the reformist solutions of the past twenty-five years have not made any difference. Is it not then irresponsible to continue to advocate these reforms as solutions to this problem? The response which simply involves a more and more furious attempt at reforms in language and practice can only be diagnosed as an example of the 'Gadarene complex': everything will be all right, as long as we keep going, and keep together.

A third reaction to the Death of God theology is a common rejection of the interpretations of the situation. We shall be

15. *The Times*, 10 February 1970.

looking briefly at these interpretations in a moment, but there is no doubt that these men have expressed views which are open to a variety of criticisms, both theological and philosophical. They have proposed solutions which seem to be more problematic than the original problems. They have not always made clear the reason why their diagnosis of the situation should involve the cure they propose, or which is worse. As one critic has put it, 'this theology is more than a diagnosis. It is also a prescription, and a prescription which offers the disease as the cure. . . .'[16] Unfortunately, those who have criticized the solution offered by the Death of God theologians have not offered any other solution themselves. They seem to make the mistake of thinking that in disposing of the false *solution*, they have thereby shown the original *analysis* of the situation to be false. But no matter what criticisms are made and sustained, Robert Adolfs' analysis of the situation still stands. Those who dispose of the Death of God solution are still faced with giving their own interpretation of and solution to the present problem.

In this book we are exploring the possibility of a secular faith in Christ, in face of the impossibility of belief in God. The difficulty in approaching this subject is that belief in God has hitherto been supposed to be the central element in Christianity. It is for this reason that the Death of God theology has made no impact whatsoever on the Church. The reformist theologies (those of Robinson, Cox, *et al.*) may not have made much difference to the life of the Church, but at least they can be discussed. However, as already noted, in a very fluid situation in which almost everything can be discussed and questioned, the one thing which cannot be debated *within* the Church is the existence of God. The Death of God theology has therefore made no impact, since it is based on precisely that one premise, atheism, which is the

16. E. W. Shideler, 'Taking the Death of God Seriously', in *The Meaning of the Death of God*, ed. Murchland, p. 113.

sole topic which cannot be questioned. There are apparently no insights from this theology which can be extracted and used within the Church, because it all stems from an unacceptable premise. The debate about God is, strictly speaking, still not a debate about the existence of God. Those who contribute to the debate are not willing to take this responsibility seriously *within* the Church. It is assumed that the debate takes place only between the Church and those outside.[17]

Yet this is part of the situation in which we live. Belief in God is not only impossible for the vast majority of people today, it is also found to be impossible for a growing number of Christians. Since the Death of God theologians addressed themselves to the same situation as the one identified in this book, it is appropriate that something should be said about their solutions. We shall consider the positions of Thomas Altizer and William Hamilton. The position of Paul Van Buren is different, and he does not qualify as a Death of God theologian. He will be discussed in Chapter 7.

THOMAS ALTIZER AND THE INCARNATION

Altizer's full-length study, *The Gospel of Christian Atheism*,[18] was first published in 1966, towards the end of the period of maximum exposure of the views of the Death of God school. The standard response to it has been to say that while it is neither gospel nor Christian, it is most certainly atheism. My own view is quite the opposite. It has a claim to be Christian, and in the terms of the analysis of the present

17. This debate between Christians and atheists has gone on interminably, but it reached a new level when on *Monty Python's Flying Circus* (BBC-Television, 12 October 1969), a Catholic bishop and a humanist academic decided to settle the matter in the ring. The result of the age-old debate was declared as: God exists, by two falls to one submission.

18. T. J. J. Altizer, *The Gospel of Christian Atheism*, Collins, London, 1967.

situation in which we find ourselves, it may well offer hope, but I doubt very much whether it qualifies for the accolade of atheism. It might be convenient indeed to present Altizer's views in these three categories: Christian, Gospel, Atheism.

One of the most irritating features about the attacks which have been made upon Altizer, condemning his work as unchristian, has been that they are made by people who seem oblivious of the obligation to present Christianity· at a universal level. That is to say, they are content to discuss Christianity within the seminary, or within the diocese, and certainly within the Church. But what of the vast majority of people in the world who are not Christian, and who are never going to be Christian as long as Christianity is conceived of in traditional–parochial terms? Altizer goes too far when he declares that 'Never before has Christianity been called upon to assume a universal form',[19] but all credit to him that he is at least recalling Christians to conceive of a form in which Christianity might once again be a world option. Those who criticize him must make sure that they do not present Christianity in a form which simply appeals to intellectual Anglo-Saxons or to the decreasing number of people who can conceive of a supernatural being.

These are in fact the two options which Altizer sees set before Christians today. We can refuse to acknowledge the situation in which we find ourselves. We can blame the majority of people in the world for not accepting Christianity. We can even call for a massive revivalist campaign: back to God, back to church, back to religion. But this religious Canutism is really not a live option. However we analyse it, the cultural situation in which we find ourselves effectively prevents the majority of people from being religious. A strange reversal indeed if the Body of Christ should be reduced to The Society of the Preservation of Religion. Since it

19. Altizer and Hamilton, *Radical Theology and the Death of God*, p. 35.

is clear to Altizer that the secular culture is not going to disappear, that the clock is not going to be turned back, he rather courageously decides to break with that option which is really no option, and to seek a new form for Christianity. Far from representing the rejection of Christianity, this attempt exhibits more faith in the potential world-wide application of Christianity than do those who are content to remain with a form which effectively prevents the vast majority of people in the world from coming to terms with it.

The dilemma therefore is whether to try to preserve and re-establish religious belief and a religious way of looking at the world, or whether to seek another form of Christianity appropriate to our secular age. Stated thus, only the second option is a valid one. But once that decision has been taken, it must be undertaken with all possible consistency. Thus Christians must take seriously the critiques of religion mounted in the last century. Religion can be an inhibiting factor, preventing the fulfilment of human and social potentialities. But more is demanded than that. It was in the nineteenth century that atheism diagnosed the death of God. Now, if Christians are called to reject every religious interpretation of life, they too must affirm the death of God. They must 'will the death of God',[20] to remove any last vestige of the religious. The great danger to this new journey of faith is the petrification which overcomes those who, like Lot's wife, set out always looking back. But if Christians accept the atheist critique, even affirming the death of God, how are they to be distinguished from the atheists? It is at this point that Altizer is perhaps most original.

True, every man today who is open to experience knows that God is absent, but only the Christian knows that God is dead, that the death of God is a final and irrevocable event, and that God's death has actualized in our history a new and liberated humanity.[21]

20. ibid., p. 30.   21. Altizer, *The Gospel of Christian Atheism*, p. 111.

Those who live outside the Christian tradition know that there is no God present to them, but they do not know what to make of the situation. But those who are Christians understand precisely why there is no present God. The explanation of the present situation is revealed in Christ. And paradoxically, Altizer tells us, we should see that God died in becoming man.

We shall return to this point in a moment, but we should note that however unorthodox it may at first appear, there can be no doubt that it is Christocentric. Everything, even the death of God, is to be understood in terms of the revelation in Jesus Christ. Altizer is a student of the history of religions, and while we should perhaps assume that he would establish an eclectic relationship between Christianity and other world religions, we find, on the contrary, that once again he attempts to be unequivocally Christian. Previously we were offered two options: to continue the present ineffective attempt to conserve a religious approach to the world, or to press forward to a secular (but still Christian) faith. Now Altizer cuts off the former option by saying that it characterizes the way of the oriental religions, and is finally incompatible with Christianity.

The way in which Altizer establishes this schematic division is open to methodological objections. The most obvious is the way in which he represents the western tradition over against the eastern. Christianity alone is taken to represent the west. Judaism and Islam are specifically set aside. Yet even if this is decided on the grounds that Christianity has been the dominant religious influence in the formation of western secular culture, it is not clear that Christianity in turn has been free from the influence of, for example, Jewish legalism or the Islamic holy war. On the other side, Altizer concentrates upon eastern mysticism with the implication that all the great religious traditions of the east have the same cultural impact in one important respect. Such considerations aside, however, Altizer attempts to show that there are two ways of attaining and preserving the sacred. If the secular movement of the west has so concentrated attention upon the profane that we have lost contact with the sacred, then perhaps we might follow the eastern way in order to regain the sacred. Altizer, ever the dialectical thinker, declares that 'an absolute negation of the profane is identical with a total affirmation of the sacred'.[22] But this negation of the profane is just not an option for western society. Of course individual westerners may drop out of the secular culture, possibly by making their homes in the east, but western society is founded upon the affirmation of the profane, and we cannot go back. There are too many elements which are good in the western 'Yes'-saying to the profane world, and we are not justified in saying 'No' to them.[23] We cannot reject our secular way for the sake of returning to a primordial relationship with the sacred. The alternative is to press on through the affirmation of the profane, to see whether in *this* direction we might somehow go on to a new awareness of the sacred.[24]

It is one of the merits of Altizer's position that he focuses attention on what constitutes the decisive difference between Christianity and the other world religions (even including Judaism and Islam) – namely the Incarnation. Altizer's whole position depends on his exposition of the Incarnation. This is another reason why his work, while certainly unorthodox, has a claim to be Christian. Indeed, it is Altizer's view that Christian theology has not taken seriously the full

22. ibid., p. 38.

23. We might think of technology and the manipulation of the natural world, the development of medicine and the overcoming of endemic disease, the awareness of the obligations of social justice . . .

24. The only analogy which springs to mind which might make this approach more credible comes from a generation ago, when pilots on early supersonic downward dives discovered that survival and success lay in pushing forward instead of pulling backward.

implications of the Incarnation. I take this to mean that, ironically, theology has concentrated attention on the problems connected with saying that Jesus of Nazareth was both God and man. But the main point of the doctrine is surely that, if it is true, we are being told something revolutionary not about a man but about God. Christianity is distinguished from other religions not because its prophetic leader was more than a man, but because it offers a completely new and staggering doctrine of God. This revelation of God is literally embodied in the Incarnation. But there is more to the Incarnation than the life of Jesus. It has a cosmic dimension: the doctrine of the Incarnation expresses the revelation of God's way with the world and the whole of human history. Thus, as we have already seen, the death of God, without reference to the Incarnation, simply means the cultural fact that for modern men there is no present God. But in the light of the Incarnation the death of God is seen not as a random cultural event, but as the outworking of God's way of dealing with his creation. Altizer is not presenting us with the traditional view of the Incarnation, but there is no doubt that he is striving to appreciate it in ways which, by comparison, make the traditional interpretation of the doctrine of the Incarnation look insensitive and truncated.

We may look at Altizer's view of the Incarnation under two headings: the implications for our doctrine of God and the implications for eschatology. It has proved impossible to construct a credible formula for speaking about the Incarnation, at least in traditional terms. To say that Jesus was both God and man is not the answer to the problem but simply the way of *stating* the problem. It is not just that the conceptual framework made a solution no solution at all, but, so far as Altizer is concerned, that the doctrine of God was incompatible with the idea of Incarnation. That is to say, while the Incarnation should have led to a revision of the doctrine of God, to a view of God that would have been compatible with

Incarnation, the impasse has been reached in dogmatics because theology tried to speak of Christ by using a pre-incarnational view of God which was also pre-Christian. Instead of meaning by Incarnation that our whole doctrine of God has to be reformed in the light of Jesus Christ – thus yielding a Christian view of God – Incarnation has simply meant that the existing, non-Christian, view of God remained intact. Altizer does not go into this point in such detail, but I take it that this is his meaning. The revelation of God in Christ has therefore been taken to mean that the God who was already known simply became a man. But this is to get Incarnation the wrong way round. Incarnation means that our view of God must now be revised in the light of our knowledge of Jesus Christ. Only this revised conception of God is compatible with Incarnation. This I take to be the basic reason for the failure of theology to come up with a viable way of speaking of God becoming man.

Thus, in a negative sense, the Incarnation marks the death of the old God. The revelation in Christ makes it clear that the old God, essentially a Hellenistic and oriental deity, has no place in Christianity. It is a good thing that the old God is dead, though of course this has considerable importance for the Church, in so far as our doctrine of God has been largely an unreformed pre-Christian view of God. Altizer, under the influence of William Blake, can even refer to this God as Satan. But it is not only the false God who dies because of what is revealed in the Incarnation. The Incarnation marks the death of the true God also. The true God is not identified by Altizer in any detail, but we must assume that he is the God revealed increasingly in the Old Testament. Of course the final revelation to some extent negates the Old Testament understanding of God, but then the higher doctrine of God in exilic times negated the cruder doctrine of God in other parts of the Old Testament.[25]

25. This does not mean a continuous upward purification of the

It seems to me that what Altizer is saying is that in our own time, in a secular age, we are being led to see, perhaps for the first time, what the Incarnation was about. This is a paradoxical situation, for it means that the Word of God comes to us precisely at the moment when God is absent. But we must be guided by this Word, even when it negates much of what we have believed about God. The challenge to Christians is to speak now in the light of the Incarnation, and not simply in the light of a religious tradition. 'Only a theology unveiling a new form of the Word, a form that is present or dawning in the immediate and contemporary life of faith, can be judged to be uniquely and authentically Christian.'[26]

It is often said that the Death of God theology stems from the tradition of Karl Barth. In an important sense this is true. Barth distinguished very clearly between the popular idea of God, even within the Church, and the true God of the Bible.[27] But Barth only sought to re-establish a proper doctrine of God, and a *biblically* religious view of the world. It is at this point that Altizer, for all his indebtedness to Barth, breaks with him, especially with his Christocentricity, because this attempt to restore a religious view, as opposed to a Christian view, is precisely what Altizer rejects. He goes as far as to say that 'many American theologians consider

---

idea of God. In many respects the classical prophets present us with a much more sensitive understanding of God than the views expressed in, for example, the Greek period of Judaism.

26. Altizer, *The Gospel of Christian Atheism*, p. 18.

27. In an address given during the First World War, Barth drew attention to the disparity between the God whose name was invoked to justify both capitalism and war, and the God of the Bible. 'This god is really an unrighteous god, and it is high time for us to declare ourselves thorough-going doubters, sceptics, scoffers and atheists in regard to him. It is high time for us to confess freely and gladly: this god, to whom we have built the tower of Babel, is not God. He is an idol. He is dead.' (*The Word of God and the Word of Man*, trans. Douglas Horton, Harper, New York, 1957, p. 22.)

Barthianism as a necessary but frightful detour from the true task of theology'.[28] It is not Barth's rejection of the false God, or his stress on Christ, but his neo-supernaturalism which is incompatible with the task to which Altizer is committed. The Incarnation represents the collapse of radical transcendence into radical immanence. The God who was not only remote from the world, but always somehow against the world, has come to an end.

To explain the implications of all this, Altizer turns to the doctrine of *kenosis*, the self-emptying of God referred to, for example, in Philippians ii, 6–11. Traditionally this has been taken to refer to Jesus, but if we understand the Incarnation rightly, kenosis is the revelation of the way in which we must now speak of God. The error of traditional theology, which led to the Chalcedonian impasse, was to think of Jesus in kenotic terms, while still thinking of God in the old pre-Christian supernaturalist terms. But if Jesus is the definitive revelation of God, then we can only speak of God in kenotic terms, the terms of the incarnation. 'An authentically kenotic movement of "incarnation" must be a continual process of Spirit becoming flesh, of Eternity becoming time, or of the sacred becoming profane.'[29] The conclusion is therefore that with the Incarnation the old distinction of sacred and profane, spirit and flesh, eternity and time, has been overcome. But it is dialectically overcome. That is to say, we now live in a culture when the sacred has actually become profane. There is no going back on this historical process, if only because this would be to try to reverse the Incarnation. It is for this reason that Altizer wishes to press forward to see whether the sacred can be regained. The possibility that it might be regained remains, since the sacred has only been dialectically negated by the profane, and not simply replaced by it.

28. Altizer and Hamilton, *Radical Theology and the Death of God*, p. 32.   29. ibid. p. 154.

I have maintained up to this point that Altizer's position, though not orthodox, has a claim to be Christian, especially since he is able to point to dimensions involved in the Incarnation not normally taken into account in traditional theology. Altizer further establishes his claim to represent a consistently Christian position when he goes on now to speak of eschatology. Once again he might even claim to be more Christian in his theology than most, since while eschatology has been recognized in our own century as the central theme of the preaching of Jesus, it has not been a characteristic theme in the theology of orthodoxy.

Eschatology is another distinctively Christian theme among world religions, at least as represented in Altizer's scheme (and this time it would not distinguish Christianity so clearly from Judaism). Altizer maintains that the eastern tradition – which by this time he regards as best representing the 'religious' way of looking at the world – is concerned with the Beginning, the primordial sacred before the profane. Christianity, now understood as a non-religious view of the world, is concerned with the End, the achievement of the *eschaton* at the end of a historical process. He therefore sees the eastern 'religious' tradition as an attempt to regain the primordial, while the Christian tradition should be seeking to press on to achieve the eschatological. The distinctive interpretation of eschatology in Altizer is of course that the nature of the *eschaton* is also defined by the revelation of God in the Incarnation. Traditional theology has not only preserved a pre-Christian God, in face of the Incarnation, but has inevitably conceived of that same God as being there in the *eschaton*. This traditional view therefore somehow implies that the whole of human history since the life of Jesus is without revelatory significance. The security of faith therefore lies in the past. Altizer regards Kierkegaard as 'the real creator of modern theology'.[30] and therefore feels that faith

30. ibid., p. 27.

has to be continually renewed in the experience of the present and the anticipation of the future (*eschaton*).

It might therefore even be said that Altizer's work is a contribution to the current theology of hope. In a time when Christianity as a religion is in decline, and there are no hopeful signs for its future, he can give grounds for hope that Christian faith may not only be maintained, but dynamically renewed – indeed, hope that it may reach a new richness and universality. This is why his work deserves the title 'gospel'. At a time when men are saying that God is dead, Altizer says that only Christians know what this really means. The death of God is in the providence of God, and until we live this out we can have no hope for the future: 'we must celebrate the death of God as an epiphany of the eschatological Christ'.[31] We come thus not only to a true understanding of the biblical faith in the Incarnation, but to a proper assessment of our secular (profane) culture and the direction in which we must now move. Our brief study of Altizer's position seems to confirm the claim he makes that his work is both Christian and gospel.

It is the thesis of this book that the Christian, and the Christian alone, can speak of God in our time; but the message the Christian is now called to proclaim is the gospel, the good news or glad tidings, of the death of God.[32]

But the puzzling question which remains is not whether it is a Christian gospel, but whether it can possibly be described as atheism, and if not, how we are to understand Altizer's position.

Some basic criticisms must be raised against Altizer's position, but with the proviso in mind that no criticism is intended to contest the preliminary analysis of the critical situation in which Christians find themselves today, and that those who criticize must indicate a willingness to address themselves to the same issues.

31. ibid., p. 141   32. Altizer, *The Gospel of Christian Atheism*, p. 15.

The first point concerns the claim that God is dead. Altizer and Hamilton have offered some ten definitions of how the phrase is commonly used. Most of the definitions would indicate what I have been calling 'reformist' positions. That is to say, the phrase 'death of God' is used as Barth uses it, to speak of the death of a false god, or as Robinson uses it, to speak of a need for a new way of speaking about God, or a new way of worshipping God. The phrase is used very often by people who believe in God themselves, but strive to find new ways of expressing belief in God or expressing themselves in worship of God. God is there, if we can only find a way of thinking, speaking, or acting. This is the reformist position. To use the phrase in this way is to speak about man rather than God.[33] Indeed Gabriel Vahanian, whose book, The Death of God,[34] introduced the phrase into contemporary theology, is to be counted among the reformists here. In that book he was concerned with the post-war religiosity of America which he interpreted not as a sign that the people had faith in God, but rather that they were dead to God.[35] In fact the phrase 'death of God' is of no use to reformists. Those who believe in God cannot use it consistently. It is always a false god, or a false way of speaking about God, that is condemned. The reason for using the phrase at all in such cases is, I take it, simply because it has a certain curiosity value for Christians and non-Christians. With-it parsons could advertise a sermon with that title, and be sure of attracting a few unsuspecting souls. Then, the doors being shut,

33. 'It is more a commentary upon the present predicament of man than upon God ...'. (The Meaning of the Death of God, ed. Murchland, p. xii.)

34. Gabriel Vahanian, The Death of God, George Braziller, New York, 1961.

35. Vahanian might even have been used as an example of those who finally deny the possibility of atheism. e.g. 'God is not necessary, but he is inevitable.' ('Beyond the Death of God', in The Meaning of the Death of God, ed. Murchland, p. 12.)

these poor people would find that only the title was different, and the sermon still appealed to the God of the religious tradition.

The phrase 'death of God' is not properly used by reformists, nor does it properly apply to traditional atheism. Altizer and Hamilton propose one definition which they say describes their own position, the so-called radical position. Used in their sense it means 'that there once was a God to whom adoration, praise and trust were appropriate, possible, and even necessary, but that now there is no such God'.[36] In fact, as we shall see, this definition looks as if it might have been put together by William Hamilton, but Altizer has subscribed to it. Christian atheism therefore is defined as the loss of God. There once was a God, and now there is not. The corollary, I take it, is that there is nothing we can do to bring that God back again. Without that corollary the radical position would simply be another reformist position.

Now the question is whether Altizer is quite so radical on *this* issue as he is on the re-interpretation of, for example, the Incarnation. We have already seen that for him the death of God means the death of the eastern 'religious' God. It means the death of false conceptions of God, also characteristic of the Christian tradition. But he moves beyond the reformist position when he says that it also means the death of the true God.

The radical Christian proclaims that God has actually died in Christ, that this death is both a historical and cosmic event, and, as such, it is a final and irrevocable event, which cannot be reversed by a subsequent religious or cosmic movement.[37]

This would indeed represent the position defined above as the radical position. There was a God, and now there is not – and God will not return. However, there is evidence in

36. Altizer and Hamilton, *Radical Theology and the Death of God*, p. 14.
37. Altizer, *The Gospel of Christian Atheism*, p. 103.

Altizer's writings that he may not in fact hold this consistently radical position. For example, he regards the present time as an interim period.

Consequently the theologian must exist outside of the Church: he can neither proclaim the Word, celebrate the sacraments, nor rejoice in the presence of the Holy Spirit. Before contemporary theology can become itself, it must first exist in silence.[38]

Radical theology calls Christians to be faithful to the new Word which is breaking in, but through faithfulness to it – and this is the basis of describing Altizer's position as 'gospel' – there is hope of something in the future. 'A profane destiny may yet provide a way to return to the God who is all in all, not by returning to a moment of the past, but by meeting an epiphany of the past in the present.'[39]

The conclusion therefore comes as a surprise. Altizer is addressing himself to one problem only, how can western men regain the sacred without turning back from their secular culture? His work is after all an alternative to that of Mircea Eliade. But a concern for the sacred might be considered a peculiarly religious concern for any man. It would seem that for all his hard words against Barth, Altizer is still very much within the Barthian orbit. The 'religion' that he rejects is, after all, only some forms of religion (mainly oriental). He is still concerned primarily with providing 'a way to return to God'. But this is an extraordinarily reformist position for one who was taken to be almost out of sight of traditional theology.

Once this is said, certain other puzzling, or disappointing,

38. Altizer and Hamilton, *Radical Theology and the Death of God*, p. 30

39. ibid., p. 33. I refer to the last two questions with some hesitation, since they come from an essay 'America and the Future of Theology', which was published in 1963, whereas *The Gospel of Christian Atheism* was published in 1966. I use them not simply because the essay was republished in 1966, but because I think this view is integral to Altizer's whole position.

features fall into place. To speak as Altizer does is to adopt a mythological mode of expression. In the exposition of Altizer I have spoken of God's revelation of himself, or rather of our increasing understanding of the nature of God. We do not say that God was despotic or racialist in the Old Testament, but that men were as yet insensitive to his true nature. It is a mythological mode of expression therefore to speak about God becoming a man, and even of God dying. Similarly the idea that God awaits us in the future sounds like a continuing cosmic drama in which a supernatural being (the one rejected by Altizer) decides to intervene in history. We have already seen, in the work of Ogden and Macquarrie, how difficult it is to find a non-mythological way of speaking about God. Altizer always seems to me to be in danger of falling into the position he has condemned, namely, anticipating at the end the God who was known earlier. Indeed his whole eschatology is mythological too, as if he anticipated an encounter with God after a specific historical period.

It might be thought that Altizer's work would be of interest to those who — whether Christian or non-Christian — could not believe in God. In this respect it is even more disappointing. To call his work gospel, good news, we should have to ask : for whom is it good news? Stated thus, it is clear that Altizer is addressing Christians who have an experience of loss, and who wish to regain the presence of God.

He is present to us only in his absence, and to know the absent or the missing god is to know a void that must be filled with despair and rebellion, an *Angst* deriving from a *ressentiment* that is itself created by an inability to bear a full existence in the present moment.[40]

But this kind of word must be addressed to only a very few people today. It is not addressed to those who still believe, or to those whose disbelief has already been described above by

40. Altizer and Hamilton, *Radical Theology and the Death of God*, p. 137.

Adolfs as *not* involving despair or rebellion. Altizer's work, surprisingly, is really addressed to those who were religious, and wish to be so again. He offers nothing at all for the large and increasing number of people who have no feeling of loss, despair or rebellion. Altizer's whole position rests on the desire to establish the sacred again. And this is the fundamental weakness of his case. The culture in which we live embodies the fact that in a secular age the distinction between sacred and profane has no value. Altizer is wrong to think that in the Incarnation the sacred was dialectically negated, and may yet reappear. In the Incarnation the idea of speaking about sacred and profane was rendered meaningless.

Of particular interest for the position being developed in this book is the fact that Altizer claims that in the Incarnation transcendence is collapsed into immanence. On the whole this kind of statement does not affect our position, since transcendence normally seems to mean supernatural. The supernatural collapses into the natural. And yet this does highlight another weakness in Altizer's position. Altizer tends towards what might be called a positivism of the natural. Having eliminated the supernatural, he leaves himself no way of distinguishing between different options in what is left. Earlier we made a preliminary distinction between an immanent way of life, which followed the natural inclinations of man, and another more demanding way of life committed to transcendent values. Neither of these ways is concerned with supernaturalism, and yet Altizer does not give himself any grounds for such a distinction. The result is that Altizer is forced into a very quietist view of secular culture. The way to reach the sacred is to say 'Yes' to the secular world. But once that is said, it is clearly too crude a position to be realistic. Our secular culture is a very ambiguous one indeed, and saying 'Yes' to it could more easily lead to the demonic than to the divine. I am not convinced that Altizer does in fact free himself from a mythological supernaturalism, but even when he appears to do so, at least for a time, his positivism of the natural makes it impossible for him to distinguish aspects in the secular culture to which Christians might say 'Yes', and other aspects to which they might say 'No'. So that when Altizer speaks of transcendence collapsing into immanence, he does not threaten the position being developed in this book, but rather creates major problems for himself.

The final point which might be made about Altizer's work, in relation to this book, concerns the place of Jesus. As already noted on several occasions, Altizer certainly attempts to be Christocentric. The Incarnation not only reveals God to us, but indeed becomes the pattern of God's way with man and the pattern of man's response to the secular culture. Yet what we miss is any attempt to speak of Christ as the pattern for Christian living, either in personal or social ethics. This is related to the last point, in which we noted Altizer's quietist attitude towards the secular culture. But it goes beyond that point. Harvey Cox has been accused of making a virtue of necessity in dealing with our secular culture, always making the surprising discovery that what *is* is precisely what *ought* to be, but Altizer does not even discuss the elements of the secular culture. Thus Christians are encouraged to become completely secular. But this is to get the problem the wrong way round. It is not a question of how Christians can be secular men, but how men can be Christian in a secular age. How does 'Yes'-saying by a Christian differ from 'Yes'-saying by a non-Christian? Above all, how might Christians adopt a secular attitude, and yet try to change the situation? Not how can they make the situation religious (again) but how can they make it more Christian? Altizer is aware of the difficulties involved in speaking of the historical Jesus, but he relates this to the death of God.[41] He also blocks off any

41. 'The disappearance of the historical Jesus is but a particular expression of a far deeper reality, the death of God.' (Altizer and

attempt to substitute a supernatural Christ for a supernatural God.

There is a great deal of original and suggestive material in the work of Altizer, and while he lays himself open to criticism from those who occupy more orthodox positions, he is to be congratulated for attempting to deal so creatively with a problem which they, too often, do not take with sufficient seriousness.[42]

I do not wish to criticize him for not being orthodox, but I must criticize him for not being radical enough. He does not consistently live up to his own definition of radical theology. But more disappointing than that, at a time when some Christians are investigating *how* to be Christians in a secular age, Altizer, while nominally advocating this, actually turns attention away from the present towards the future. He claims to be overcoming the traditional dualism in theology, but the irony is that he overcomes a proper dualism only to present us with a false one. That is to say, he overcomes the justifiable dualism which we have been presenting in this book in the terms transcendence–immanence, but he ends up

---

Hamilton, *Radical Theology and the Death of God*, p. 128.) The only way in which this might make sense would be by considering the part which historical consciousness has played in the development of a secular culture. cf. 'King Midas, legend says, everything he touched turned to gold. For modern man everything, the whole of reality, turns to history.' (G. Ebeling, *Word and Faith*, trans. James W. Leitch, Fortress Press, Philadelphia, 1963, p. 363.) Also, Friedrich Gogarten's cryptic statement that 'What is not historical is for modern man not real.' (*Verhängnis und Hoffnung der Neuzeit*, quoted by Ebeling, loc. cit.)

42. The best short introduction to the Death of God theology is Thomas W. Ogletree, *The 'Death of God' Controversy* (S.C.M. Press, London, 1966), which presents a very comprehensive survey of the positions of Hamilton, van Buren and Altizer. Unfortunately Ogletree's criticisms tend to be from a traditional point of view, and do not illuminate Altizer's failure as a *radical* theologian, but rather how he differs from the orthodox position.

with his own version of the old sacred–profane division.

Altizer is without doubt a radical thinker, but because his radicalism is set in the context of an investigation of a traditional concern we must conclude that he is an old-fashioned reformist at heart. He does not provide any help in presenting the Christian faith to those who cannot believe in God.

WILLIAM HAMILTON: THEOLOGIAN IN WAITING

We have been concerned throughout this book with religious experience as the grounds for belief in God. How we interpret our experience – whether religious or not – depends to a considerable degree on the society and culture within which we live. But at the end of the day, we have to be satisfied that the interpretation is appropriate and adequate. One of the difficulties in dealing with the work of Altizer is that for much of the time he is not dealing with matters which we could conceivably experience, for example, when he deals with the cosmic implications of the death of God at the Incarnation, and also in the dialectical reaffirmation of the sacred which may take place in the future.

When we turn to William Hamilton we are dealing not simply with a change in style – though the change is frankly a great relief – but with a change in basic material. Hamilton engages in a good deal of analysis of his own personal situation, in the belief that when he has been frank and honest about what he experiences and believes this may be of some use to others. One of the most fascinating pieces of theology which I have read in recent years is not really a theological treatise at all. It is Hamilton's rather autobiographical essay 'Thursday's Child'.[43] Over a period I have discussed this essay with groups of lay people, of very mixed social and intellectual backgrounds, but of no theological training. The

43. Altizer and Hamilton, *Radical Theology and the Death of God*, pp. 95–101.

results are always the same, and quite amazing. Earlier I pointed out that *Honest to God* had come as a therapeutic experience to many Christians, who had not felt able to admit (even to themselves) that they could not believe certain things which were thought essential to being a Christian. It is clear to me that 'Thursday's Child' has precisely the same effect. This may come as a surprise to parish ministers and even theologians, for lay people are not always willing to be honest about such things. They are certainly very reluctant to acknowledge that they have lost the belief in God which they had as children or adolescents. In fact such discussion groups, if care is not taken, can take on the atmosphere of testimony night at a gospel hall. The difference is of course, that in the present circumstances, in a new mood of honesty and with not a little courage, people sometimes feel constrained to say that they do *not* believe in God. I wonder how many Christians there are who suffer yet from 'dishonesty and schizophrenia' because they wish to remain Christians but are afraid to face the fact, or admit it to others, that they no longer have any grounds in their experience for saying that they believe in God.

I believe that William Hamilton has done theology and the Church a great service by saying honestly where he finds himself. He has incurred even more abuse and criticism than John Robinson, simply because he has raised as an issue the one topic on which no debate is allowed within the Church. The result has been that Hamilton has been largely alienated from other theologians, and has not been able to enter into the constructive debate that he had hoped to provoke. Constructive debate is necessary, because he does not present us with a fixed or final position. Thursday's child, as we all knew at one time in our lives, 'has far to go', and Hamilton has been left to find his own way. A good deal has been made of the fact that he is becoming more and more radical, that his position as one of the leaders of the Death of God school was much more extreme than the views expressed in *The New Essence of Christianity*, published only a few years earlier.[44] But when we look at the book and the later essays, we see a basic continuity, in which the 'soft' use of the phrase 'death of God' is not completely overtaken by the 'hard' use. The continuity and ambivalence can be seen in presenting the two positions as they appear in relation to four themes.

1. The death of God is referred to in the book not in a reformist sense, i.e. not in relation to a false God or a false way of thinking about God, but as the death of the real God. 'I am not here referring to a belief in the non-existence of God. I am talking about a growing sense, in both non-Christians and Christians, that God has withdrawn, that he is absent, even that he is somehow dead.'[45] Hamilton does not speculate about the death of God as a cosmic event: the phrase is used to describe the experience of being deserted by God. 'If Jesus can wonder about being forsaken by God, are we to be blamed if we wonder?'[46] The idea of the death of God does not dominate the book, but it does provide the context in which it is written. In a time of confidence, doctrine is expanded and peripheral issues taken up with enthusiasm, but Hamilton claims to be speaking in a time when the central tenets of Christian faith are in question, and when therefore it is natural to concentrate on what it is that constitutes the essence of Christianity. 'We are reduced to fragments, partial vision, broken speech, not because of the unbelieving world "out there", but precisely because that unbelieving world has come to rest within ourselves.'[47]

2. The fact that even in a time of the absence of God, Hamilton is asking such questions indicates that he is still a Christian, or at least wishes to be one. Yet this period of absence

44. William Hamilton, *The New Essence of Christianity*, Darton, Longman & Todd, 1966. (First published in 1961.)
45. ibid., 53-4.   46. ibid., p. 57.   47. ibid., p. 28.

can only be an interim one. Either the experience of God returns, or Hamilton must cease to be a Christian. It is a period of waiting, in which faith becomes hope that God will in fact return. Of course he may not be there when he is wanted, and may well be there when he is not wanted, but this is the reality of 'this absent–present disturber God'.[48]

3. The problem then is to keep faith till God returns. But we must be sure that it is the Christian God, or we shall wait in vain. Hamilton is guided to some extent in his analysis of the present age by his reading of contemporary literature. Partly from this, and no doubt from his own background, he focuses upon a particular problem for theology, the problem of evil. Although his concern with this problem is real, I take it that the problem is symptomatic of a concern with a God who is not altogether Christian. We noted in dealing with Altizer that it might be claimed that, strange to say, the Church has not paid enough attention to the Incarnation. At least theology has not understood that the Incarnation is not about Jesus, but about God. It does not tell us anything about Jesus we did not already know, but it tells us a great deal about God which was not already known. We can see Hamilton taking up the same kind of position, not in the terminology of Altizer, but under the influence of Bonhoeffer. As I understand him, Hamilton is saying that the problem of evil also contributes to the death of God, but that it should not, since the traditional understanding of this problem depends on a view of God which is not Christian. The God we are dealing with is one revealed at the cross. In contrast to this, the God who is at the heart of the problem of evil is a God whose divinity should be rejected by Christians. 'To say that Jesus is Lord is to say that humiliation, patience, and suffering are the ways God has dealt with man in the world, and thus are also the ways the Christian man is to deal with the world.'[49]

48. ibid., p. 47.   49. ibid., pp. 102–3.

4. This leads us on to the final point. If it is the Christian God for whom we wait, then there is only one way in which to wait, and that is by keeping faith with the revelation in Christ. We shall only come to God again if we live out in the world his way of dealing with the world. Hamilton therefore ends with a chapter on 'The Style of the Christian Life'. I cannot say this is a particularly striking or exciting outline for a Christian life style. One element in it which may be surprising in the light of Hamilton's later position is his stress on the continuation of worship. 'One can perhaps become a Christian without prayer, but surely one cannot stay Christian without it.'[50] This recalls us to the fact that the period of God's absence must be but an interim one. Even when God is absent the life style must also be a worshipping one. 'All we know is that somehow our style of life must make room, in our world of noise and movement, for the silence, the waiting, the withdrawal of the life of prayer.'[51] Keeping faith with God in the absence of God must be a balance of contemplation and action.

Radical Theology and the Death of God reflects Hamilton's pilgrimage since his early book. The essays cover the period 1963–6, and the same themes appear as before.

1. While in the book Hamilton looked for the return of God after an interim period, in the essays we find a more aggressive assertion of 'not-having'. In the parables of Jesus, even while the master is away and the stewards are faithful, even though the timing of his return is uncertain, there is no question about the existence of the master. The William Hamilton Mark-II position is that he no longer has grounds for believing in God at all. This was to some extent anticipated in the earlier book, where he maintained that the traditional view of God, the Wholly Other, lends itself finally to the conclusion that the God who is totally removed is just not there after all. In our illustration from the parables, what is

50. ibid., p. 122.   51. ibid., p. 123.

the difference between a master who is not going to return, and no master at all? And yet this is not just a sophisticated atheism, 'atheism dressed in a new spring bonnet'[52] (Though possibly an Easter bonnet?) The Death of God position, by the radical definition already quoted is 'that there once was a God to whom adoration, praise and trust were appropriate, possible, and even necessary, but that now there is no such God'. The difference is marked by a sense of loss. It is not the position of those who have never known God, nor that of those who still know him. It is not even the position of *The New Essence of Christianity* which was characterized by the absence of God, but the absence of the 'absent–present disturber God'. The denial of God is not the intellectual denial of the possibility of God, but the denial that the God previously known is known any longer. 'It is really that we do not know, do not adore, do not possess, do not believe in God.'[53]

Yet if it is possible to distinguish this position both from atheism and from other 'waiting for God', 'eclipse of God' positions, is it really anything new? A standard response to the Death of God theology has been that it is just a new name, not for atheism, but for what in the history of devotion has been called 'the dark night of the soul'. Those who wish to interpret it in this way are free to do so, since, like the test of prophecy, only time will tell. If anything, however, the signs are not favourable for such an interpretation. The dark night has normally overcome individuals, whereas now it is overtaking whole generations. Hamilton goes further than this, in a well-known statement. 'We are not talking about the absence of the experience of God, but about the experience of the absence of God.'[54] Such an assertion is open, of course, to the traditional objection that we cannot directly observe the absence of an entity, but Hamilton is

52. Altizer and Hamilton, *Radical Theology and the Death of God*, p. 40.   53. ibid., p. 40.   54. ibid., p. 40.

referring to the sense of loss involved in the death of God. The analogy is not the departure of a loved one, but the death of a loved one. He maintains that this experience of loss may be painful for some, but not for others, but in each case there is a void, a disappearance.

2. It is difficult to believe that Hamilton does not place special significance on this particular loss. Clearly the loss of a pair of gloves is annoying, but trivial. The loss of a child or parent can be a shattering experience. But I suspect Hamilton relates the loss of God to the deepest existential level, in which the experience is the loss of that reality which both created and sanctioned the meaning and direction of life. And yet since the life can remain without the sanction, there is a sense in which the continuation of the life maintains the reality which appears to have gone.

However that may be, it is not altogether surprising that Hamilton is not entirely consistent in maintaining that God has gone forever. 'Our waiting for God, our godlessness, is partly a search for a language and a style by which we might be enabled to stand before him once again, delighting in his presence.'[55] We therefore see the theme of waiting, which played a central part in the book, now appearing once again. And indeed the references to finding new ways of speaking and acting sound positively reformist. When he says that while waiting, 'we pray for God to return',[56] he returns to the theme of finding a style of life which includes a place for prayer, the theme which occupied him in the final chapter of the book. In this respect he has not moved at all, in the essays, from the position of the book. Indeed he can even reiterate that 'waiting here refers to the whole experience I have called "the death of God"',[57] which is a return to the 'soft' use of the phrase.

3. The influence of Bonhoeffer is increasingly seen in the essays. The religious premise is rejected, so that whether God

55. ibid., p. 53.   56. ibid., p. 58.   57. ibid.

is to be found or not, even the true God cannot be found as 'our need-fulfiller and problem-solver'.[58] In his later essays he makes it clear that he goes further than Bonhoeffer, in declaring his alienation from worship, from preaching and the sacraments. He has no interest in the renewal movements within the Church which are concerned with the Church. In this respect he seems to take a more radical line than Bonhoeffer's 'secret discipline', but also his own position on the necessity of prayer.

4. The greatest stress in the essays is put on ethics, the style of Christian living. The waiting must not be a religious waiting (dark night of the soul?), but a waiting on God in the form of being Christ to the neighbour. If in the book faith became hope, now 'faith has collapsed into love'.[59] Altizer might be said to focus attention upon Jesus Christ, and indeed his position cannot be understood except as an exposition of the Incarnation. In their joint introduction, Altizer and Hamilton say that 'The radical theologian has a strange but compelling interest in the figure of Jesus'.[60] This reads more like Hamilton, since Altizer has little interest in the man Jesus, least of all in his ethical significance. Yet Hamilton is far from simply advocating a walking in the footsteps of the Master. He reckons the present time to be one of confusion between Christology and ethics.

We may finish this study by referring to two points from 'Thursday's Child'. God has gone, but the Christian life remains. Yet just as in the book Hamilton warned against a pre-Christian conception of divinity, so he now returns to the same theme, in the context of the Church. Since Hamilton cannot take part in public worship, and is not concerned with Church renewal movements, he might be expected to admit that he is alienated from the Church. Far from it. The radical theologian 'has an overwhelmingly positive sense of being in and not out; even in his unbelief he is somehow

58. ibid., p. 52.　　　59. ibid., p. 48.　　　60. ibid., p. 16

home and not in a far country'.[61] I take this to mean that the radical theologian still feels very much part of the body of Christ, since he strives to embody this life style. But he also feels at home in a world from which God has disappeared, because it is precisely in the world and not in the self-centred Church that Christ is to be found. So that being alienated from the least Christian parts of the life of the Church is a positive gain to the radical theologian.

The second point, which follows from this, is that the radical theologian, who now has no other concern than the way of Christ, is free to discover anew the true significance of the 'man for others'. Thus once again, in the essays as in the book, Christ becomes the norm by which divinity is judged. Speaking of this concern for the neighbour, he says, 'This may be the meaning of Jesus' true humanity and it may even be the meaning of his divinity, and thus of divinity itself. In any case, now – even [though] he knows so little about what to believe – he does know where to be.'[62]

I have already indicated the importance of 'Thursday's Child', and indeed the whole of Hamilton's work. He has very honestly and courageously given us an analysis of just what it is that he does not believe, as well as what he does believe. I have only two points to make. One is a defence and the other a criticism.

The defence concerns the familiar question:[63] with what justification can a radical theologian put such emphasis on Jesus? Such questions sometimes range beyond alternatives, such as Socrates and Ghandhi, to Hitler. Hamilton tries to answer this question seriously, but I am not at all sure that he should feel this to be particularly relevant to his own position. Is it not true to say that this question can be put with equal force to everyone who confesses that Jesus is Lord? Why Jesus? Nor I think does belief in God make any

61. ibid., p. 100.   62. ibid.
63. e.g., Ogletree, *The 'Death of God' Controversy*, p. 36.

significant difference here. After all, do we confess faith in
Jesus because he is the Son of God, or do we give him this
title because he justifies our faith in him? Once again we
must say that the dogmatic assertion that Jesus is the Son of
God is not revealed. The assertion is the orthodox interpretation of what is revealed in Jesus. But why this interpretation
is appropriate is just as pointed a question, directed towards
the man who believes in God, as the question directed against
Hamilton's *post mortem dei* faith in Jesus.

The criticism must be prefaced with a final assessment. In
the course of this present book, we have been concerned with
those who wish to commit themselves to the way of Jesus,
'the way of transcendence', even though they cannot believe in God. William Hamilton might therefore appear to
occupy precisely that position, and to be well placed to give
us great assistance. Of course there is a great deal of value
in his work, but his position is significantly different from
the one which concerns us. Like Altizer, he can justifiably
claim to occupy a Christian position, though he does not
proclaim it as a gospel. But, as in the case of Altizer, we must
question whether it really is a form of atheism at all. Certainly *The New Essence of Christianity* provides us with a
'soft' use of the phrase 'death of God', speaking of an
'absent–present' God. It might be argued that *Radical Theology and the Death of God* provides us with a 'hard' use
of the phrase 'death of God'. This 'hard' use would be based
on atheism, i.e. on the contention that while there was a
God in the past, thinking and acting must now be done without reference to such a being. Yet the theme of 'waiting'
undermines the credibility of his 'hard' use of the phrase. It
is to be found in the essays just as much as in the book, and
since it is found in an interview with Ved Mehta in 1966,
we should not be over-eager to characterize Hamilton as an
increasingly radical theologian.

I think a lot of people nowadays *make* it without believing in

God, and without despairing about not believing in God, so God may be dead or gone. I mean the Judaeo-Christian God. But I am still waiting and hoping for God to rise up again.[64]

The suspicion that Hamilton's position is not really based on the 'hard' use, corresponding to the second definition of 'death of God' already quoted, does not simply arise from his continued compromising of it with the 'waiting' theme. It could be argued that in this he is simply inconsistent, swinging between the soft and hard uses. It could be argued that he actually has two incompatible positions, and that his later one is increasingly the hard one. But the evidence against his atheism does not rest solely upon the 'waiting' theme. It is to be found, for example, in the last quotation given from 'Thursday's Child'. There he returned to the theme expressed so ably in his earlier book, namely the way in which Jesus redefines divinity. Not simply, let it be noted, how we might re-interpret the so-called divinity of Jesus in a secular manner appropriate to the time of the death of God, but how the life of Jesus illuminates the meaning 'of divinity itself'. We have already noted that he can speak of trying to find new ways of speaking about God, and acting responsibly before God. In this respect his work is a striking kind of reformist theology. But it should not be understood as Christian atheism. It is really a very interesting form of secular theology, and nothing more – or should we say nothing less.

Our present study concerns the possibility of addressing those who cannot believe in God, and challenging them with the 'way of transcendence'. The work of William Hamilton represents a reformist position, if slightly more extreme than *Honest to God*. He is concerned with the problem of how a Christian who has lost God may still keep faith. This is much more limited and introspective concern than ours.

64. V. Mehta, *The New Theologian*, Penguin Books, Harmondsworth, 1968, p. 69.

THE MEANING OF THE DEATH OF GOD

We are told that there is a lot of radical theology about these days. The trouble, as we have discovered, is trying to catch sight of it. Theologians and vicars can claim to be radical on all sorts of issues, but when it comes to the non-credo, the affirmation of the death of God, they come to the point where they must admit they are not radical. Radical theology 'persists in making use of the phrase "death of God", in spite of its rhetorical colour, partly because it is a phrase that cannot be adapted to traditional use by the theologians to-day'.[65] Hamilton focuses on this phrase as the parting of the ways. Those who can really use this phrase and mean it, are divided off from those who use it in various reformist senses. But it is clear from our examination of the views of Altizer and Hamilton that even they do not qualify as Death of God theologians, not even by their own definition of the position. Far from being men who know that God will never again appear, both Altizer and Hamilton are men who hope, in one way or another, that God will reappear. Altizer hopes that through 'Yes'-saying to the secular world we may yet come to a new epiphany of the sacred. Hamilton hopes that if in the time of the death of God we keep faith with him by embodying the life of Christ, then he may yet return. The fact that this is not a misrepresentation of the Death of God movement is to be seen in Dorothee Sölle's book, *Christ the Representative: an essay in theology after the 'Death of God'*[66] Dr Sölle speaks of the present time of the absence of God as a time when he needs to be represented before us. 'Either we can assume that God's absence means he is dead, and so seek or create a substitute for him. Or we can regard

65. Altizer and Hamilton, *Radical Theology and the Death of God*, p. 22.
66. D. Sölle, *Christ the Representative: an essay in theology after the 'Death of God'*, trans. D. Lewis, S.C.M. Press, London, 1967.

his absence as a possible mode of his being-for-us.'[67] Despite the sub-title of the work, it is clear that the last thing envisaged by Dr Sölle is that God might actually be dead, i.e. that he will never again be experienced.

To this extent it is difficult to see not only why such an emotive phrase as 'the death of God' should be used, but also difficult to see why these theologians should be considered radical. And here is the irony of the matter. Altizer and Hamilton are considered as radicals because of what they say about God. But while they are very radical and most helpful in other aspects of their work, the irony is that in their doctrine of God they are relatively conservative. They might be thought of as radical if they pursued their analysis that men today just cannot believe in God, and that therefore they must find a secular form of Christian faith. They might even make a claim to be radical if they sought revolutionary new ways of conceiving of God. But the irony is that both Altizer and Hamilton hope for the *same* God to return as the God who has recently disappeared. They certainly make it plain that the God in whom Christians should believe must be a *Christian* God, and this has been brought out in our discussion of Altizer on the Incarnation and Hamilton on Jesus' redefinition of divinity. But once that is said, it is precisely this God who is anticipated in the future.

What possible justification is there then for using the phrase 'death of God' at all? Whether God is absent or present, both Altizer and Hamilton speak within a theological context. The familiar taunt gets it right except for one word: '*While* there is no God: Jesus is his only Son.' And this describes the positions of Altizer, Hamilton and, *a fortiori*, Dorothee Sölle. This 'while' means that the whole discussion about this interim period of the absence of God still takes place *coram dei*, in the presence of God. The master of the house, as in the parables, has gone away, but nothing has

67. ibid., p. 131.

changed. It is his house, and the stewards must be faithful to him.

Despite the protestations to the contrary, does the phrase 'death of God' actually mean anything? Alternatively, who has the right to claim orthodoxy in its use? The with-it parsons may use it as a revamped intro to an old theme. The popularizing theologian may use it to show that he is in touch. But it would seem that not even the radicals use it in a meaningful and consistent way. Gabriel Vahanian might be seen making his way forward to claim custody of the phrase: did he not introduce it into contemporary theology?

There is only one man in the modern era who has exhibited a consistent and meaningful use of the phrase. It is appropriate that this man, Friedrich Nietzsche, was the one who introduced it into common usage. It has not been developed since his day. To the contrary, it has been trivialized and cheapened from the meaning and significance it had in his exceedingly powerful use of the phrase. It is appropriate now to turn to Nietzsche, not simply because he knew the meaning of the death of God in a way that no contemporary theologian does, but because it is in his work that our problem receives its most dramatic expression.

CHAPTER 4

Nietzsche and the Godless World

THE work of Friedrich Nietzsche (1844–1900) may be re-regarded as the most powerful and sustained of the great nineteenth-century critiques of religion. It is perhaps of some significance that in approaching these critiques we must make a conscious effort to avoid the pervasive but distorting associations normally regarded as the key to their interpretation. As Feuerbach (see Chapter 7) is all too often understood through Barth's attack on Schleiermacher, as Marx is fended off through fear of communism, so in the popular mind Nietzsche has been discredited by association with German fascism. Further, his works are not only extensive but labyrinthine, strident and polemical, often haughty and assertive. We know that he was insane when he died, and mentally ill for ten years before that, but there is always the suspicion that this condition may already have been developing during his active life as a writer. So long as we think of him as one of the great sinister figures of the last century, the prophet of the most demonic of movements in the present century, then even if he has something to say to us, we shall not hear it.

Fortunately this view of Nietzsche is both unjustified and misleading. We are no more likely to be converted to fascism by reading Nietzsche than to Stalinism by reading Marx. Ironically, it seems there is a strong case to be made for saying that Nietzsche was opposed to the sentiments and philosophy which paved the way for National Socialism. It has even been suggested that a general revulsion from the policies and views of the Nazis has coincided with a revival in interest in Nietzsche.[1]

It is more common now to see Nietzsche's association with Aryanism through a relationship which he later repudiated, and through a calculated distortion of his work by his editor. The relationship was with Richard Wagner, during the period 1869–76, when Wagner was at the height of his powers and influence. Nietzsche was fascinated by him, but the final break was on these precise grounds, the singleness of mind with which Wagner sought power and influence. Nietzsche the philosopher–psychologist could not have had a better subject for the embodiment of the 'will to power'. Hitler was an admirer of the work of Wagner, with good reason. In his later operas his heroes are increasingly men who set themselves above the conventions of society, who create their own standards of truth and morality. No one who wanted to associate the work of Nietzsche with the Aryan philosophy took seriously Nietzsche's rejection of Wagner and all forms of German imperialism.

In the last few years of his life Nietzsche was cared for by his sister, Elisabeth, and she managed to gain sole rights to the publication of his works. The only major work which has

1. 'The destruction of Nazi Germany – and with it not merely the dream of a thousand-year *Reich* but also the actuality of a seventy-five-year Reich might have meant the destruction of Nietzsche too: what it in fact meant was the destruction of the pseudo-Nietzsche, the mythological figure invented by the George Circle and by the Nietzsche Archive with the collaboration, active and passive, of the German academic world; invented too, it must be said, by Nietzsche himself in his last months of semi-sanity. The cataclysm which wrecked the pseudo-Nietzsche was also responsible for the revival of the real Nietzsche: the reawakening of interest in him was closely connected with the recollection that the spiritual void of the 1940s was not merely prophesied in his philosophy but was actually its presupposition: Nietzsche *started* from the point Europe had just reached.' (R. J. Hollingdale, *Nietzsche: The Man and His Philosophy*, Routledge & Kegan Paul, London, 1965, p. vii.)

been seriously affected by this arrangement is *The Will to Power*, which is not a single work by Nietzsche, but a collection of aphorisms edited by his sister. But more damaging for the *interpretation* of his works was the persistence with which she tried to associate Nietzsche with German nationalism and even with the anti-Semitism of her late husband. Bernhard Förster had been one of the leaders of this movement, and an admirer of Wagner. Walter Kaufmann has written a very vigorous attack upon the attempts to associate Nietzsche with the nationalist sentiments and Aryan ideology, especially the part played by Nietzsche's sister.

If one wanted a symbol of his sister's unfitness for her later role as his apostle, one might find it in the name which she assumed in this capacity : Förster-Nietzsche. The irony of this name suggests almost everything that could be said against her : the gospel she spread was indeed Förster first and Nietzsche second.[2]

I have thought it worth mentioning these points concerning Nietzsche and the Nazi movement because we must have the record before us if we are to approach his work in a receptive, sympathetic, though critical, frame of mind. Yet we must not be swept along by Kaufmann's arguments. Of course he is right to say that *historically* Nietzsche broke with Wagner and expressly repudiated the developing Aryan and anti-Semitic ideology of the day. Of course it is historically correct to say that he later specifically denied that Wagner could be seen as the hero type of his work (e.g. Zarathustra). But, nonetheless, there are fundamental elements in the works of Nietzsche which were congenial to the Nazis. To be sure, Nietzsche rejected both German imperialism and Aryan racialism, yet as we shall see, his work was anti-democratic and characteristically elitist. Nationalism and racialism aside – granted they are not insignificant factors – his work did encourage and guide National Socialism. This

2. Walter Kaufmann, *Nietzsche: Philosopher, Psychologist, Antichrist*, Meridian Books, World Publishing Co., New York, 1956, p. 50.

against Kaufmann's perhaps too frantic attempt to defend Nietzsche. And against Hollingdale, the suggestion that the 'real' Nietzsche has been discovered in a post-fascist Europe would have to be further examined. When Hollingdale's book was published in 1965, there were signs, which have become more apparent since, that Europe has not rid itself of fascism. Many of the elements which combined to endear Nietzsche to Germans in the 1920s and 1930s are once again present in Europe today. Nietzsche was not a proto-Nazi, but we should not be uncritical of his elitist views, nor indeed of the general implications of his philosophy.

THE REVALUATION OF ALL VALUES

Not all critics of Christianity have been religious at some time in their lives, but as we might expect, the most able critics have very often come from Christian homes – a surprising number from clerical families. Kaufmann frequently describes Nietzsche as a 'protestant' atheist. His criticism of religion refers particularly to the Lutheran tradition, which he knew best. But before examining such criticism, something must be said about his atheism.

We cannot describe how Nietzsche became an atheist: perhaps he never came to a belief in God at all. The characteristic of his position, however, was not simply a rejection of religion but rather the seeking out of the implications of atheism for the whole of human life. Religious people often assume that atheists live in exactly the same world as they do, except that the atheists do not worship God. Religious or non-religious, they can admire, praise, criticize or condemn the same things. This, as a matter of fact, can and does happen, but Nietzsche raised the question whether or not it should. In moral and aesthetic matters it might be said that for the religious man, God is the source and guarantee of trans-subjective standards. While a non-religious man might unthinkingly accept that there are such standards of judgement and evaluation, Nietzsche asks whether he has any right to accept them without the divine sanction. Thus the difference between the world of the religious man and the world of the non-religious involves more than the loss of a supernatural being. For Nietzsche it involves the loss also of every moral landmark and every aesthetic point of reference.

This point has of course been disputed, especially in the 'morals without religion' debate. But the issue for Nietzsche is not simply one of logic. Arguments could be found for continuing to adopt the same value system as before, but this would always be suspect, very much a justification after the event. The characteristic of the work of Nietzsche here is the traumatic experience of the collapse not only of a religious way of looking at the world – which he probably never fully accepted – but also the collapse of all metaphysics. Not the disappearance of the world, but its collapse, so that the laborious and painful process of building must begin this time on a new basis. The point is easily made in philosophical terms, but it is typical of Nietzsche that to express the existential dismay of living in a world without God he should turn to metaphor.

We have quit the land and gone on board ship. We have cut off the bridge behind us – more than that, the land behind us. Now, little ship, be careful. Alongside you lies the ocean. True, it does not always roar, and sometimes it stretches out as silk and gold, like a pleasant dream. But there will be times when you will realize that it is infinite and that there is nothing more dreadful than infinity. Oh, the poor bird that felt itself free but now beats against the side of the cage. Alas, if you should be seized by homesickness for land, as if there had been more freedom there – and there is no 'land' any more.[3]

'The Gay Science' is the name which Nietzsche gives to

3. 'Die fröhliche Wissenschaft', *Nietzsche's Werke*, Alfred Kröner Verlag, Stuttgart, 1921, Vol. 5, p. 162.

his philosophy, but there is a kind of desperate gaiety about it. Thrust out of a religious world in which he could be commanded, yet Nietzsche still found himself answerable. He was still responsible and free, and had to discover a completely new basis of judgement. This was his task, the 're-valuation of all values'. He was not a nihilist, nor was he immoral. He had to find a new standard of judgement, now that the divine standard had been removed.

It was therefore his atheism which led him to criticize Christianity, but particularly this necessity of having to begin again. Neither Feuerbach nor Marx felt this particular form of alienation. In so far as Marx had any interest in discussing morality, he purported to approve of original Christian ethics, by which standards he then criticized contemporary Christian practice. This is the tradition of holding up the example of Jesus to condemn the witness of his followers. But Nietzsche was committed to a more thoroughgoing reconstruction of the value system than any such ethical eclecticism. If he could find a new basis for evaluation then it would in all probability lead him to criticize the Christianity of all periods and even the ethics of Jesus himself. Thus his final *magnum opus* was to be *Revaluation of All Values*. Although incomplete, we know its course, and in particular we have the first part, *The Antichrist*. The task Nietzsche set himself was an ambitious one, which he did not complete, and which we may doubt whether, given time, he ever would have completed. But his position was an original one, so far as it went. It broke with Christianity, and also presented an elitist view of humanity, which, as I have suggested, was congenial to fascism.

The understandings of man offered by religion and by Idealism were rejected by Nietzsche, but fortunately for him a new way was opened up at precisely that moment. 'Nietzsche was aroused from his dogmatic slumber by Darwin, as Kant had been by Hume a century earlier . . ."[4] Yet his acceptance of the theory of evolution and his use of it were complex. On the one hand he saw that man, related in some sense to the apes, is simply an animal, albeit of an advanced type. This meant that there could be no non-natural sanction for human judgements on morals or aesthetics. But on the other hand, Nietzsche was more consistent than most of his contemporaries, who associated evolution with the idea of progress. If there is no God, then, for Nietzsche, there is neither eschatology nor teleology. He refused to replace God with an historical process which was 'leading' somewhere. This view of 'making sense' of life, giving it meaning and purpose, he regarded as an illegitimate hang-over from a religious view of the world. In his acceptance of Darwin's theory, then, Nietzsche was forced to give a natural basis for values, but in rejecting teleology he was forced to give an a-historical view of value. 'The *goal of humanity* cannot lie in the end but only *in its highest specimens.*'[5]

To say that man is an animal of an advanced type is not a new departure in philosophy; it is normally stated to shock us, but then quickly qualified in so many ways that, with relief, we see that man is not understood as an animal at all. We might expect Nietzsche to insist that man is indeed an animal, without qualification, but even he goes on to enter a qualification. Man also has a potentiality for self-realization. To be sure, very few men actualize this potential. Perhaps they do not care to; more often society prevents them. This is the basis of Nietzsche's elitism. He has no interest in the mass of people who do not strive to actualize this potential. His sympathies are entirely with those who wish to go 'beyond'. The man who strives thus to go beyond the normal, the customary, the average, is the Superman or Overman

4. Kaufmann, *Nietzsche: Philosopher, Psychologist, Antichrist*, p. 142.   5. Quoted by Kaufmann, ibid., p. 127.

(*Ubermensch*).[6] The 'goal of humanity' is not in the future, but in the appearance of 'the higher men'.

We should not allow our natural interest in this terminology to disguise from us the fact that it is inconsistent with Nietzsche's general premises. The terms 'super' and 'higher' represent value judgements which Nietzsche is making, without any proper basis for them. He deals with the Higher Men in *Thus Spake Zarathustra*. They should have power and authority, instead of those who usurp it at present. Nietzsche admires them, but the present leaders simply disgust him. Yet Nietzsche does not show how the individuals he singles out, though different from the average person, are qualitatively superior to the average. Or rather, even when he has described the characteristics which distinguish the higher men from the average, he does not show why these characteristics should be regarded as superior, more worthy. Nietzsche is in danger here of introducing a non-natural factor into the situation.

His attempt to overcome this problem is found in the development of the concept of 'the will to power'. The unity of his previous position had been his concentration upon the natural, rejecting any dualism with a supposed supernatural realm. The sub-title to Kaufmann's book includes the description of Nietzsche as a psychologist, and he certainly was a very shrewd observer of men and human motivation. The crude concept of nature had not proved to be a consistent enough basis for his revaluation, and he turned therefore towards the internal drives which make some men strive to 'go beyond' themselves. The advantage of this concept was that it seemed to describe something inherent in human nature. Everyone lives by this drive, though it takes many forms. Yet even here Nietzsche sees the new unity divide once again. Previously nature had been divided into nature

6. Both versions sound odd to our ears, the first suggesting a children's fantasy, the other a grade in a coal-pit.

and 'true' nature. Now the will to power is seen to have two basic forms. Or rather, it can provide the driving force for man to overcome himself, if properly harnessed, or it can be used simply at the natural level to gain power over others. For Nietzsche the 'goal of humanity', the superman or the higher men, involves using the will to power, but using it to go beyond the average, accepted view of human life. 'Man is something that must be surpassed.'[7]

It is on this basis that Nietzsche mounts his criticism of Christianity. 'What is good? All that augments the feeling of power, the will to power and power itself in man. What is bad? All that stems from weakness.'[8] There are different ways of using the drive of the will to power, but for Nietzsche the greatest error is its rejection. He sees this drive as the one which has determined the selective aspect of evolution. The drive can be harnessed for good or ill, but to reject it is fatal. And this is where he criticizes Christianity, for in it he finds the will to power replaced by 'sympathy' and 'pity'. So, in more dramatic form, Zarathustra, when he meets the Ugliest Man, is overcome first of all by pity, and therefore weakness. But he pulls himself together, and becomes stern again. The Ugliest Man pleads for help. He is being persecuted, but worst of all, he is being pitied. Zarathustra has heard that God died in a strange way. 'Is it true, what they say, that pity choked him?'[9] The last pope is able to describe the scene as the old God existed, 'world-weary, will-weary till one day he suffocated of his all too great pity'.[10] Sympathy and pity represent the rejection of the will to power. They not only foreshorten man's capacity for creativity, but, in running contrary to nature, they have

7. 'Also Sprach Zarathustra', *Nietzsche's Werke*, Alfred Kröner Verlag, Leipzig, 1923, Vol. 6, p. 388.

8. 'Der Antichrist', *Friedrich Nietzsche*, Carl Hanser Verlag, Munich, 2nd revised edition, 1960, Vol. 2, p. 1165.

9. 'Also Sprach Zarathustra', p. 377.   10. ibid., p. 379.

disastrous consequences: 'where the will to power is deficient, degeneration comes about'.[11] It represents a reversal of evolution. 'Wherever the will to power declines, no matter in what form, then there is always a physiological retrogression, decadence.'[12] Nietzsche, as we have seen, does not believe in automatic progress for the human race, but without the will to power there can be no achievement. Hence the danger of Christianity is that it destroys the motive power under which the superman, or the higher men, can appear.

This is no longer the familiar 'Christian' criticism of Christianity, the charge that the Church is not living up to the standards of Jesus. Nietzsche could make that distinction, but in fact it is not relevant to his criticism. Or rather, we might say that in so far as the Church has very often in its history forsaken the ethic of Jesus for the way of unethical political and social manipulation, Nietzsche should approve of Christianity precisely when it is *least* Christian. 'Christian is the hatred of the *senses*, of the joys of the senses, of joy in general.'[13] It is world-renouncing, it is No-saying, and it exhibits 'lack of faith in the "higher men"'.[14] For Nietzsche, Jesus called men to follow his example, but Paul has perverted Christian living into the life of faith, which is a substitute for a life of struggle. Faith represents weakness of will, just as conviction represents weakness of logic.

Although Nietzsche began by trying to construct a new basis of evaluation quite apart from religion, it becomes clear in *The Antichrist* that as a rule of thumb, whatever Christianity approves of must be rejected, and its opposite espoused. The revaluation of all values therefore becomes 'the attempt undertaken with all resources, with all instincts, with all genius, to bring about the triumph of the *opposite* values, the *noble* values'.[15] The revaluation has already begun simply because Nietzsche and other 'free spirits' have appeared.

11. 'Der Antichrist', pp. 1167–8.   12. ibid., p. 1177.
13. ibid., p. 1181.   14. ibid., p. 1189.   15. ibid., p. 1233.

In this account I have been concerned to show the general application of Nietzsche's critique to Christianity. His understanding of the Bible or Christian faith and practice could be challenged at almost any particular point, but the overall point that he wishes to make could probably be consistently maintained, even when these specific issues had been resolved. His main point concerns the 'goal of humanity', and the inhibiting effect which religion has and will always have on human development. Once again we turn from Nietzsche's more direct statements to his dramatic, metaphorical presentations of the matter. The issue is brought to a head in Nietzsche's discussion of the Death of God.

Before leaving this discussion, however, two final points might be made. The first concerns the question of Nietzsche and fascism – again. It is not difficult to see the strong appeal in his work to those who regarded sympathy and pity not only as inappropriate in the fascist 'crusade' (though the cross was a distorted one) but as a positive danger to the cause. Nor were all of those who adopted this attitude outside the Church. We might adapt Kaufmann's words on Elisabeth Förster-Nietzsche to say that the so-called 'German-Christians' were German first and Christian second. The other point concerns Nietzsche's philosophy of 'eternal recurrence', which he defined as the doctrine of 'the unconditional and infinitely repeated circulation of all things ...'[16] Although Nietzsche regarded this as one of the central contributions of his philosophy, comparable to the will to power, I cannot see that it plays a formative role in his work. It is connected with Nietzsche's own personal history, with an experience which came to him in 1881 and which might be described as mystical or quasi-religious.[17] Its relevance to us is not the highly speculative metaphysical doctrine, but

16. *The Birth of Tragedy*, quoted by Kaufmann, *Nietzsche: Philosopher, Psychologist, Antichrist*, p. 275.

17. *Ecce Homo*, quoted in Kaufmann, ibid., p. 179.

rather Nietzsche's insistence that 'The goal of humanity cannot lie in the end but only in its highest specimens.' With his rejection of religion, Nietzsche also rejected all forms of teleology. That is to say he rejected the notion that individuals and particular moments of history are 'made significant' by reference to the historical process as a whole. The particular has its own significance, apart from the general, or it has no significance at all. It is along this line that I think Nietzsche's teaching on eternal recurrence might be interpreted, leaving aside the speculative aspects. In this Nietzsche does represent a further criticism of religion whenever it tends to undervalue the particular and the present, subsuming them in a grand view of 'salvation history' or regarding this vale of tears as without lasting significance. Clearly those who live at an early stage in any such historical process are at a disadvantage, and Nietzsche provides a valid reminder that we must not allow any such metaphysical view to rob an individual either of significance in his own time, or fulfilment in his own terms.

THE DEATH OF GOD

We began our examination of Nietzsche with his recognition of the fact that when God is removed, the universe of meaning, significance and value collapses. It is illegitimate to continue to occupy the same structure when the foundation and justification for it have been removed. Nietzsche was at first oppressed by the recognition of this fact, and later overjoyed by his success (at least to his own satisfaction) in establishing a new basis for meaning, significance and value. The crisis for Nietzsche can be expressed directly or metaphorically, and perhaps the most famous dramatic presentation of it involves his use of the concept of the 'death of God'.

One of the most important of Nietzsche's aphorisms forms a background to this discussion. 'It is our taste which now decides against Christianity, not our reason.'[18] In passing, we should note its significance for any discussion between religious men and atheists. If atheism were the conclusion of a rational argument then there would always be the possibility of producing a sufficiently plausible counter-argument that atheism would give way to theism. But Nietzsche says that his atheism, and, he hints, the atheism of a host of moderns of his time, is not a matter of argument. Religion is simply no longer a live option. This makes any attempt to revive religion as a live option a very much more complex process than the construction of a good argument. Nietzsche does not reject Christianity because of historical questions about the Bible. Nor is it a moral rejection because Christians do not practice what they preach. Granted that at various times in history belief in God has been a very prominent feature of European culture, Nietzsche is not concerned to take on the interminable discussions about what our ancestors believed, and why. That is their concern. I take it that Nietzsche did not believe there ever was a God, but the thing that concerns him now is that there is no longer such an option. He chooses to state this in a colourful and dramatic way. The death of God describes a quasi-historical event, a cultural fact rather than a logical conclusion. Something has happened in nineteenth-century Europe, something about the way people think and behave, the relationship they have to themselves and their understanding of the natural world. All these factors have combined to produce a cultural event, the death of God, and all those who have participated in the making of this cultural event are responsible for the death of God.

Nietzsche was, above all, a dialectical thinker, and this applies to his treatment of the death of God. I should like to

18. 'Die fröhliche Wissenschaft', *Nietzsche's Werke*, p. 168.

quote two passages which deal with this theme. In both he begins by speaking of the terrible consequences of the death of God, consequences so unthinkable that it is hardly surprising that, though the event has taken place, men are willing neither to discuss it nor accept it. But the second part of each passage deals with the new possibilities opened up by the death of God. Nietzsche's treatment of the theme is therefore dialectical in this sense, that he presents the death of God in its negative significance, as the end of the world as we know it, but immediately follows it with a positive interpretation of the event as the clearing away of the old in preparation for the new world.

The first passage is headed 'What our Cheerfulness Signifies':

The most important of more recent events – that 'God is dead', that the belief in the Christian God has become unworthy of belief – already begins to cast its first shadows over Europe. To the few at least whose eye, whose *suspecting* glance, is strong enough and subtle enough for this drama, some sun seems to have set, some old, profound confidence seems to have changed into doubt: our old world must seem to them daily more darksome, distrustful, strange and 'old'. In the main, however, one may say that the event itself is far too great, too remote, too much beyond most people's power of apprehension, for one to suppose that so much as the report of it could have reached them; not to speak of many who already knew what had taken place, and what must all collapse now that this belief had been undermined, – because so much was built upon it, so much rested on it, and had become one with it: for example, our entire European morality. This lengthy, vast and uninterrupted process of crumbling, destruction, ruin and overthrow which is now imminent: who has realized it sufficiently today to have to stand up as the teacher and herald of such a tremendous logic of terror, as the prophet of a period of gloom and eclipse, the like of which has probably never taken place on earth before? . . .[19]

19. 'Die fröhliche Wissenschaft', English translation by Thomas

This is the first part of the passage, dealing with the negative, destructive aspects of the death of God. Few people have understood the consequences of the 'logic of terror', and fewer still want to hear about it. But there are already in the world at least a few like Nietzsche, who not only recognize the event and its negative significance, but can see beyond the 'period of gloom and eclipse'.

Even we, the born riddle-readers who wait as it were on the mountains posted 'twixt today and tomorrow, and engirt by their contradiction, we, the firstlings and premature children of the coming century, into whose sight especially the shadows which must forthwith envelop Europe *should* already have come – how is it that even we, without genuine sympathy for this period of gloom, contemplate its advent without any *personal* solicitude or fear? Are we still, perhaps, too much under the *immediate effects* of the event – and are these effects, especially as regards *ourselves*, perhaps the reverse of what was to be expected – not at all sad and depressing, but rather like a new and indescribable variety of light, happiness, relief, enlivenment, encouragement, and dawning day? . . .[20]

Even those who understand the significance of the event, or perhaps only those who truly understand it, have no need to despair, for the event which destroys one world invites the creation of another. The final section is a very important statement of this tentative hope, suppressed by realism about the new situation.

In fact, we philosophers and 'free spirits' feel ourselves irradiated as by a new dawn by the report that the 'old God is dead'; our hearts overflow with gratitude, astonishment, presentiment and expectation. At last the horizon seems open once more, granting even that it is not bright; our ships can at last put out to sea in face of every danger; every hazard is again permitted

Common, *The Complete Works of Friedrich Nietzsche* ed. Oscar Levy, George Allen & Unwin, London, 1910, Vol. 10, pp. 275–6.
   20. ibid.

to the discerner; the sea, *our* sea, again lies open before us; perhaps never before did such an 'open sea' exist.[21]

Although the death of God – the disappearance of the sanction for existing meaning and value judgements – brings immense problems, problems which most men cannot face, yet the death of God for Nietzsche means the liberation of man. When the safe, secure and known world is destroyed it is a traumatic experience, but for those who can accept it, the opportunities are as unbounded as the sea. But note the realism also: 'granting even that it is not bright'. The death of God does not make life easier or more pleasant. There are hazards and dangers. But ... and it is with this 'but' that the modern age begins, 'the sea, *our* sea, again lies open before us ...'. For the first time man is completely on his own, and not until that situation arose could man become man. Nietzsche believed religion to be an illusion, based on projection. And not until the illusion is broken, till God is dead, can man emerge as man.

I should now like to quote at length the more familiar passage dealing with the death of God, for the significance of the death of God involves more, for Nietzsche, than the liberation of man. This passage is called 'The Madman'.

Have you ever heard of the madman who on a bright morning lighted a lantern and ran to the market-place calling out unceasingly: 'I seek God! I seek God!' – As there were many people standing about who did not believe in God, he caused a great deal of amusement. Why! is he lost? said one. Has he strayed away like a child? said another. Or does he keep himself hidden? Is he afraid of us? Has he taken a sea-voyage? Has he emigrated? – the people cried out laughingly, all in a hubbub. The insane man jumped into their midst and transfixed them with his glances. 'Where is God gone?' he called out. 'I mean to tell you! *We have killed him* – you and I! We are all his murderers! But how have we done it? How were we able to

21. ibid.

drink up the sea? Who gave us the sponge to wipe away the whole horizon? What did we do when we loosened this earth from its sun? Whither does it now move? Whither do we move? Away from all suns? Do we not dash on unceasingly? Backwards, sideways, forwards, in all directions? Is there still an above and below? Do we not stray, as through infinite nothingness? Does not empty space breathe upon us? Has it not become colder? Does not night come on continually, darker and darker? Shall we not have to light lanterns in the morning? Do we not hear the noise of the grave-diggers who are burying God? Do we not smell the divine putrefaction? – for even Gods putrefy! God is dead! God remains dead! And we have killed him![22]

We see in this passage the same negative aspect of the dialectic of the death of God. The coordinates of our world of meaning and value have been removed, so that we do not know one direction from another, or whether there is any longer a higher and lower. The source of light has come to an end, and though for a short time life goes on as if nothing had happened, yet increasingly there will be confusion and anxiety. In the second part of the passage we move to the other aspect, the positive significance of the death of God, but this time with a quite different conclusion before us.

How shall we console ourselves, the most murderous of all murderers? The holiest and the mightiest that the world has hitherto possessed, has bled to death under our knife, – who will wipe the blood from us? With what water could we cleanse ourselves? What lustrums, what sacred games shall we have to devise? Is not the magnitude of this deed too great for us? Shall we not ourselves have to become Gods, merely to seem worthy of it? There never was a greater event, – and on account of it, all who are born after us belong to a higher history than any history hitherto![23]

Not this time that the death of God means the liberation of man to become man, but the obligation laid upon man to

22. ibid., pp. 167-9.   23. ibid.

become more than it was previously conceived that man could become. Those who, in creating the new cultural event, have become the murderers of God, find themselves in the place of God. Whatever was previously ascribed to God must be ascribed to man. He must create and direct and judge himself and his world. And it must be *his* world. The passage ends with the theme of incredulity which came in the negative section of the 'Cheerfulness' passage previously quoted.

Here the madman was silent and looked again at his hearers; they also were silent and looked at him in surprise. At last he threw his lantern on the ground, so that it broke in pieces and was extinguished. 'I come too early,' he then said, 'I am not yet at the right time. This prodigious event is still on its way, and is travelling, – it has not yet reached men's ears. Lightning and thunder need time, the light of the stars needs time, deeds need time, even after they are done, to be seen and heard. This deed is as yet further from them than the furthest star, – and *yet they have done it!*' – It is further stated that the madman made his way into different churches on the same day, and there intoned his *Requiem aeternam deo*. When led out and called to account, he always gave the reply : 'What are these churches now, if they are not the tombs and monuments of God?'[24]

From all this it is not difficult to see why Nietzsche called his philosophy 'the gay science'. The way is not pleasant, but, he claims, there is hope and joy at the end. Perhaps this is why Zarathustra says, 'I should only believe in a God who would know how to dance.'[25] It is with Zarathustra that Nietzsche pursues this theme of the Madman : not just that man becomes man when God is dead, but that man must become more than man has ever been before or been conceived to be.

The new challenge, when God is dead, is man and his potentialities. Thus Zarathustra : 'I teach you the Superman. Man is something that must be surpassed. What have you

24. ibid.   25. 'Also sprach Zarathustra', p. 58.

done to surpass?'[26] To what end have they turned their attention and applied their creativity?

God is a conjecture: but I do not wish your conjecturing to reach beyond your creating will. Could you *create* a God? – Then, I pray you, be silent about all Gods. But you could well create the Superman. Not perhaps by yourselves, my brethren! But into fathers and forefathers of the Superman could you transform yourselves: and let that be your best creating.[27]

Just as few men can recognize the new historic situation, fewer still will themselves be able to take advantage of it. We have already seen that Nietzsche recognized that only a tiny minority of men ever realize their potential, to surpass the expected, the average level. Those who do are the 'higher men', and Zarathustra has a special word for them. As long as they are immersed in the normal life of society, they will never emerge from the average kind of existence of the market place. There is a levelling process there, whereby everyone is equal before God.

Before God! – Now however this God has died! You higher men, this God was your greatest danger. Only since he lay in the grave have you again arisen. Now only comes the great noontide, now only does the higher man become – master! Have you understood this word, O my brethren? You are frightened: do your hearts turn giddy? Does the abyss here yawn for you? Does the hell-hound yelp at you? Well! Take heart, you higher men! Now only travails the mountain of the human future. God has died: now do *we* desire – the Superman to live.[28]

Nietzsche used the phrase 'death of God' not to describe an experience, but to draw attention to the implications of living without God. In this respect his position is more rele-

26. ibid., p. 13.
27. 'Thus Spake Zarathustra', English translation by Thomas Common, *The Complete Works of Friedrich Nietzsche*, ed. Oscar Levy, George Allen and Unwin, London, 1909, Vol. II, p. 99.
28. ibid., p. 351.

vant to our study than are the positions of the Death of God theologians. But two aspects have to be distinguished. Like Marx, Nietzsche believed that Christianity, as a religion, had an inhibiting influence on man. Thus the death of God was not a bad thing. This suggests that a secular faith in Christ, from which belief in God has been excluded, might well escape many of the valid nineteenth-century criticisms of religion.

But there is a second aspect to be considered, of more direct relevance to our discussion. This has to do with *The Antichrist*. Nietzsche is not simply rejecting the Christian religion. He is rejecting Christ, and the way of Christ. *His* proposal for the way, the truth and the life for men is in calculated opposition to Christian faith in Jesus Christ. We shall return to this point in the final chapter, for it is of fundamental importance. In the meantime it is clear that living without God can be anti-Christian. But under what conditions could living without God still be Christian? We shall discuss this question in Part 2.

PART TWO

LIVING WITH TRANSCENDENCE

CHAPTER 5

The Christian Dilemma

THIS book is written out of concern for Christians and non-Christians, caught up in the current dilemma of Christian faith. Christianity is a world religion. This might be said in the way that a department store could claim to have branches everywhere. But Christianity has a mission to the whole world, so that even if it is not present in every part of the world, it should be. That is to say, it has a world reference, not by geography but by its own theology. Either Christianity is for everyone, or it is not Christianity. Christians are too often content to enjoy their religion, neither propagating it in their society nor actively spreading it throughout the world, but this is a Christian failing: Christianity is not simply a faith for Anglo-Saxons, for those of the west, for those of a class, income or educational level.

The dilemma is that today Christianity can neither be universally preached, nor universally heard. In the Introduction it was claimed that belief in God is a condition which cannot be complied with at will, and without this prior condition, men today are not allowed to become Christian. If they should lose belief in God, they are not allowed to remain Christian. Yet we have reached a cultural position where fewer and fewer people can believe in God. Belief in God and faith in Christ have not always gone together. Clearly millions of Hindus and Muslims believe in God but have no faith in Jesus as the Christ. In the history of the Church, the fact that the vast majority of Jews believed in God, but did not accept Jesus as the Christ, caused much heart-searching. But for the first time in our history the position is reversed. There are men today who want to believe in

Christ, yet are unable to believe in God. Alternatively there are Christians who can no longer believe in God, and yet who have not lost their faith in Christ.

What is to be done about this new situation? In Part 1 we reviewed various responses to the dilemma. In Chapter 1 we saw that it is impossible to insist that any particular experience be given a religious interpretation. Nor does there seem to be any way of offering non-believers a way of coming to belief in God. Is this not a most extraordinary thing, that belief in God is the *conditio sine qua non* of becoming a Christian, and yet the Church has no idea how to lead men to belief in God? We saw also that in face of this practical atheism, there is a tradition within the Church of denying that there really can be such a thing as atheism. This is no doubt a very satisfying position for those who do believe in God, but for those who wish to become Christian, and find no possible way of believing in God, the logic of the argument does not square with the reality of the situation.

In Chapter 2 we looked at two outstanding attempts to reform our thinking and speaking about God. There are logical objections to each of these proposals, but the practical defect is that while they may be of interest to believers who no longer consider the traditional language adequate, they do not enable non-believers to believe. It is not an inadequate conception of God which prevents (or terminates belief), but the inability to identify at all anything in experience which could legitimately be called God.

Chapter 3 dealt with more general reforms, including the liturgical renewal, the ecumenical movement, *aggiornamento* and other structural alterations to the household of faith. But while they may well make for a richer religious experience and a corporate Christian life, they do not make belief in God any more possible, either for those who have lost belief, or for those who never had any. This is true also of the Death of God theology, which really only makes sense to those who can anticipate the return of God. As we have seen, only Nietzsche, living in a world without reference to God, understood the true implications of the death of God.

How are we then to respond to the present crisis confronting the Church? There are five possibilities. The first is to pay no attention. This is the most probable response. It involves organizing the Church as a religious society.[1] Numbers are made up by running a Sunday School and hoping that at least some adolescents will take up full membership. On the other hand it involves no evangelism of those outside the Church. If they do not want to come and join, that is up to them. This response reflects the present life of the Church, and there is no doubt that it is the most convenient way. On purely statistical grounds the Church will be a tiny minority in the land by the end of the century. But what kind of faith does this reflect? It is a tacit rejection of the commission to convert the whole world, and an acceptance of the fact that most people find nothing in Christianity for them. It also represents the ignoring of the possibility that the form of Christianity presently embodied in the Church may be defective. In the Introduction, it was suggested that the vast majority of people in this country today have never actually had the chance to choose for or against Christ. Does this possibility not merit investigation? Those who propose radical changes are often accused of being defeatist. Far from it. Those who envisage the possibility that men might once again choose for or against Christ have at least as much faith in the power of Christ as those who assume that the majority have already rejected him consciously and deliberately. This is the first possible response to the crisis in which we find ourselves. I regard it as no response at all, and indeed to a large extent the attitude responsible for the crisis in the first place. It will be tragic if the Church faces the present crisis

1. cf. William Pickering, 'Religion – a Leisure-time Pursuit?' see above, p. xii.

in this way, but I have no doubt that this will be the most probable response.

The second possible response is the reformist one we have already outlined. Those who, unlike the conservatives just mentioned, wish to reform the Christian religion as we have it, believe that it is still possible that modern men might become Christian. A great deal of effort and thought has gone into these reforms, and the result has been frustration. The reason for this has already been indicated. All these reforms presuppose God. They are based on the assumption that by various changes in religion, men can be brought to identify God in their lives, and worship him meaningfully. There is nothing logically wrong with this approach. It has been a creditable response to the crisis. What would be less responsible would be to continue to put faith in such reforms long after it has become clear that reforms of this sort are just not meeting the situation. We have already examined two attempts to reform our conception of God, and noted possible criticisms which can be raised against them.

One final criticism could be added. It is not a philosophical or theological point, but is perhaps more important in its own way than any intellectual criticisms. If in response to the present crisis we attempt to reform Christianity, then the new form must be comprehensible to ordinary folk. It may seem a rather non-academic point, but people must be able to know what it is they are giving their lives to. Nor is intellectual paternalism in order. That is to say, it will not do to assure ordinary folk that, even if they do not understand the new conception of God, at least the experts understand. The words of Martin Kähler, originally applied to the historical problem, apply now to the ontological, that 'in relation to the Christ in whom we can and should believe, the most learned theologian must have a place no better and no worse than the simplest Christian'.[2] The most objectionable aspect

2. Martin Kähler, *Der sogenannte historische Jesus und der*

of sophisticated reforms is that they very often lead towards a subtle dishonesty. For example, the preacher deals with a biblical theme. He expects his congregation to understand it in the straightforward way. But he himself, with historical and philosophical awareness, cannot accept what he expects them to accept. Thus in the sermon he either does not believe what he preaches, or more often, uses the familiar words but means by them something quite different from their normal meanings. I cannot help but think that the reforms proposed by Ogden and Macquarrie would inevitably produce this situation. The difference now is not that they think that what ordinary people believe is inadequate, they believe it to be actually wrong (especially belief in God as a supernatural being). My non-academic objection to their positions is that they would have to produce in each case a form of their understanding of Christianity which would be comprehensible to ordinary folk, which could thus become the basis of the decision whether or not to become a Christian. It will not do to allow things to go on much as they are, with a small band of intellectuals secretly knowing that the vast majority of Christians misunderstand what Christianity is about, yet allowing this misunderstanding to continue. Above all it will not do, if it is the present form of Christianity which is preventing others from becoming Christian. The main point is, however, that the reformist solution is just not working, has not been effective for over a generation, and therefore must be regarded as quite inadequate.

We now turn to three other possible responses to the present crisis. They will be dealt with in the next three chapters. The first I have called a pluralistic approach to the problem; the second is a reductionist solution; the third involves examination of the subject of theology.

---

geschichtliche biblische Christus, 2nd edition, A. Deichert, Leipzig, 1896, p. 73.

CHAPTER 6

Agenda for Pluralism

ONE of the O.K. words of the 1960s was 'pluralism', signi-
fying in a negative sense that coexistence which civilized
communities expect from those who occupy comparable or
competing positions which are not to be reconciled. Positively, pluralism refers to the richness experienced in the life
of a community when different positions make their contributions, and none is allowed to overcome, dominate, or sup-
press the others. One possible response to the present crisis is
to advocate Christian pluralism. Could the traditional believers not coexist in the Church with the radical non-
believers? Could we not welcome into the Church those who
professed faith in Christ, but could not find a way to believe
in God? Above all, could this not lead to a revitalization of
the Church, and to a richness of insight and experience not
exhibited at present? What would be the characteristics of
such a community?

CONDITION OF MEMBERSHIP

We know that faith does not vary in proportion to the confession of faith. That is to say, very long credal statements
do not indicate new depths of faith, but rather new levels of
controversy. The merit of a detailed confession of faith is
that it expresses with increasing clarity what is entailed in
the fundamental 'essence' of faith. The weakness of lengthy
confessions is that they make each subsequent interpretation
of faith as essential as the early elements. It is to be noted
that in our own time there is a move to return to the essential
statements of faith which unite and reconcile, rather than to

those which polemically define and divide. The pluralism to which I have referred is to be seen therefore in the minimum statement which is required of Churches as a condition of membership of the World Council of Churches: 'The World Council of Churches is a fellowship of Churches which accept our Lord Jesus Christ as God and Saviour.'

A further return to essentials would be required in the new situation envisaged in which traditionals and radicals would be found in the Church. It has often been pointed out that a very early form of profession of Christian faith was simply, 'Jesus is Lord'.[1] In so far as *kyrios* is the LXX word for God himself, it would be misleading to say that the formula 'Jesus is Lord' could be the basis of a secular faith in Jesus. Historically, however, it would seem that this use of *kyrios* was not intended in the confession. It provides a courageous and defiant alternative to the confession of total submission required within the Roman Empire, in the formula *Caesar kyrios*. If 'Jesus is Lord' is set over against 'Caesar is Lord', clearly we have a possible way of speaking meaningfully of a secular faith in Jesus. The confession 'Jesus is (my) Lord' is not primarily an ascription of divinity to Jesus, but a statement of intent to live the life commanded by Jesus. Paradoxically, the statement 'Jesus is *kyrios* (=God)' does not say any more, and may *commit* the person making the statement to *less*. In a pluralistic community there would be in practice no difference in commitment between those who used this confession in a secular and those who used it in a religious sense. Indeed, a community whose sole basis was this confession might in fact be enriched by those who joined solely to live out the appropriate life.

It is interesting to note that what distinguishes Christians from non-Christians today is normally that Christians believe in God (or at least, have done so until recently). But this is not a distinctively Christian belief. What distinguished

1. I Corinthians xii, 3.

the earliest Christians was their faith in Jesus. Belief in God would hardly have set them apart from other Jews. The early Christians were called those of 'the Way',[2] because what they believed constituted a new way of living. Indeed, even in the second century, this tradition is preserved and re-affirmed in the words attributed to Jesus by which he declares himself to be 'the way'.[3] The point is, once again, that although this can have religious connotations, in *practice* there is no difference between a traditionalist who believes Jesus is 'the way ... to the Father', and the radical who believes that Jesus is 'the way'. This is the spirit of pluralism.

THE BODY OF CHRIST

Earlier this century, Reformed and Protestant theologians vied with each other to see who could claim to be more Christocentric than the rest. Today the name of the game is ecclesiology : the object, to see who can claim to be giving a deeper significance to the Church. I have no interest in this game. 'The body of Christ' is not a way of speaking about the Church, but a way of speaking about the community of those committed to the way of Christ. It is tempting to say that the body of Christ is present wherever there are committed Christians, but this is misleading, for it might give the impression that 'the body of Christ' is some mysterious substance. A more dynamic way of speaking is to say that wherever men and women are committed to the way of Christ, they embody his life.

When put in this sense, what has been said in mystifying ways becomes true in realistic ways. The Christian Church, if it can be thought of in terms identical with a community of men and women who strive to embody the life of Christ, does become the real presence of Christ.

Truly, I say to you, whatever you bind on earth shall be bound

2. Acts ix, 2. 3. John xiv, 6.

in heaven, whatever you loose on earth shall be loosed in heaven. Again I say to you, if two of you agree on earth about anything they ask, it will be done for them by my Father in heaven. For where two or three are gathered in my name, there am I in the midst of them.[4]

Ultra-Protestant scholars, conscious of the abuses to which this has been put in the past, have been appalled by this passage.[5] But it does form part of the proclamation of Jesus as the Christ that when Christians meet, they embody the life of Christ.

But what are the characteristics of this life the Church is to embody? The list might be long indeed, but certain characteristic elements spring to mind. The Church, if it embodies the life of Christ, must be a caring-healing community. I have never forgotten the words of a Jewish psychiatrist in a large city hospital, who claimed that if he could find a caring community of people, many patients would not need to enter hospital. The Church just does not embody the life of Jesus, to whom those in need flocked. The Church, if it embodied the life of Christ, would embody the dialectic of judgement and grace. It is sometimes said that those who do not believe in God hold that 'man is the measure of all things'. This just is not so. Those who confess that Jesus is Lord of their lives, whether they believe in God or not, hold that *Christ* is the measure of all things. This is a fundamental aspect of the secular meaning of saying 'Jesus is Lord'. Gentle Jesus was gentle with those who needed care and healing, but he was quick to denounce and condemn others. And who were the others? If anything, they were, although formally religious, precisely those who lived as though man were the measure of all things. In religious terms sin is the refusal to

4. Matthew xviii, 18–20.
5. The whole of Matthew Chapter 18, is of course open to doubt on critical grounds, since it represents a concern for the government of the Church as a continuing and not an eschatological community.

'let God be God',[6] but in secular terms sin is the refusal to let Jesus be Lord. The presence of Jesus represents judgement on sin, and the Church, if it is the real presence of Jesus today, must also pronounce judgement on those things which deny the Lordship of Christ. But it is a dialectical word, because to those who acknowledge the justice of judgement there comes the grace of forgiveness.

Of course I should dispute that *going* to church is constitutive of being a Christian, but I am certain that no one can be a Christian for long if he cuts himself off from the rest of the Body. This is my experience in the Church and in the Iona Community. It is in responsible association with other Christians that judgement and grace come to us. Surely this secular understanding of being a Christian, part of the embodiment of Christ, is not less Christian than a religious understanding? Again, I think a pluralistic understanding may enrich the life of the Church. In my own community we challenge each other continually on our mutual commitments to seek peace, political and social concern, economic responsibility. I know of no local congregation which demands such commitments. But if the Church also included radical Christians, whose *sole* concern in being Christian was to embody the life of Christ, nothing less demanding would satisfy them: not the Sunday morning praise, not the Thursday evening indoor game night.

We have not yet mentioned the fact that there was a certain inevitability that one who embodied such a life was bound to be persecuted and crucified. The Church, as the embodiment of the life of Christ, will be a community of love. Now love today is rightly seen as a celebration of life,

6. 'Man is by nature unable to want God to be God. Indeed he himself wants to be God, and does not want God to be God.' (Martin Luther, 'Disputation Against Scholastic Theology, *Luther's Works*, ed. and trans. Harold J. Grimm, Muhlenberg Press, Philadelphia, 1957, Vol. 31, p. 10.)

but in an evil and unjust world, love is also, as Theo Westow has said, an attack on our own self-interest. Are we as Christians in the habit of damaging our careers, our status, our respectability or our circumstances for the sake of being part of a prophetic–compassionate community? The pluralism I am advocating could hardly make the Church less the embodiment of Christ than it is at present, and I argue that it could very well make it more truly the real presence of Christ in the world.

ENABLING LEADERSHIP

It was contended in the last section that the 'high' doctrine of the Church has not been high enough, since it has been deceived into mistaking mystification for realism. The Church needs leadership, but the same mystification has obscured the real character and demands of leadership. I know many young men who have wished to commit themselves to full-time service of the Church, but are completely disillusioned and frustrated with the role they are expected to play. They find themselves 'set apart' from the Body of Christ, and, ironically, largely cut off from the grace which comes from being closely associated with other Christians. Instead of working shoulder to shoulder with others they find themselves standing six feet above their heads, dressed in the costume of another age. It is not that they fail in the job given to them, but that they are required to do the wrong job. The radical pluralism which I am envisaging, far from representing a threat to them, would actually be the most exciting prospect for the clergy in living memory. We cannot even conceive of how a man or woman ordained to enabling leadership would go about enabling the Church to be the embodiment of the life of Christ. But it would to my mind be one of the most dynamic, exciting, rewarding and creative careers in a modern society. As it is, ordination is a passport to limbo and candidates for ordination turn reluctantly to seek other ways by which they may embody the life of Christ.

Many other issues could be taken up to indicate the new character that a pluralistic approach to Christianity might have. But why continue on this line when it is too unrealistic for words? It cannot be realistic so long as Christianity is viewed religiously. Radical Christians who cannot believe in God would only be allowed into the Church (or allowed to remain in it) as second-class believers, Gentiles of the outer court. The kind of Church I have been envisaging involves several lines of reform which have already been attempted. They have failed because, in the reformist tradition, they have been joined to the strictly religious view of Christianity, the first condition of which is belief in God. Pluralism cannot be established as long as Christianity is regarded in a primarily religious manner. What then are the two remaining possible responses? Since the crisis is caused by the problem of non-belief in God, we must address ourselves more directly to this issue. One solution would be to devise a way in which men could once again come to belief in God. The evidence of the last one hundred years is that we have no way of bringing a significant number of men to belief in God. As Altizer points out, the most promising way to do this would be to reverse the process of secularization which has made belief in God impossible. Apart from the fact that this is impossible, he is right in judging it to be undesirable. Some leading theologians today admit that modern men are quite right to reject belief in the God of traditional theism. They themselves propose other ways of thinking about God, but it seems more likely that a more radical solution must be attempted.

I have no doubt that if there is a solution to the problem it lies in a secular understanding of Christianity. In the past twenty years there has been a good deal of secular theology. It has not changed anything. The reason for this is not hard to find. Secular theology has, like any other theology, been based on the assumption that Christianity involves belief in God. Hence the failure. It might be very interesting stuff, but since it assumes that belief in God is necessary, it can hardly be relevant to dealing with the problem of belief in God. Secular theology has been of great interest to those who believe in God, but is no more relevant than the most conservative or traditional system to those who do not believe.

If there is a solution then, it will have to be a secular understanding of Christianity which deals specifically with the problem of God. The first possibility is a re-interpretation of Christian theology which eliminates God. If this could be consistently maintained, it would solve the problem of God simply by eliminating the problem. This is the solution by reduction. It has a distinguished history in modern theology, and we shall examine three expositions of the reductionist tradition in the next chapter.

CHAPTER 7

The Reductionist Solution

LUDWIG FEUERBACH:
'THE ESSENCE OF CHRISTIANITY'[1]

FEUERBACH is regarded as the most significant critic of Christianity in the nineteenth century, but among theologians this judgement is often made on the wrong grounds. His significance stems from the impact which Feuerbach had on Marx.

> The *positive*, humanistic and naturalistic criticism begins with Feuerbach. The less blatant Feuerbach's writings, the more certain, profound, extensive and lasting is their influence; they are the only writings since Hegel's *Phenomenology* and *Logic* which contain a real theoretical revolution.[2]

Feuerbach was responsible in large measure for turning European critical philosophy from idealism to historical materialism.

This is not, however, the context in which he is normally judged by theologians, who come to Feuerbach already influenced by the work of Karl Barth. It was Schleiermacher who claimed that 'Man is born with the religious capacity as with every other',[3] Feuerbach claimed that 'the secret of

1. *Das Wesen des Christentums* (1841), English translation by George Eliot, Harper & Row, New York, 1957. For recent accounts of Feuerbach's philosophy, see especially E. Kamenka, *The Philosophy of Ludwig Feuerbach*, Routledge & Kegan Paul, London, 1970, and H. F. Reisz, 'Feuerbach on the Essence of Religion', *The Journal of Religion*, Vol. 49, No. 2 (April 1969), pp. 180–92.

2. The third of the *Economic and Philosophical Manuscripts* (1844) included in *Karl Marx: Early Writings*, ed. and trans. T. B. Bottomore, C. A. Watts, London, 1963, p.64.

3. Schleiermacher, *On Religion: speeches to its cultured despisers*, p. 124.

theology is anthropology',[4] and Barth concluded that Feuerbach represents the logical outcome of the tradition of theology from Schleiermacher.[5] Unfortunately this has been regarded as 'dealing with Feuerbach'. Barth was neither interested in Feuerbach nor prepared to discuss Feuerbach in Feuerbach's own terms. His real interest was in attacking the theology of Schleiermacher, which he regarded not only as the major alternative to his own theology, but as an all pervasive and insidious influence on modern theology. Feuerbach attempts to reduce theology to anthropology, to demonstrate that talk about God is 'really' talk about man. Barth therefore held Feuerbach up as a warning to theologians of what happens to those who set out on the way of Schleiermacher. Having thus used Feuerbach, Barth assumed that he could then revert to his own theology. 'But is that really to overcome Feuerbach? Is it not just evading the discussion with Feuerbach and his disciples when theology goes on to speak about God, quite unconcerned, as if nothing had happened?'[6] Feuerbach deserves more attention in our own time than he has been given. He cannot be understood in terms of the debate between liberal and neo-orthodox theology. His work not only contains many penetrating criticisms of religion, but it represents the first great attempt to reduce theology to anthropology, talk about God to simply talk about man.

Feuerbach is not an easy writer to deal with, partly because his position resembles the 'really' form of argumentation to which we referred in dealing with John Baillie. Christians claim to be speaking about God, but according to Feuerbach, they are 'really' speaking about themselves. Feuerbach was an atheist, but unlike most atheists he did not reject

4. Feuerbach, *The Essence of Christianity*, p. 270.

5. K. Barth, *From Rousseau to Ritschl*, S.C.M. Press, London, 1959.

6. W. Pannenberg, 'Typen des Atheismus und ihre theologische Bedeutung', *Grundfragen systematischer Theologie*, Vandenhoeck & Ruprecht, Göttingen, 1967, p. 351.

theology in rejecting God. What theologians say is (largely) true, but they mistake their subject. 'The beginning, middle and end of religion is MAN.'[7] The fact that there is no God simply meant that theological statements had been mis-applied. Taken in their traditional sense they were worthless, often positively misleading. But by making them refer to man instead, Feuerbach claimed to have 'found the key to the cipher of the Christian religion . . .'.[8]

While it is true that theology *also* refers to man, we here face a radical reduction when it is claimed that theology *only* refers to man. Talk about God is reduced to talk about man, without remainder. Actually this extreme position is quali-fied in various ways, but it does focus on the principle by which Feuerbach attempts to appropriate the valuable ele-ments of Christianity, even while rejecting the God reference. In passing we might notice that he does not begin by arguing about the existence of God. It does not seem to occur to Feuer-bach that he might even argue about the possibility of God. But if he does not base his case on an argument, in the second half of the work he does say some very revealing things about why he cannot accept the traditional belief in God. Through-out the book he uses the word 'God', but in his own way, compatible with his reduction. But for him the God of reli-gious belief is one quite distinct from God, external to man and the world. 'The existence of God must therefore be in space – in general, a qualitative sensational existence.'[9] Ap-parently, what is real must have objective existence, suscep-tible to sensory experience. Feuerbach adopts an empirical position with regard to the existence of God, and finds that by this standard divine existence does not pass muster. 'The existence of God is essentially an empirical existence, with-out having its distinctive marks, it is in itself a matter of experience, and yet in reality no object of experience.'[10] As

7. Feuerbach, *The Essence of Christianity*, p. 184.
8. ibid., p. xxxvi.   9. ibid., p. 200.   10. ibid.

we shall see, his own interpretation of theology would not stand up to such empiricism. Even so, Feuerbach's reduction is important because today many Christians cannot believe in the God of traditional theism, and there is no doubt that both in the Bible and in most of the history of the Church, men have believed in a God whose existence could be demonstrated empirically – at least in the sense that *God* could demonstrate his own existence if he so chose.[11] So that, for quite different reasons, Feuerbach does address himself to the same problem as the one which faces us. How can we find a viable way of appropriating the Christian tradition, without *necessarily* accepting the traditional belief in God?

Feuerbach was one of the most prominent left-wing Hegelians of his day, and this meant, appropriately, that he had a dialectical relationship to Hegel's work. He took over the concept of 'alienation', but, like Hegel's other critics (e.g. Marx, Kierkegaard and Nietzsche), he did not share the master's confidence that alienation was about to be overcome in the contemporary cultural synthesis. Feuerbach is not explicit on this point, but it seems that he viewed religion not as the cause of alienation, but as a symptom, and in some measure a further aggravation of it. He further, though inconsistently, seems to have believed that his elimination of religion (focused on belief in God) would lead to the overcoming of alienation. I do not wish to discuss Feuerbach's criticism of religion, which is for the most part a very penetrating and justifiable analysis of ways by which religion has both inhibited man from action and distorted man's knowledge of himself and his relationship to the world. It is in this area that Feuerbach laid the foundations for Marx's criticisms of religion. But these criticisms simply form part of Feuerbach's motivation for reducing theology to anthropology, before further damage is done. Yet when all that is

11. This might be referred to as 'the Elijah school of religious empiricism'.

said, he has provided no basis for his assumption that the reduction of religion would lead to the overcoming of alienation. In so far as religion is a symptom of alienation, the cause must lie elsewhere. While Marx pursued this problem increasingly into the field of economics, Feuerbach does not deal with the problem of the underlying causes of human alienation.

In our discussion of Feuerbach, we simply take over his use of the word anthropology, though of course this could be misleading, since he means the study of man in a contemporary rather than a primitive setting. But Feuerbach does venture into the field of modern anthropology, in claiming that the function of religion in primitive times corresponds to his interpretation of its 'real' subject: 'religion is man's earliest and also indirect form of self-knowledge'.[12] We have already noted the influence of Feuerbach on Marx. Buber has acknowledged his indebtedness to Feuerbach for his I–Thou analysis (though Feuerbach would no doubt disapprove of the way in which he has developed it). But Feuerbach also seems to anticipate Freud when he speaks about God as human projection. Feuerbach has an apparently ambiguous attitude toward this projection. On the positive side he approves of it. He adopts the deist–rationalist position that revelation is the appropriate mode by which unenlightened people may come to truths which can be established directly by reason. This is why he refers to the knowledge gained through religion as 'indirect'. He does not dispute that this is real knowledge, but his negative view of religion stems from the fact that religion goes beyond self-knowledge in what he calls 'religious objectivism'.[13] Thus the religious man not only uses the projection as a convenient means of gaining self-knowledge, he actually takes seriously the existence of God. And it is here that Feuerbach comes closest to

12. Feuerbach, *The Essence of Christianity*, p. 13.
13. ibid., p. 204.

speaking of alienation. 'Religion is the disuniting of man from himself; he sets God before him as the antithesis of himself.'[14] In this objectivization, man creates God in his own image. The reduction may be restated thus: while in the traditional view the 'essence of Christianity' was the Christian teaching on God, in Feuerbach's terms the 'essence of Christianity' is the Christian teaching on man.

No religion has ever conceived of its God as being despicable, unworthy (cf. worth-ship), evil or immoral. If man creates God in his own image, the content of 'God' will clearly be the sum of all human virtues. Thus for Feuerbach, if we examine a religion it will reveal a great deal – but about the believers, not about a divine being. 'That which I recognize in the understanding as essential, I place in God as existent: God is what the understanding thinks as the highest.'[15] Unfortunately this observation is true in the sense that, at least in the 'higher' religions, men have always thought of God as being very much like themselves. Yet from his atheistic starting point, Feuerbach was unable to draw the other conclusion, that men conform to, or at least nominally approve of, the standards demanded by God. For Feuerbach, God represents the deification of the essence of man. It is for this reason that he considers Christianity to be valuable, since over a long period it has come to discover, by various empirical means, what is after all the essence of man.

The corresponding danger, already mentioned, is developed under the analysis of religion as basically a striving for wish-fulfilment. To believe in God is to have a God. To wish to be immortal is to be immortal. 'The resurrection of Christ is therefore the satisfied desire of man for an immediate certainty of his personal existence after death – personal immortality as a sensible, indubitable fact.'[16] No one could

14. ibid., p. 33.
15. ibid., p. 38. Cf. '... the measure of thy God is the measure of thy understanding.' (ibid., p. 39.)   16. ibid., p. 135.

reasonably accuse Feuerbach of examining the New Testament evidence by the historical critical method – or of examining the evidence at all, for that matter. I suspect that if
theologians made such cavalier statements, they would be
sharply brought back to a careful discussion of evidence.
Feuerbach's criticism of this characteristic of religion (wish-
fulfilment), is not that it is concerned with an illusory divine
being, but rather that it further alienates man from his essence
and inhibits his activity. Man is content to allow God to be the
essence of what man should be, while not himself expecting
to achieve that essence (indeed this grasping equality with
God is specifically regarded as the epitome of sin). Man is
also content to be the recipient of God's grace, rather than to
strive for himself.

The fundamental dogmas of Christianity are realized wishes
of the heart; – the essence of Christianity is the essence of human
feeling. It is pleasanter to be passive than to act, to be redeemed
and made free by another than to free oneself; pleasanter to make
one's salvation dependent on a person than on the force of one's
own spontaneity; pleasanter to set before oneself an object of
love than an object of effort; pleasanter to know oneself beloved
by God than merely to have that simple, natural self-love which
is innate in all beings; pleasanter to see oneself imaged in the
love-beaming eyes of another personal being, than to look into
the concave mirror of self or into the cold depths of the ocean of
Nature; pleasanter, in short, to allow oneself to be acted on by
one's own feeling, as by another, but yet fundamentally identical being, than to regulate oneself by reason.[17]

If we were considering Feuerbach's criticism of religion, then
we should have to take this passage very seriously, to determine to what extent unconsciously Christians have been content to 'continue in sin that grace may abound'.[18] Has the
assurance of forgiveness made us insensitive to the effect on
others of our egocentricities? We could answer Feuerbach

17. ibid., p. 140.   18. Romans vi, 1.

with countless examples of Christians who have given their lives for others, in work which unbelievers were not prepared to do. His criticism is too sweeping, though not altogether wide of the mark. But, as before, he has neglected to take into account the dialectical movement by which God not only represents the essence of man, but belief in God provides an additional motivation for embodying the essence of man. It has yet to be shown even in our own time that the elimination of religion leads to a more morally sensitive or socially active society.

The argument for reduction because of wish-fulfilment is not a strong one, but let us continue to examine what Feuerbach hopes to achieve thereby. In calling his method interpretation and reduction, we have stressed the point that he does not wish to reject Christian doctrine, nor does he wish to excise great parts of it. The major feature which he wishes to eliminate is of course belief in a supernatural being. But then, as has been pointed out, that is one of the concerns of many different types of theology today.

An obvious objection to a projection interpretation of religion is the disparity between the image of God and our common understanding of man. 'Man – this is the mystery of religion – projects his being into objectivity.'[19] If religious belief were simply that a being exists who could qualify for the title 'Mr Average Man' it is difficult to see why such a projection would take place, and of course Feuerbach would have no interest in such belief. According to the theory, only certain human characteristics are projected, constituting the ideal man or the essence of man. As we have seen, for Feuerbach 'God is what the understanding thinks as the highest'. It is one of the disturbing things about Feuerbach that he can without difficulty incorporate well-known phrases from traditional theology, but placing them in a setting in which Anselm, for example, appears to support his reduction. 'That

19. Feuerbach, *The Essence of Christianity*, pp. 29–30.

which is the highest for man, from which he can make no further abstraction, which is the positive limit of his intellect, of his feeling, of his statement, that is to him God – *id quo nihil majus cogitari potest.*'[20] But unlike Anselm, Feuerbach maintains that each species can conceive of nothing higher than itself. Hence, man is the highest possible conception for man.

But Feuerbach still leaves himself open to a charge of trivializing rather than reducing theology. After all, even a perfect man, wise, virtuous, strong and so forth, would not justify the projection which it is claimed is at the heart of religious belief. Pursuing Anselm's definition, if religion is concerned with 'a being than which no greater can be conceived', then it is surely concerned, rightly or wrongly, with something more than the ideal man. Feuerbach is forced to agree, and with this, it might be claimed, his attempt to reduce theology to anthropology is seen to fail. But even so, he does have a 'being' to be substituted for God, and that is 'the species'. As already indicated, he believed that each species can conceive of nothing higher than itself. No argument is brought forward to support this rather extraordinary assertion, but Anselm's definition, which is no longer applied to the traditional God, but which would be trivialized if made to refer simply to an ideal man, is taken over and applied to the human species.

All divine attributes, all the attributes which make God God, are attributes of the species – attributes which in the individual are limited in the essence of the species, and even in its existence, in so far as it has its complete existence only in all men taken together. My knowledge, my will, is limited; but my limit is not the limit of another man, to say nothing of mankind; what is difficult to me is easy to another; what is impossible, inconceivable, to one age, is to the coming age conceivable and possible. My life is bound to a limited time; not so the life of humanity.

20. ibid., p. 198.

The history of mankind consists of nothing else than a continuous and progressive conquest of limits, which at a given time pass for the limits of humanity, and therefore for absolute insurmountable limits. But the future always unveils the fact that the alleged limits of the species were only limits of individuals. . . . Thus the species is unlimited; the individual alone limited.[21]

Feuerbach undertook to demonstrate that talk about God is really only talk about man. He has failed to make good this promise, since the image of the claimed projection is not in fact man, even ideal man. At that point he seems to bring forward a new undertaking, namely, to demonstrate that talk about God is really talk about the human species. The obvious advantage, given his empirical approach to the question, is that there can be no doubt of the existence of the human species. But this must be set against the fact that the human species is if anything less like the image of God than an ideal man. An *ideal* human species might be as difficult to cope with as a supernatural God, but Feuerbach speaks only of the actual species. He is committed to equation by quantification. That is to say, the love of God, or his justice or mercy, are somehow equated with the total sum of imperfect acts of human love, justice or mercy. Not only is this quite unsatisfactory, but in the same terms could we not seek to quantify individual acts of human bestiality, hatred, genocide, cruelty and injustice?

From all this we see that Feuerbach, although critical of Hegel, always remained loyal to idealism, if not a form of Absolute Idealism. This inconsistent halting between two ways led to the rejection of Feuerbach by both Marx and Engels. 'But not only did philosophy remain for him an impassable barrier, an inviolable holy thing, but as a philosopher, too, he stopped half-way; the lower half of him was materialist, the upper half idealist.'[22]

21. ibid., pp. 152–3.
22. F. Engels, *Ludwig Feuerbach and the Outcome of Classical*

If Feuerbach's reduction appeared at first sight to be a form of demythologizing[23] it finally becomes simply trans-mythologizing.

It therefore appears that Feuerbach's project does not provide us with the answer to our problem, the quest for a new basis for Christianity compatible both with traditional religious faith and with radical secular faith in Christ. The most obvious defects, in this respect, may be summed up under two headings. In the first place, Feuerbach did not pay enough attention to alienation. This is surprising, since his reduction of Christianity is connected with his assertion that 'religion is the disuniting of man from himself; he sets God before him as the antithesis of himself'. But if it is man that is alienated from man (according to Feuerbach's 'key to the cipher') what is the basis of the antithesis? Religion seems to be at times only symptomatic of alienation. His lack of interest in this whole question seems to justify Barth's recalling the criticism of Ehrenberg that Feuerbach was a 'true child of his century', a 'non-knower [*Nichtkenner*] of death', and a 'miss-knower [*Verkenner*] of evil'.[24] There is a lack of realism about this part of Feuerbach's work, above all his failure to seek the causes of the fundamental division within human existence. Feuerbach at times seems to realize that

---

German Philosophy, Lawrence and Wishart, 1947, p. 49. In the light of the lengthy quotation on the species given above, it may be that Marx broke with Feuerbach on the right point, but for the wrong reason, e.g. Thesis VI: 'Feuerbach resolves the essence of religion into the essence of *man*. But the essence of man is not an abstraction inherent in each particular individual. The real nature of man is the totality of social relationships.' ('Theses on Feuerbach', ed. T. B. Bottomore, and M. Rubel, *Karl Marx: Selected Writings in Sociology and Social Philosophy*, Penguin Books, Harmondsworth, 1963, p. 83.)

23. cf. Bultmann's claim that 'myth should be interpreted not cosmologically, but anthropologically . . .'. (*Kerygma and Myth*, Vol. I, p. 10.)

24. 'An introductory Essay', *The Essence of Christianity*, p. xxviii.

there is a real basis of alienation apart from religion, a real division (in his terms) objectified in religion. 'God is his *alter ego*, his other lost half . . .'[25] This is certainly closer to the biblical view, that man *as he is* is lost, but if it is taken seriously it makes nonsense of Feuerbach's romanticizing about the species, which then becomes the sum of lost individual lives.

The second obvious defect in *The Essence of Christianity* is that Christ does not have a definitive place in the reduction. Christian faith, whether in its traditional (religious) form or in its more radical (secular) form, sees Christ as the place where alienation is overcome. In the terminology of this book, Christ is the way of transcendence, in contrast to the way of immanence which characterizes the lives of individuals and the existence of the species. We should of course note that Feuerbach can speak of Christ as ideal man.

Christ is the ideal of humanity become existence, the compendium of all moral and divine perfections to the exclusion of all that is negative . . . not regarded as the totality of the species, of mankind, but immediately as one individual, one person.[26]

Yet we should not overestimate such statements. This turning to Christ cannot have the significance that it would have had if Feuerbach had taken alienation and being 'lost' seriously. It is also inconsistent with his focusing of attention on the species rather than on the ideal man. Finally, in a work published two years later, he made a rather revealing point when he claimed that Protestant theology had in any case (presumably since Schleiermacher) taken up the very reduction he advocated : '. . . it is no longer *theology* : it is in

25. Feuerbach, *The Essence of Christianity*, p. 195.
26. ibid., p. 154. Cf. 'The Incarnation is nothing else than the practical material manifestation of the human nature of God.' (ibid., p. 50.) Feuerbach is also able to refer to the common saying of the Fathers: 'He was made man that we might be made God.' (Athanasius, *De Incarnatione*, section 54.)

essence only *christology*, i.e. religious anthropology'.[27] He confuses christology, which is, properly speaking, a Christian view of God, with a religious way of speaking about man. Feuerbach's reduction could be successful, in so far as even the God of the Christian tradition has been simply the sum of human virtues raised to the highest conceivable degree. But he fails to reduce Christianity to its essence, mainly because he has not understood to what extent the Christian view of God is incompatible with what men commonly envisage as the goal of human existence.

R. B. BRAITHWAITE: AN EMPIRICIST'S VIEW OF THE NATURE OF RELIGIOUS BELIEF[28]

Philosophy and theology have been consciously brought into relation throughout the history of European thought. That tradition had long been established in Greece before Christianity began to spread out into the Roman Empire. It was inevitable that this new religion would also be brought into relation with the philosophy of the day. It was assumed that philosophy and theology were concerned with the same great issues, though their resources might be different in some respects. This assumption, which went largely unchallenged until the beginning of this century, is no longer shared by those who stand in the analytical tradition which stems from G. E. Moore. Philosophy and theology were for a time still consciously related, but in a negative way, consisting of a philosophical critique of theological assertions. It was one of the great merits of Professor Braithwaite's lecture that he

27. Feuerbach, *Grundsätze der Philosophie der Zukunft*, ed. Gerhart Schmidt, Vittorio Klostermann, Frankfurt am Main, 1967, p. 35.

28. Cambridge University Press, 1955. References below are from the reproduction of this Eddington lecture, as reprinted in *Christian Ethics and Contemporary Philosophy*, ed. Ian T. Ramsey, S.C.M. Press, London, 1966.

attempted to make a positive contribution to the under-standing of religious assertions. We shall look more closely at his lecture in a moment, but a characteristic contention throughout is 'that the primary use of religious assertions is to announce allegiance to a set of moral principles'.[29]

It is on this basis that Braithwaite qualifies as one who has proposed a reductionist solution to the problem which faces us in this book. Briefly, his solution is that religious as-sertions are 'really' moral assertions. This reduction is for-mally similar to the solution proposed by Feuerbach, though Braithwaite would no doubt shudder to find himself in such company. Feuerbach undertook his reduction because, while he could not believe in the supernatural aspects of religion, he still believed Christianity embodied something of value. His reduction was the means by which he wished to appropriate the more empirical aspects without having to accept the supernatural features. I do not believe it would be particularly illuminating to make a strained comparison be-tween these two philosophers, but since they are being classed together here, it might be noted in passing that Braithwaite's attitude is not so very far removed from that of Feuerbach. Although reducing religion to morality is quite unacceptable to religious believers, we should remember that this repre-sented a considerable advance on the Logical Positivist position prevalent between the wars: 'Compared with the empirical austerity of twenty years ago, Professor Braithwaite is extravagant ...'.[30] To say that religious assertions have any meaning at all was a most enlightened view. But, apart from their agreement that there is something valuable in Christianity, Braithwaite goes beyond Feuerbach, in that he

29 ibid., p. 63.

30. Ian T. Ramsey, in his contribution to the 'Discussion' follow-ing Braithwaite's lecture (ibid., p. 84). Of course Ramsey, now Bishop of Durham, does not agree with Braithwaite's reduction, and com-pletes the sentence, '... but is he extravagant enough?'

actually wants to find a way by which he can be reckoned a Christian, though an empiricist. He responds to his critics by saying 'it would have been disingenuous of me to conceal the fact that, according to the view of religious belief given in the lecture, I count myself a Christian'.[31] Braithwaite's reduction, therefore, is an attempt to speak positively about religious belief, and to indicate a way in which those who do not or cannot believe in God as a supernatural being might still be able to call themselves Christian.

Braithwaite begins his lecture by adopting the logical positivist approach to religious assertions: 'the meaning of any statement is given by its method of verification'.[32] For the purpose of this lecture he is concerned, not with the truth or falsity of religious assertions, but with what it would mean for them to be true or false. Since religious assertions do not satisfy the verification principle, they cannot be shown to be true or false. The logical positivists therefore ruled them to be strictly meaningless. This conclusion was applied to other assertions, such as moral or aesthetic judgements. With this, analytical philosophy found itself in a position remarkably like that of the neo-idealists at the turn of the century. It may be that Moore did not in fact refute idealism, but he pointed out that when philosophers reach conclusions contrary to our experience, there is a *prima facie* case for saying that it is their logic rather than our common experience which is at fault.[33] The debate concerning the meaning of

31. 'Discussion', ibid., p. 89.   32. ibid, p 54.

33. There could hardly be a greater contrast in positions than between those of Moore and Heidegger, and yet on the question of the reality of the external world they refuse to answer the question set by traditional philosophy. Both have specifically noted Kant's deploring of the fact that there exists no proof of the world outside of us. Both, from quite different standpoints, simply deplore such a concern. 'I can prove now, for instance, that two human hands exist. How? By holding up my two hands, and saying, as I make a certain gesture with the right hand, "here is one hand", and adding,

moral assertions continues, but there is no debate about whether they are meaningful. Logical Positivism has been rejected, not only because the verification principle is itself ruled out as meaningless in its own terms, but because it runs counter to our common experience.

The strange thing about Braithwaite's opening section is that he begins by applying the Logical Positivist principle to religious assertions, as if the verification principle were still regarded as valid. He draws back from accepting the positivist conclusion that religious assertions must be rejected as meaningless, by referring to the comparable case of moral statements. In the case of moral assertions, he accepts the position of Wittgenstein in the *Philosophical Investigations* (published posthumously only two years before Braithwaite's lecture), that the meaning of a statement is given by the way in which it is used.[34] The obvious objection to this procedure is that if the Logical Positivist position is shown to be inadequate with respect to moral assertions, it is also inadequate with respect to religious assertions. And further, the new principle taken over from the later Wittgenstein applies as much to religious as to any other assertions. It is difficult to avoid the conclusion that the opening section of the lecture has been invalidated, and that Braithwaite should now begin again, but without the narrow positivist limits imposed on the meaningfulness of religious assertions. This

---

as I make a certain gesture with the left, "and here is another".' (G. E. Moore, 'Proof of an External World', *Philosophical Papers*, George Allen & Unwin, London, 1969, pp. 145–6.) Compare this Johnsonian response to Heidegger's dismissal of the sceptical tradition of continental philosophy. 'The "scandal of philosophy" is not that this proof has yet to be given, but that such proofs are expected and attempted again and again.' (Heidegger, *Being and Time*, p. 249.)

34. Apart from the sections to which Braithwaite directs our attention, the most explicit example is: 'the meaning of a word is its use in the language'. (L. Wittgenstein, *Philosophical Investigations*, trans. G. E. M. Anscombe, Blackwell, Oxford, 1963, section 43.)

is an important point, since the rest of the lecture continues on the assumption that religious assertions do not in fact assert anything except an attitude. That is to say, in the true reductionist tradition, assertions about the supernatural, or even the natural world, are 'really' assertions about attitudes of the speaker. Braithwaite does not simply accept the Wittgenstein position, but insists on turning it to serve his continuing empiricism.

The meaning of any statement, then, will be taken as being given by the way it is used. The kernel for an empiricist of the problem of the nature of religious belief is to explain, in empirical terms, how a religious statement is used by a man who asserts it in order to express his religious conviction.[35]

How then would Braithwaite deal with the following quite fictitious example? An officer, during jungle warfare, had reason to believe that a vital bridge was about to be attacked by guerrillas. Only after he had ordered an artillery strike did he discover that the group wiped out were not enemy soldiers, but refugee women and children. From that day, over twenty-five years ago, till quite recently, he has borne the crushing guilt of their deaths. He made a full report at the time, and was completely exonerated. But neither that nor his attempts to provide compensation to the relatives took away his guilt. Neither his family nor his psychiatrist were able to help him. Quite recently, though he had never been a particularly religious man, he was converted to Christianity. Now he realizes what is meant by the confession of faith (religious belief) in 'the forgiveness of sin'. He says 'Jesus Christ died for my sins.' Here we have a religious belief, and according to Wittgenstein's principle we could discover what it means if we took the trouble to become familiar with the Bible and with the history of the doctrine of the atonement. Corresponding to it, we also have its cash value, that a man who believes it has lost his guilt. Hands up those who

35. Ramsey, op. cit., p. 59.

are feverishly asserting that it can all be explained psychologically. Why feverishly? Is it because this example conflicts with an existing world-view which excludes such connections? Of course if you can *demonstrate conclusively* that it was wish-fulfilment, I shall be most impressed, especially since he had had the same wish for twenty-five years, during which time he was offered forgiveness by a dozen different routes. But that is not today's problem. Braithwaite has said that he is not at the moment concerned with the truth or falsity of religious assertions, but with their meaning. It is my contention that Braithwaite has allowed Logical Positivism to rule out an assertion such as 'Jesus Christ died for my sins', and for that matter the concepts of sin and guilt. He has then allowed Wittgenstein to rule out Logical Positivism. But, finally, Braithwaite proceeds from the positivist conclusion, to find another way in which religious assertions might be meaningful? Yet if Logical Positivism has been repudiated, why must we find another way in which religious assertions might be meaningful? Why, through a modern, neutral, functional analysis, might we not establish what they mean – without of course being committed to their truth or falsity?

Braithwaite's reductionism applies also to morals, and he next proceeds to an examination of the meaning of moral assertions, in part because a good deal of the theology of the higher religions is concerned with moral issues, but also because his 'explanation' of how moral assertions function provides him with his key to the meaning of religious assertions. He adopts a conative rather than a simple emotive theory, claiming that when a man says that a certain action is right, 'what is primary is his intention to perform the action when the occasion for it arises'.[36] There may or may not be emotions involved in this intention, but these are not the primary element. Thus the moral assertion is not a proposition about the world but a statement of intent. But in

36. ibid., p. 60.

accordance with the previous discussion, the meaning is backed up by an empirical examination.

This account is fully in accord with the spirit of empiricism, for whether or not a man has the intention of pursuing a particular behaviour policy can be empirically tested, both by observing what he does and by hearing what he replies when he is questioned about his intentions.[37]

Since this account of moral assertions is to be the basis for the discussion of the meaning of religious assertions, it is necessary to point out a grave defect in the analysis. It is not Braithwaite's empiricism that is objectionable, but his continuing positivism.

We should expect of a moral man that he would display moral integrity. If he acknowledges certain moral principles, then we should expect him to act in accordance with them. This is the empirically testable side of morality. Braithwaite is quite right in saying that the moral man intends to act in accordance with these principles. And should we not accuse such a man of hypocrisy if he acknowledged these principles, yet had no intention of acting in accordance with them? Braithwaite even points out that a moral man will on occasion fall short of his intention. He merely *mentions* this in passing, but it may in fact be that he has underestimated a significant pointer to the nature of morality. After all, we have many different kinds of intentions. I may intend to stop at a garage and put petrol in my car. If, perhaps because there is a cold gusting wind, I drive past the garage, then I shall have failed to carry out my intention. But it is of no significance, and to speak of 'failing' to carry out the intention gives it an importance it does not deserve. It is the distinctive nature of the intention to carry out a *moral* action, that if I fail to do so, I feel that I have done something wrong, that I am guilty, or to blame. I have failed, but not in something so relatively trivial as my intention. My failure is in-

37. ibid., p. 60.

curred in respect of the moral principle which I intended to act out. There are two points here. The first is that the guilt, blame or failure is a consequence of not acting as I intended, but it is not incurred simply through not keeping the intention, but because of the moral implications of not keeping it. The second point follows from this, namely that the failure is important because there was a reason for the intention in the first place. I intended to act in accordance with a moral principle, and the significance of the failure is a function of the seriousness of the moral principle rather than a function of my intention.

Perhaps this might be illustrated by an example from a different field. A man might assert that he loves his wife. On her birthday he buys her flowers. Assuming that on investigation it is found that he is married, did buy flowers, (for his wife), and that she likes flowers, then we might say that his action provides empirical evidence of his love for his wife. But it would be quite ludicrous to say that buying flowers *is* his love for his wife. Braithwaite, as already quoted, maintains that when a man claims that a certain action is right, 'what is primary is his intention to perform the action when the occasion for it arises'. But this is to get things the wrong way round. What the man means is that this action is right, whether or not he himself fails to perform it. He is asserting that the action should be done (and certainly not its opposite), because it should be done. This is the weight of the language of 'should' and 'ought'. We feel a responsibility for doing the action, even though we cannot give any reason for this sense of responsibility. It is open to any philosopher to dispute whether we should [*sic*] act on this basis, but once again, Braithwaite is discussing only the meaning of the moral assertions, not their truth or falsity. The empirical test applies only to whether a man acts in accordance with his stated intentions.

The main point at issue is whether we should concentrate

attention on the stated intention, or on the grounds of the intention. The fact that this is the issue is confirmed by Braithwaite's conclusion.

> The advantage this account of moral assertions has over all others, emotive non-propositional ones as well as cognitive propositional ones, is that it alone enables a satisfactory answer to be given to the question: What is the reason for my doing what I think I ought to do? The answer it gives is that, since my thinking that I ought to do the action is my intention to do it if possible, the reason why I do the action is simply that I intend to do it, if possible. On every other ethical view there will be a mysterious gap to be filled somehow between the moral judgement and the intention to act in accordance with it: there is no such gap if the primary use of a moral assertion is to declare such an intention.[38]

It is for this reason that, even with respect to his discussion of morals, Braithwaite's reduction represents a form of positivism. He must at all costs eliminate the 'mysterious gap' between the judgement and the intention. He does eliminate the gap, but the cost is very high indeed. He eliminates with it all moral judgement. On the basis of this analysis there is no difference between the assertions 'It is wrong to kill', and 'It is wrong to buy a black car in a hot climate', except that the first displays the intention to refrain from murder, while the second an intention not to buy a black car in a hot climate. If any grounds were given for the assertions, this would immediately introduce a 'mysterious gap' in the former between the judgement and the intention. But without grounds, it is difficult to see how any assertion could be referred to as a moral one.

It is not difficult to see how Braithwaite uses his conative account of moral assertions to throw light on the treatment of religious assertions. He claims that they are to be understood 'as being primarily declarations of adherence to a

38. ibid., pp. 60–61.

policy of action, declarations of commitment to a way of life'.[39] Moral assertions are primarily expressions of the intention to follow a moral principle (though it is not now clear how Braithwaite can still use this phrase). Similarly, religious assertions are really expressing the intention to follow a certain policy of behaviour. This brings us immediately to the same point of conflict as in the account of moral assertions. Granted that true religion involves commitment, i.e. that it affects behaviour, is it not also true that the intention to behave in a certain way is based on some other (religious) grounds? It is just this point that Braithwaite disputes.

> To say that it is belief in the dogmas of religion which is the cause of the believer's intention to behave as he does is to put the cart before the horse: it is the intention to behave which constitutes what is known as religious conviction.[40]

But this does not make any sense. In practice the believer may not carefully distinguish between his change in belief and change in behaviour, but there is no doubt that change in behaviour, to be significant, must have grounds. Μετάνοια is the basis of the resolution to adopt a new policy of behaviour. Are we not to assume that 'intention' in this context refers to a purposive and rational reorientation?

I have indicated that I consider Braithwaite's account of moral assertions to be inadequate precisely at the point where he thinks it strongest, namely, it 'requires no reason for my doing what I assert to be my duty ...'.[41] Similarly, his account of religious assertions is inadequate at just the point of supposed strength, that 'it connects them to ways of life without requiring an additional premise'.[42] Braithwaite's famous example is that the assertion 'God is love', which he takes to 'epitomize' the assertions of the Christian religion, must be taken to indicate the asserter's intention

39. ibid., p. 61.   40. ibid., p. 62.
41. ibid., p. 63.   42. ibid.

'to follow an agapeistic way of life.'[43] This takes us to the heart of the reduction, since it does indeed eliminate the 'additional premise', as in the account of moral assertions it eliminated the 'mysterious gap'. We also see the outworking of the Logical Positivist position with which the lecture began. It is now assumed that the asserter could not possibly be speaking about God. Further, it is also clear why, although the lecture purports to deal with 'An Empiricist's View of the Nature of Religious Belief', Braithwaite is concerned throughout with religious assertions. We shall return to this point later. The immediate point is that just as he has eliminated any reason for calling an assertion moral, so he has now eliminated any reason for calling an assertion religious.

Braithwaite admits that there may be argument about the proper description of the Christian way of life: he favours the agapeistic form, as described in 1 Corinthians xiii. Christians might be forgiven some surprise at the speed with which attention is focused on Christianity as a way of life. Of course it does involve a way of life, but we must reject the reductionist view that it is defined as a love-ethic or any other ethic. As we have seen already, early Christians distinguished themselves by asserting that 'Jesus is Lord'. While at first sight this might seem to support Braithwaite's view, we must reaffirm the seriousness of the title 'Lord'. A Jewish disciple might intend to copy everything that his master did.[44] But no Christian presumed to do what Jesus had done.

43. ibid.

44. 'It is not enough to learn the words of a rabbi, but necessary to live with him, so as to absorb his thought and copy his every gesture.' (W. D. Davies, *The Setting of the Sermon on the Mount*, Cambridge University Press, 1964, p. 455.) This reflects a very long tradition in Israel, in which the disciple or protégé learns in a servant role. cf. Joshua is described as the 'servant' of Moses, מְשָׁרֵת (LXX παρεστηκὼς). Rabbi Joshua ben Levi exemplifies this tradition when he says that 'all manner of service that a slave must render to his master a student must render to his teacher, except that of taking off his shoes'. (Quoted by Davies, *loc. cit.*)

To identify Christianity with following a Jesus ethic is precisely the mistake of the nineteenth-century Christian liberalism which reduced Jesus to a great moral example. The assertion that 'Jesus is Lord' is intended in the first instance to say something about Jesus. The way of life appropriate for Christians is the *response* to this affirmation. But this is to indicate the 'additional premise', the 'mysterious gap', the elimination of which Braithwaite regards as the main contribution of his conative account of moral and religious assertions. Even the examples chosen by Braithwaite show an unbalanced view of Christianity, perhaps deliberately slanted towards Christianity regarded primarily as a way of life. He mentions the Good Samaritan, but had he considered the parables of Buried Treasure, or the Unjust Steward, he would have encountered the disturbing fact that the teaching of Jesus is fundamentally eschatological, and cannot always be made the basis of a moral way of life.[45]

45. In this respect Braithwaite occupies the position of the nineteenth-century liberal theology already referred to, and exemplified in Adolf Jülicher's definitive work of the period, *Die Gleichnisreden Jesu* (Vol. 1, 1899, Vol. 2, 1910). Jülicher was not influenced by the Weiss–Schweitzer *konsequente Eschatologie*. His contribution to the development of the study of the parables was that he broke with the long-established method of allegorical interpretation. Unfortunately he then tried to find in them examples of general moral maxims. Thus Buried Treasure (Matthew xiii, 44) is taken to mean that we should sacrifice the lower good for the higher. But on closer inspection, we see that the story is about a piece of trickery and deceit. It describes the singleness of mind appropriate to the decision about the Kingdom, but it cannot be made the basis of a universal *moral* axiom. Braithwaite might also be forgiven for thinking that the parables of Jesus outline a moral code, since the early Church tried to interpret them in this light. The most disastrous example of this project is to be seen in the series of expansions to the story of the Unjust Steward (Luke xvi, 1–8 and 9–13). Once again a fundamentally immoral action is taken to exemplify the singleness of mind appropriate to the time of judgement. It is impossible to convert the originally eschatological story into an edifying moral one.

The final point to which we must refer in this lecture concerns the way in which Christianity is to be distinguished both from morality and from other religions. Braithwaite's proposal is that the distinction is not so much in the behaviour but in the stories associated with the adopted behavioural policy. Being a Christian involves both the intention to live according to Christian moral principles and the associating with this intention of the Christian stories. These stories, it appears, are mainly the biblical narratives. Once again we see Braithwaite turning away from the concept of belief. Being a Christian involves 'entertaining' the stories. There is no need to believe them – and at this point he specifically returns to the verification principle. Even if they are not believed, at least they are of psychological help in carrying out the behaviour intended.

This position is unsatisfactory for several reasons. In the first place we might compare it with a famous definition of Christianity offered by Schleiermacher: 'Christianity is a monotheistic faith, belonging to the teleological type of religion, and is essentially distinguished from other such faiths by the fact that in it, everything is related to the redemption accomplished by Jesus of Nazareth.'[46] Christianity is not distinguished by the stories which Christians 'entertain', but because these stories express beliefs about the world or about history. Above all, the beliefs refer to something which happened in the events surrounding the life of Jesus of Nazareth. Christians are distinguished not by entertaining certain stories, but by believing certain things. That this is so has been recognized from the formulation of the first *credo*. These beliefs are the grounds for the Christian way of life.

In the second place, the discussion requires to be clarified by distinguishing between different uses of the inclusive term 'story', and, for that matter, 'belief'. The Elijah cycle includes stories which may be 'entertained' rather than be-

46. Schleiermacher, *The Christian Faith*, p. 52.

lieved. But the story of Israel from the Exodus to the Restoration cannot simply be entertained. If it were shown to be substantially different from the way in which it has been represented in the Bible this would have a corresponding effect on the content of Christian belief. What could be said on the basis of the biblical narrative could not be said on the basis of a completely different history. In particular this applies to the gospel narratives. We might entertain the account of Jesus at the marriage at Cana, or even the Transfiguration, in the sense that we had doubts about the historicity of aspects of these stories. But should we come to doubt whether a man existed about whom such stories could appropriately be told, then this would have a corresponding effect on the content of Christian belief. There are stories which can be valuable although historically problematic. There are other stories which, while certainly not to be taken literally, must have some relationship to historical events and experiences. Braithwaite's term 'entertain' does not emphasize sufficiently the necessity of maintaining some relationship between faith and fact if Christianity is to be a truly historical religion.[47]

Braithwaite summarizes his position by saying that 'a religious belief is an intention to behave in a certain way (a moral belief) together with the entertainment of certain stories associated with the intention in the mind of the believer'.[48] There are certain objections of a philosophical nature and some very basic theological objections, to this position. It is a positivist form of reduction which eliminates rather

47. To avoid giving this point a disproportionate amount of attention, we cannot pursue it further, but it is the basic issue in the quest of the historical Jesus, which, in its old and new forms, has been going on for two hundred years. The issue also involves the related project of demythologizing. Cf. J. Macquarrie, 'A New Kind of Demythologizing?', *Studies in Christian Existentialism*, S.C.M. Press, London, 1966, in which Braithwaite is compared with Bultmann.

48. Ramsey, op. cit., p. 71.

than reinterprets the problematic areas of Christian faith. It does not provide us with a satisfactory basis upon which traditional Christians and radical Christians might meet.

PAUL M. VAN BUREN: 'THE SECULAR MEANING OF THE GOSPEL'[49]

With the publication of Wittgenstein's *Philosophical Investigations*, a positive and potentially creative phase of the relationship of philosophy and theology in England was made possible. Unfortunately there has been little interest in this debate among continental theologians. Correspondingly, English theology has continued to be little influenced by continental theology. We have had the unhappy position of late in which new and exciting developments have taken place in England and on the Continent, but with very little awareness of either group of developments by the other. The characteristics of the contemporary theological scene correspond. Thus in England the theological issues which are put under scrutiny are normally rather old-fashioned ones, such as the traditional proofs, the problem of evil, or the concept of eternal life. Yet on the Continent the great issues of hermeneutics, hope and eschatology are not treated in the light of the real advances in linguistic analysis. In recent years there has been some attempt to bridge this gap,[50] but when van Buren wrote his remarkable book he was breaking new ground. In theology the pace was set by the German writers, and yet English analysis was still largely concerned with traditional problems. It is to his credit that van Buren saw that this situation was unsatisfactory, and sallied forth with the motto, 'let fools rush in where Angles fear to tread'.[51]

49. S.C.M. Press, London, 1963.
50. e.g. R. W. Jenson, *The Knowledge of Things Hoped For*, Oxford University Press, New York, 1969.
51. Van Buren, *Theological Explorations*, p. 83.

Unfortunately, van Buren did look rather foolish but only because he undertook to do what had to be done, and what those who were in a better position to do had not cared to attempt.

We shall not be concerned to summarize or even comment on the whole of the book, but van Buren's method is of special interest, since he provides us with one of the most interesting examples of reductionism to date. Originally within the Barthian camp, indeed a doctoral student under Barth, he is one of the post-war theologians who have come to reject the familiar Barth–Bultmann division as properly defining the contemporary agenda for theology. But unlike the continental theologians who have tried to take account of the contributions of both of these men, van Buren has also tried to incorporate the contribution of analytical philosophy. The fact that he has not always been able to combine the insights of Barth, Bultmann and Wittgenstein is hardly surprising, but he does challenge us to do the job more satisfactorily.

Van Buren begins with the question: 'How may a Christian who is himself a secular man understand the Gospel in a secular way?'[52] What he means by 'secular' becomes clear as the book develops, but the main point is that it is incompatible with belief in the God of traditional theism. Like Hamilton's writing, van Buren is presenting us with a work which is, in the last analysis, autobiographical. The secular man is Paul M. van Buren. Hence the seriousness of the question. What if, because of the secular culture in which we live, a man should no longer be able to affirm the existence of God, and yet still want to remain a Christian? The solution is by a reduction, from what van Buren calls 'God-statements' to 'man-statements'. We must find a method by which we can translate Christianity from one language to the other, or rather show how it retains its value and force

52. Van Buren, *The Secular Meaning of the Gospel*, p. xiv.

when its subject is changed from God to man. How can the religious meaning of the gospel be translated to yield the secular meaning? 'Either "being a Christian" is something "religious" and quite distinct from secular affairs, or Christian faith is a human posture conceivable for a man who is part of his secular culture.'[53] Van Buren claims that the translation can take place through the application of linguistic analysis, in the tradition of the later Wittgenstein, and he specifically refers to the famous dictum that 'the meaning of a word is its use in the language'.

However, the key to the understanding of van Buren's work is not Wittgenstein but Braithwaite, and we shall be able to deal with van Buren's position largely by reference to our previous section. Indeed there is a great deal in common between the two. We criticized Braithwaite for claiming to begin with Wittgenstein, but in fact simply adding Wittgenstein's functional analysis to a previously laid foundation of Logical Positivism. This is true also of van Buren. He claims that the later Wittgenstein is fundamental to his work, yet Wittgenstein is only brought in when certain fateful assumptions of an empirical nature have been made. Throughout the book we are told that the secular involves 'certain empirical attitudes',[54] that modern man 'thinks empirically and pragmatically',[55] and that the book is based on 'certain empirical attitudes'.[56] Indeed in describing his method as it has been developed in the first half of the book, he makes a very revealing statement.

This clarification has been accomplished by a frankly empirical method which reflects the thinking of an industrialized, scientific age. It has taken certain empirical attitudes characteristic of modern thought seriously and accepted them without qualification.[57]

53. ibid., p. 17.
54. Van Buren, *The Secular Meaning of the Gospel*, Preface, pp. xiii–xiv.
55. ibid., p. 17.   56. ibid., p. 20.   57. ibid., p. 102.

It is now clear why being a secular man is identified primarily with unbelief in God.

The empiricist in us finds the heart of the difficulty not in what is said about God, but in the very talking about God at all. We do not know 'what' God is, and we cannot understand how the word 'God' is being used.[58]

But this is far removed indeed from functional analysis. Of course it is true that many people today do not as a matter of fact know how to use the word God, except as a minor ejaculation. But then there are many words which, for technical or cultural reasons, are only used by minority groups in society. Functional analysis entails the examination of how a word is used by those who know how to use it, determining the rules for its use by those who know how to play that particular game. The term 'language-game' was first used by Wittgenstein to describe the multiplicity of ways of speaking (and living), including for example giving and obeying orders, reporting an event, reading a story, telling a joke. The list ends: 'Asking, thanking, cursing, greeting, praying.'[59] Whether or not we should pray does not enter into the question of what it means to pray. Contrary to Wittgenstein's example, van Buren has not examined how the word God is used, but has simply ruled out its use. But this procedure is the one adopted by the Logical Positivists, more recently logical empiricists, when they apply the verificational principle. Van Buren claims to be aware of the difference between Logical Positivism and functional analysis, but in practice, like Braithwaite, he combines the two.

The verification principle has continued to be important, but it has another function in contemporary linguistic analysis. There are a variety of 'language-games', activities with their appropriate languages, and a modified verification principle is

58. ibid., p. 84.
59. Wittgenstein, *Philosophical Investigations*, section 23.

now used to ask what sort of things would count for an assertion and what sort of things would count against it.[60]

This position might be taken to reflect the procedure of Antony Flew in 'Theology and Falsification',[61] but not the method of Wittgenstein. Just as the Logical Positivists set up scientific language as the model to which all speaking must conform, so van Buren has chosen the language of empirically oriented, pragmatic, modern, secular man. His model may be considerably less precise than that of the Vienna Circle, but it is no less a form of positivism. In dealing with Braithwaite we said that it was not his reductionism but his positivism which is objectionable. So now we must be on our guard throughout the remainder of van Buren's book. His reduction of what is left may or may not be satisfactory: that remains to be seen. But his reduction can never be wholly satisfactory for precisely that reason, that it concerns only what is left. In *The Secular Meaning of the Gospel*, we are involved in two kinds of reduction. In the first certain dimensions of theology are arbitrarily (by positivist assumptions) cut off. Whatever they meant, they are not allowed to mean anything today. Having cut off these dimensions, which might easily be the most significant, he then employs to the remainder the now familiar God-to-man reduction.

It will be clear that, as it stands, van Buren's position is much more radical than the Death of God theology. 'Today, we cannot even understand the Nietzschian cry that "God is dead!" for if it were so, how could we know? No, the problem now is that the *word* "God" is dead.'[62] It is for this reason that he is considered here and not in connection with Altizer and Hamilton. His position is much more consis-

60. Van Buren, *The Secular Meaning of the Gospel*, p. 15.

61. *New Essays in Philosophical Theology*, ed. A. Flew and A. MacIntyre, S.C.M. Press, London, 1955.

62. Van Buren, *The Secular Meaning of the Gospel*, p. 103.

tently radical than theirs. Indeed, in the light of what has just been said, it might well be claimed that he is not a radical theologian at all, since he has adopted a form of positivism. Not that such a charge would dismay van Buren. When asked by Ved Mehta if God was not indispensable to Christianity he said, No. But clearly Mehta's traditional question did not properly illuminate van Buren's fundamental concern. 'I am trying to raise a more important issue: whether or not Christianity is fundamentally about God or about man.'[63] He has more recently used the phrase 'Christological humanism' to focus on his central concern.[64] The secular meaning of the gospel will therefore be a way (unfortunately positivist in some respects) of speaking about man, from a perspective given by Jesus of Nazareth.

This leads us back again to Braithwaite, whose position is outlined by van Buren almost without criticism. Certainly there is no criticism of the view that Christian faith means an intention to act in a certain way. It seems clear, however, that van Buren did not altogether understand the implications of Braithwaite's position, if only because he still attempts to find a basis on which a man might choose to be a Christian. Such 'grounds' for action are specifically eschewed by Braithwaite. The solution is to hand, for to Braithwaite's position van Buren — whose work is never marred by any failure of nerve — confidently adds a pinch of 'blik' from R. M. Hare,[65] and a modest dose of discernment commitment from I. T. Ramsey.[66] Thus 'Easter faith was a new perspective upon life arising out of a situation of discernment focused on the history of Jesus'.[67]

Van Buren rejects the view that theological statements are

---

63. V. Mehta, *The New Theologian*, p. 76.
64. Van Buren, *Theological Explorations*, p. 132.
65. Response to Flew's essay already noted above.
66. Ramsey, *Religious Language*, S.C.M. Press, London, 1957.
67. Van Buren, *The Secular Meaning of the Gospel*, p. 132.

cognitive. They do not make cosmological assertions. As we saw in Braithwaite's essay, they are verified simply by checking up to see whether or not a man's speech, and above all, his conduct, correspond to his profession. But in taking up this position he leaves himself open to the same criticism which is made of Braithwaite. Worse than that, van Buren seems to come under the criticism of Braithwaite's position without fully benefiting from the simplicity of the position. Thus in the example just quoted, a new perspective upon life is entailed in Easter faith, but Easter faith is actually faith in Jesus. That this is so seems to be conceded in the second part of the statement, that the discernment situation is the basis or grounds for faith. We should conclude therefore that for van Buren, as in our discussion of Braithwaite, there is a gap between belief and action. The two are not identical. Action is the expression of belief, and belief the grounds of action. But if this is the case, then the verification principle can no longer be taken as one of the twin principles in van Buren's work of translating.

Statements of faith are to be interpreted, by means of the modified verification principle, as statements which express, describe, or commend a particular way of seeing the world, other men, and oneself, and the way of life appropriate to such a perspective.[68]

I do not think van Buren has reached a consistent position here. He is claiming to agree with Braithwaite, but there is some evidence that he has not fully accepted this view. In any case the principle just enunciated is open to the same criticism as that made of Braithwaite. As we saw then, it is possible to verify whether a man loves his wife or not by discovering how he acts towards her – the specific example was that of buying flowers. But the buying of flowers is not identical with loving his wife. Thus van Buren's principle might be very illuminating in searching out what is entailed in any

68. ibid., p. 156.

statement of faith, and in verifying whether or not a man's conduct is commensurate with his beliefs. But it would be, once again, a form of positivism to identify the actions possibly entailed in the belief, and the belief itself. The most striking example of such an identification comes from van Buren's treatment of the double commandment.[69] He quotes Bornkamm's comment on this passage: 'Surrender to God now ... [means] a waiting and preparedness for the call of God, who calls us in the person of our neighbour. In this sense the love of our neighbour is *the test of* our love of God.'[70] To this van Buren replies: 'Precisely. If love for the neighbour is the test of "love for God", then by the verification principle, it is the meaning of "love for God". What is "being ready for God" other than being ready for the neighbour?'[71] In the light of what has been said we need not press this point any further, except to say that like Braithwaite's 'agapeistic' way of life, van Buren has given us the secular entailment of the gospel, but he has not shown that there is nothing more to be said about the love of God.

So far we have spoken of that part of van Buren's work which corresponds to the opening sections of Braithwaite's essay, the empiricism and the account of morals. When we turn to the specifically Christian part of van Buren's work we find that it has, not surprisingly, much in common with Braithwaite's emphasis on 'the story'. It is here, as indicated, if anywhere, that van Buren says he has some reservations about Braithwaite's position. What these amount to is not made clear, but it looks as if van Buren's previous neo-orthodoxy forces him on to regard the Jesus story still very much in kerygmatic terms. It may be a question of degree, but I suspect he wishes to emphasize the fact that a man is

69. Matthew xxii, 34ff.

70. G. Bornkamm, *Jesus of Nazareth*, Hodder & Stoughton, London, 1960, p. 111, italics added.

71. Van Buren, *The Secular Meaning of the Gospel*, p. 183.

grasped by the kerygma, which gives him a total orientation for life. 'In saying that Jesus was Lord over the whole world, they indicated that their perspective covered the totality of life, the world, and history, as well as their understanding of themselves and other men.'[72] This means more than doing good to one's immediate neighbours: 'faith is not based simply on a picture of the historical Jesus, but the historical Jesus is indispensable for faith'.[73] It may be for this reason that van Buren is not happy about Braithwaite's more tentative position that the believer 'entertains stories'. I do not think van Buren ever escapes his memories of Basel, that in Jesus of Nazareth something actually happened, and that the events surrounding his life and death have actually changed history. Thus his second principle of interpretation: 'The norm of the Christian perspective is the series of events to which the New Testament documents testify, centring in the life, death, and resurrection of Jesus of Nazareth.'[74] In a recent lecture van Buren has laid even more stress on the power with which the story of Jesus grasps the believer, and is not simply entertained by him. He says that 'theology is the activity of men struck by the biblical story, in which they undertake to revise continually the ways in which they say how things are with their present circumstances, in the light of how they read that story'.[75]

It is often said that of the radical theologians van Buren is the cool, lucid one. No doubt there is some merit in being lucidly wrong, in contrast to the writing of Altizer, who is often too incomprehensible to be judged right or wrong. But there is no doubt that van Buren's low-key theology gives

72. ibid., p. 133.

73. ibid., p. 126. Cf. 'The historical man Jesus was not made superfluous by the Easter event.' (ibid., p. 134.)

74. ibid., p. 156. The first principle was quoted above, p. 180.

75. Van Buren, 'On Doing Theology', *Talk of God*, Macmillan, New York, Royal Institute of Philosophy Lectures, Vol. 2 (1967–8), 1969, p. 53.

the impression of plausibility. The point to note, however, is that the same fundamental problems recur for van Buren as for other theologians. At the centre is the problem of God. Van Buren cannot affirm the existence of the traditional God, and cannot find a contemporary and viable alternative way of speaking of God. His book, and its problems, flow from this starting point.

The first mistake which he makes is to give a reason why speaking of God is impossible. This inevitably leads to positivism (in this case via empiricism and pragmatism). This was not, historically, the route by which he came to the point of being unable to affirm belief in the traditional God. Although he claims that the philosophical foundations for his work are Hare and Wittgenstein, there is no doubt that the fundamental assumptions are those of Flew and Braithwaite.

If van Buren had undertaken an analysis of how the word God is used, he might have avoided the other side of the reduction, God-to-man. 'Whatever men were looking for in looking for "God" is to be found by finding Jesus of Nazareth.'[76] As previously indicated, this line of reduction provides us at most with the secular entailment of the gospel, but it leaves too many issues unexamined.

Indeed this leads us to the final criticism of van Buren, that his positivism is of the head and not of the heart. His philosophy lets him down in various ways. He has not fully understood or assimilated the positions of Wittgenstein or Braithwaite. But the impression comes through that his inconsistency is not caused simply by a lack of comprehension; it is rather caused by his feeling that he wants to say more than his ill-considered philosophical position will allow. In his two principles of interpretation he speaks of a certain 'perspective'; more recently he has been speaking of 'how we are'. Van Buren underestimates the significance of such a position. 'If you persist with your questions, asking why this

76. Van Buren, *The Secular Meaning of the Gospel*, p. 147.

picture and this story are to be taken so seriously, or why this story rather than another, he will finally say, because that is how things are.'[77] The prior issue, however, is not why *this* story, but why *any* story? Not why this discernment situation leads us to a Christian perspective, but why do we speak in the language of discernment at all?

It is not difficult to push this criticism of van Buren to an ironic conclusion. He started out to appropriate the contributions of Barth, Bultmann and Wittgenstein. He rejected Barth's neo-supernaturalism but unwittingly reintroduced the qualitative distinction between how things seem and how they 'really' are. He rejected Bultmann's demythologizing, yet failed to heed Bultmann's warning that to eliminate instead of translate is to fall into positivism. He claimed to adopt the method of Wittgenstein, yet ends up nearer the *Tractatus* than the *Investigations*. However, his failure should not be taken to give comfort to those who occupy traditional positions. Van Buren is right to point out that the old supernaturalism is incompatible with our secular culture, and that we cannot continue with this view of God.

The problem before us is the problem of God. Unless a solution is found, men will not be able to make the decision for or against faith in Christ. We have rejected the idea of ignoring the problem; we have rejected the kind of reforms hitherto regarded as possible solutions; and unfortunately we have been forced to say that pluralism will not work under the present circumstances. We cannot have a truce, with some Christians regarding others as second-class believers. In this chapter we have been examining the more radical solution : the elimination of the problem by the elimination of God.

Feuerbach, Braithwaite and van Buren all present positions which are empirically based, and as we have seen, all three are involved to varying degrees in positivism. Braithwaite's

77. Van Buren, 'On Doing Theology', *Talk of God*, p. 69.

position does not offer a viable solution to our problem. His position has a certain internal consistency, granted the positivist foundation, but it is precisely the foundation which is quite unsatisfactory even on logical considerations. Also his attempt to eliminate grounds upon which responsible action should be undertaken seems to eliminate responsibility.

In the case of Feuerbach we are confronted with a form of positivism, especially with the idea of each species being able to conceive nothing higher than itself. But his work is not a thoroughgoing positivism, since he replaces 'God' with the 'Species'. His work is no less metaphysical and if anything less viable than the theology it was supposed to replace.

Van Buren falls immediately into a form of positivism against which he struggles throughout the rest of his work. His solution to the problem of God is not so much reduction as elimination. Yet he is not so easily rid of issues involved in the use of the word 'God'. His allegiance to Barth prevents him in the end from giving up the concerns which belong to theology, even when he has given up the word 'God'.

Two points emerge from this chapter. The first is that the solution to our problem is not going to be found through resort to reduction. There are too many questions begged in this approach. I propose, therefore, that we should explore the possibility of a solution in the other direction, which might be called a solution by escalation rather than by reduction. This is the first point, and it will be the concern of the rest of the book. The second point which emerges from this chapter is that before we go any further we must make a close examination of the logic of the word 'God' and consequently the meaning of doing theology. This will be the content of the next chapter.

CHAPTER 8

The Meaning of Theology

WE have maintained since the beginning of the book that the major problem for theology, and perhaps for the Church, is the inability of the vast majority of people to believe in God. John Hick, in an essay entitled 'Religious Faith as Experiencing–As',[1] has argued forcefully for the possibility of interpreting our experience in a theistic way. This argument will be of great comfort to those who do believe in God, but the scope of the discussion is severely limited, as Hick admits, to 'an epistemological analysis of religious faith, not an argument for the validity of that faith'.[2] The vast majority of people will still not be able to interpret their experience as experience of God. And yet belief in God is regarded as the prior condition of becoming a Christian.

We have also discussed the possibility of a secular faith in Christ, which would not involve belief in God. Although the idea of a secular theology was very popular in the early 1960s, it was bound to fail, because it incorporated a fatal inconsistency. It tried to give secular expression to Christianity, but a Christianity still conceived of by reference to the traditional God of the Bible.[3]

1. *Talk of God*, The Royal Institute of Philosophy, 1969, pp. 20–35.
2. ibid., p. 35.
3. This inconsistency was taken over from Bonhoeffer, whose influence on contemporary theology has been important only on secondary issues. Bonhoeffer, for all his talk about the false 'religious premise' (*Letters and Papers from Prison*, Collins, London, 1959, p. 91), based his work on the simple religious premise of the existence of God. Although he recognized that increasingly, fewer and fewer people would be able to believe in God, he made no attempt to in-

Secular theology does not offer us a solution to our problem, since, without exception, examples of it still presuppose belief in God. That is to say, they presuppose precisely the one issue which prevents secular men from facing the challenge of Christianity.[4] Nor do we find any help in the so-called 'radical theology' of Altizer and Hamilton. Do they or don't they? And in the end they do have some kind of continuing religious premise. Finally we have looked at solution by reduction. Is it possible to eliminate the problem by eliminating the word 'God'? From our examination of examples of this course of interpretation the answer is 'No'. In the case of van Buren, in particular, the elimination of the word does not in fact solve the problem, because the prob-

---

terpret Christianity without reference to belief in God. Perhaps this was because he did not have time to pursue this line, but I doubt it. I think that had Bonhoeffer survived the Second World War he would today be quite irrelevant to our contemporary problem. He would still have had belief in God and would still have understood Christianity as impossible without such belief. In the late 1950s and early 1960s, Bonhoeffer's thought was widely discussed, but as long as belief in God is required as a prior condition of becoming Christian, we are no further forward in formulating a secular faith in Christ. We must reluctantly conclude that this inconsistency in Bonhoeffer, exploring a secular faith but holding a prior religious premise (albeit not the false 'religious premise'), has prevented contemporary theology from solving its central problem. It is for this reason that Bonhoeffer has been entirely ignored in this book. Perhaps this is the first work in contemporary theology in which Bonhoeffer has been relegated to a footnote. This may be the only way forward for theology now.

4. Pannenberg is justified in refusing to begin with the pre-Christian God of natural theology. 'The procedure of Christology, on the contrary, begins with Jesus himself in order to find God in him. In this case, in turn, the idea of God must be *presupposed* historically and in substance.' (*Jesus: God and Man*, trans. L.L. Wilkins and D. A. Priebe, S.C.M. Press, London, 1968, p. 20, italics added.) But can we today, even *within* the Church, presuppose God?

lem seems to break out in other forms. The resort to positivism is no solution even when dealing with morals, and it is still less satisfactory in dealing with theology.

It is difficult to believe that the whole Christian tradition can be dismissed completely because belief in God has become problematic. If a man cannot interpret his life as experience of God, must he then say that Christianity (indeed the whole Judeo-Christian tradition) has been founded on an error? Is it not more likely that it has been on to something real, though its description is now seen to be inaccurate, crude or misleading? This would be readily admitted: the doctrine of God has undergone many refinements since the day on which Uzzah was struck down for offering a helping hand. But it would seem that we have reached a more critical juncture in the history of the doctrine of God. *The future of Christianity is not viable unless we can find a way of presenting it which includes the old doctrine of God, but does not demand belief in God as a prior condition of becoming a Christian.*

Such a solution to the problem of God would involve taking account of the doctrine of God. This is what van Buren really fails to do. Nor does this happen by an oversight. He claims that this is the pattern of the growth in human knowledge, and points to the reduction of astrology to astronomy, alchemy to chemistry. Richard Comstock has taken up this simplistic solution.

> But could astronomy eliminate all reference to astral bodies and chemistry all reference to chemicals without destroying the integrity of their respective areas of investigation? Similarly, is a theology possible without reference to theos, the divine, God?[5]

Comstock is right, but for the wrong reasons. Van Buren's analogies are not so apt as they at first appear. No one would try to establish any connection between the astrologer and

5. *The Meaning of the Death of God,* ed. Murchland, p. 213.

the astronomer, the alchemist and the chemist. It is not just that historically there is no connection, but that, more important, their concerns were actually quite different. Above all, astrology failed (notwithstanding the popular newspaper columns on 'the stars and you'), because it was not 'on to something'. It was not primarily concerned with the stars, but with human history. It failed because there is no connection. But Comstock's analogies are not altogether conclusive either. Astronomy does not, as a matter of fact, deal with 'astral bodies'. When I read astronomy as a student, no lecturer would ever have used such an archaic expression, and certainly would have invited applause from the benches if he had spoken of 'heavenly bodies'. At one time stars were thought to be solid bodies. In a sense such astronomy *has* been given up, but this is of no consequence. Astronomers are on to something, and however revolutionary the changes in their ways of conceiving of and speaking about what it is they are on to, continuity is preserved. Comstock himself goes on to warn that etymology cannot be the deciding factor.

Etymology is not the deciding factor, and yet some kind of continuity must be preserved. Above all the issues must be preserved. If theology was on to something in speaking about God, then *that* must be preserved, although the further investigation of it may move away from the traditional doctrine of God. I do not think this has been sufficiently noted in the two theologians considered earlier, Macquarrie and Ogden. Macquarrie does not even consider the Death of God school to be radical, since 'one would hesitate to give the name of "theology" to an enterprise which has rejected theology's key word, "God"'.[6] This is further spelled out when he considers the end result of such radical thought.

He may construct a philosophy of religion (and he may even do this brilliantly), or he may construct a doctrine of man (anthropology) or a doctrine of Jesus (Jesuology) or an ethic or

6. Macquarrie, *Principles of Christian Theology*, p. 143.

a mixture of all of these, but whatever results from his endeavours, it will not be a theology.[7]

Similarly, Ogden makes the following point when he discusses van Buren's position : 'However absurd talking about God might be, it could never be so obviously absurd as talking of Christian faith without God.'[8] It would of course be tempting to put the work of Macquarrie and Ogden to their own test. They would agree that to be a Christian one must believe in God, but should one not believe in the same God that Jesus believed in? Yet neither Macquarrie nor Ogden is willing to be committed to that kind of belief. That point could be expanded, but it deflects us from the central issue. I agree with Comstock, Macquarrie and Ogden that van Buren's position is unsatisfactory. But it is not unsatisfactory simply because he does not use the *word* 'God'. Rather it is because of his positivism. He does not reinterpret the word God; he does not even inquire after its logical meaning : he simply eliminates it. Van Buren's position does not qualify as theology (and he would be indifferent to this judgement), but the disqualification is not the absence of the word God. It is rather because its absence is symptomatic of the fact that he has eliminated what it is that theology is on to. These theologians have mistaken the symptom for the disease. Astronomers tell us that if, hypothetically, we could travel to a star by spaceship, there would be nothing to see when we arrived. If you insist of course that the word 'star' refers to a solid body which twinkles, then it is as absurd to speak about this modern study as 'astronomy' as it is to do theology without speaking of the God in whom Jesus believed. The etymology can in neither case be regarded as decisive. The question is : what are we on to, and how is this study continuous with its past? Van Buren's position is unacceptable not because what he is on to is unimportant. Far

7. Macquarrie, *God and Secularity*, Lutterworth Press, London, 1968, p. 13.   8. Ogden, *The Reality of God*, p. 14.

from it. It is unacceptable because it deals with only some aspects of what theology was on to, and perhaps not even the most important aspects.

The position to which we are moving is not entirely new. Indeed, almost twenty years ago, Tillich pointed in this direction. But the climate of thought was not so radical as it is today. When he spoke of 'ultimate concern', clergymen took this up simply as a secular way of speaking about the religious God. Perhaps today we are in a better position to see what Tillich meant. We have been asking whether the word 'God' is a necessary condition of doing theology. It is not, at least, not when judged by Tillich's two formal criteria of theology:

1. The object of theology is what concerns us ultimately. Only those propositions are theological which deal with their object in so far as it can become a matter of ultimate concern for us.
2. Our ultimate concern is that which determines our being or non-being. Only those statements are theological which deal with their object in so far as it can become a matter of being or non-being for us.[9]

At the outset these may seem rather eccentric criteria in defining theological activity. But let us compare them with more familiar approaches. Theology is often assumed to be what theologians do, or what goes on in a Faculty of Theology. Certainly the word 'God' is liable to be more used in this context than in most. Yet anyone who has read theology knows that the history of dogma is at times quite arid or speculative. Some controversies about God have no conceivable existential interest for us. Similarly, biblical exegesis can be comparable with the study of any other classical texts from the ancient world. Thus 'theology' can on occasion obscure the word of God from us. It was against this failure

9. Tillich, *Systematic Theology*, Vol. I, pp. 15, 17.

to arouse a dialectical involvement with the text that Barth vigorously protested.[10]

Alternatively it might be assumed that theology is talk about God. This has already been covered in part in the last example. But the professional atheist or agnostic, not so common today, might spend a good deal of his time talking about God. Yet such mere talk would hardly justify the description 'theological'. Nor would we take very seriously the talk about God of a man who affirmed belief in God, but did nothing about it. Finally, theology is not the study of a supernatural order.

Tillich is quite right to point us not to things but to concerns. Nor is this very far away from our common view of theology. Do we not say that a woman cleans her home 'religiously'? This task becomes the focal point of her life, determining the rest of her life. Without real concern and commitment there is no theology, but the subject must be determinative for the whole of our lives. This is what Tillich means by his two formal criteria. When he speaks of being concerned ultimately with 'that which determines our being or non-being', we might today speak simply of an issue which is a matter of life and death. Now this is all right, as far as it goes. But it might be objected that such a view is always in danger of allowing theology to become trivialized. If a woman is ultimately concerned with the appearance of her home, if a man is ultimately concerned with his career, are we really to say that these are theological pursuits? Unfortunately the *short* answer is 'Yes'. It is unfortunate for different reasons in each case. If a woman were ultimately

10 'I have nothing whatever to say against historical criticism. I recognize it, and once more state quite definitely, that it is both necessary and justified. My complaint is that recent commentators confine themselves to an interpretation of the text which seems to me to be no commentary at all, but merely the first step towards a commentary.' (*The Epistle to the Romans*, trans. Sir Edwyn C. Hoskins, Oxford University Press, 1933, p. 6.)

concerned with the appearance of her home, then (in my view) she would have set her sights too low. She would have committed her whole life to something not really worthy of her potential, perhaps not compatible with morality in the areas of neighbourliness or social responsibility. In other words, theology is trivialized whenever our ultimate concern is trivial. In the case of the man whose career was his ultimate concern, the position would be more serious. We should have to examine it more closely, but it may be that such a concern would tend to be destructive; self-destructive in terms of health or even of efficiency, and socially destructive in terms of his relationship with his family and friends. Then this theology would be demonic, the commitment not to something trivial but idolatrous.

How then are we to distinguish a legitimate ultimate concern from a rather trivial one, and how are we to identify a demonic one? There is no difficulty in answering this question when we decide to pursue *Christian* theology. Tillich tells us that the criterion of deciding whether a man is a theologian or not does not depend on his having had the prescribed religious experience (pietism) or even belief in God (orthodoxy). 'Rather it depends on his being ultimately concerned with the Christian message even if he is sometimes inclined to attack and to reject it.'[11] Being a Christian means that one's ultimate concern is the Christian message. In his own distinctive terminology, Tillich then moves to define the material norm of theology as taking 'the New Being in Jesus as the Christ as our ultimate concern'.[12] I should now like to propose a definition of our subject. Christian faith means commitment, with ultimate concern, to that which came to expression in Jesus Christ. Christian theology is the systematic reflection on what is entailed in commitment, with ultimate concern, to that which came to expression in Jesus Christ.

11. Tillich, *Systematic Theology*, Vol. I, p. 13.   12. ibid., p. 56.

The meaning of these definitions will be clarified increasingly in the remainder of the book, but they are given now in order to make some preliminary points. Unlike Tillich, who stresses 'the Christian message', we have chosen the phrase 'that which came to expression in Jesus Christ'. This provides us with a certain flexibility until we can fill out what is involved. But it does mean that we are not simply concentrating attention on the historical Jesus, his message, or even the Church's message (gospel) about him. It may be that although we shall agree that this was the most important event in human history, we shall have to give our own account of what was involved in the event, how we should see and interpret its significance, in a phrase, how we should understand what came to expression. The phrase also allows us to see what happened in Jesus Christ as the culmination of the history of Israel's pilgrimage. The word 'God' does not appear in the definition, but we are determined not to resort to a reduction of theology. We have specifically rejected this path. Indeed we have set out on the contrary path of escalation. Continuing in this direction we must pursue our examination of the logic of the word 'God'.

The heading of this chapter is 'The Meaning of Theology', and it is intended to suggest that we might have some help with the problem if, unlike van Buren, we really did turn to analyse the use of the word 'God'. As long as we say that Christian theology, or Christian faith, is concerned with God, then we cannot proceed until we have established the existence of God. But, as we have already seen, there seems to be no way in which we can bring modern men to belief in God. Christians feel this to be an intolerable situation. Why? It is because the attempt to lead men to belief in God, an attempt which invariably fails, seems to suggest that the existence of God is contingent. It is for this reason, I believe, that there is such a tradition as we have previously examined, which denies that there can finally be such a thing as atheism.

The three theologians previously mentioned sharpen the issue in saying that we cannot omit reference to God because theology is about God. Yet we have just pointed out that the word 'God' does not seem to be an adequate criterion for identifying theology. We are thus faced with the problem that we know we are on to something in theology. The key word for theology is said to be God. Yet we are not in a position to make the existence of God, the presupposition of theology, contingent. The traditional solution to this problem has been to try to make the existence of God necessary. This is to be seen classically stated in the Ontological argument. More recently I think the same attempt is to be seen in the works of Macquarrie and Ogden. The effect of their arguments would be to make it as impossible to deny the existence of God as to deny one's own existence or the existence of the world. The inherent weakness of all such approaches is that there are (insurmountable) objections to the concept of necessary existence, or necessary being. Even the existence of the world is not necessary. But, such objections aside, it may be that the attempt to establish God as the presupposition of theology is itself misguided.

According to our previous discussion, the presupposition of theology is not God, but the legitimacy of having an ultimate concern. The meaning of the word 'God' then becomes the content of our ultimate concern. It is not that we should be ultimately concerned about a being called God, but that 'God' is the name of our ultimate concern. Bearing in mind what has been said about the possibility of choosing a trivial or a demonic ultimate concern, 'God' is what we mean by taking as our ultimate concern that which came to expression in Jesus Christ. This is indeed a secular faith in Jesus Christ, though as we shall see, it is not a reductionist faith. The area of dispute has passed from the existence of God to the question whether we have any right to attempt to speak in ultimate terms in this life. This whole topic is very ably discussed by Stuart Brown in his book *Do Religious Claims Make Sense?*,[13] especially through his use of Wittgenstein's suggestion that 'God' may have a grammatical rather than a matter-of-fact function in theology. Thus he concludes that if we say 'that God is what theology is about rather than the other way around, the question about the existence of God will be seen to be reducible to the question whether it is possible to speak about the terms in which human experience should ultimately be understood'.[14]

This looks like a very promising way to solving our problems. God is no longer a stumbling block preventing men facing the challenge of the cross. It is also possible to speak in such terms of secular faith in Jesus Christ. The dispute is focused on the right issue and it is not only meaningful to ask men to follow the way of the cross, it is also possible for them to do so if they so choose. It looks like a very promising way, but we must take further steps to guard against any tendency towards the same positivism which we have met in each reduction. In fact, although I believe that what has been said so far is correct, so far as it goes, I suspect it is not so much a solution to our problem as an advanced way of *stating* the problem. Before it could emerge as a real solution, some further issues must be taken into account.

13. S. C. Brown, *Do Religious Claims Make Sense?* S.C.M. Press, London, 1969.

14. ibid, p. 164. To further clarify this point it would be necessary to amend Tillich's first formal criterion of theology: not 'the object of theology is what concerns us ultimately', but 'the meaning of theology is what concerns us ultimately'. It is his use of the word 'object' which has enabled traditional theology to identify 'ultimate concern' with God.

CHAPTER 9

Secular Transcendence

THE attraction of Anselm's definition of God as 'a being than which no greater can be conceived' was not that it told men anything about God, but that it indicated the direction in which God might be found. In the previous chapters, we have said that the solution to the problem facing us will not be found in reduction, but, if at all, in escalation. The escalation will not be of the kind exemplified in Anselm. With every new discovery in knowledge of man or the natural world, the doctrine of God was further heightened; at all costs the distance between God and man had to be preserved. In the realm of piety this may be evidenced in the Middle Ages in the increasing part of the saints in mediating between heaven and earth. But with respect to dogmatics, the principle was well enunciated in Barth's radical position. He opposed the liberal tradition, which sought to present religion as a human possibility, an integral part of the life of a cultured man. The early Barth had not yet worked out a consistent position, except that he knew the point at which he was to break with this tradition.

My reply is that if I have a system, it is limited to a recognition of what Kierkegaard called the 'infinite qualitative distinction' between time and eternity, and to my regarding this as possessing negative as well as positive significance: 'God is in heaven, and thou art on earth.'[1]

What seems central to theology is the 'infinite qualitative distinction'.

We have already noted that any reductionist solution is

1. Barth, *The Epistle to the Romans*, p. 10

opposed by traditional religious belief. This is because those who believe in God are not willing to accept any system from which God is excluded (denied) or within which he simply finds a place – in which case the system is somehow greater than God. It may be that all hostility towards reduction is basically a rejection of the removal of God from his central place. But there is little doubt that this rejection also concerns a genuine dismay at what is put in the place of God. Thus, in the case of Feuerbach, the idea that the Species might replace God is rejected not simply on psychological grounds, but quite properly because the Species is completely unworthy of its new exalted position. In the case of Braithwaite or van Buren, the dismay is that nothing is put in the place of God, hence the charge of positivism. The dismay, however, might be legitimately extended to the relatively modern proposal that the word 'God' is retained, but used now as the name of something mundane. It is for this reason that it was noted, at the end of the last chapter, that this proposal, while not necessarily wrong, always tends towards positivism.

Alternatively, the redefining of the word 'God' may lead towards the concept of God being finally superfluous. I must state frankly that I am out of sympathy with Helmut Gollwitzer's attempt to re-establish the orthodox doctrine of God. It seems to me to be based on the familiar Canute-style of argumentation : to counter the rising tide of change with a more and more strident reassertion of what is *supposed* to be the case. Yet, while disagreeing with his approach, I suspect that he does raise quite valid points against Herbert Braun's position. Braun wants to maintain that there is a non-objective way of speaking about God in the New Testament. God would then not be conceived of as a being existing separate from the world.

God is the whence of my being taken care of and of my being obliged, which comes to me from my fellow man. To abide in

God would, therefore, mean to abide in the concrete act of devoting oneself to the other; whoever abides in ἀγαπᾶν abides in God (1 John iv, 16). I can speak of God only where I speak of man, and hence anthropologically.[2]

Braun is not wrong in what he says, but he does leave himself open to the criticism that he has not clarified the way in which the apparently familiar word 'God' is being used. Is he relying on some of its former connotations, while rejecting the objectifying use of the word which gave it such dimensions of meaning? Thus I believe that Gollwitzer is right to inquire whether 'God' now refers simply to human associations and social phenomena, and whether the term 'whence' can be legitimately retained when God is not conceived of as separate from man.[3]

The problem in dealing with the reinterpretation of the traditional doctrine of God is not simply the traumatic elimination of the personal God, but the more subtle difficulty of retaining the infinite qualitative distinction. If the distinction – yet to be analysed – is eliminated, then there would seem no point in retaining the word 'God' at all. Should the distinction go, then there really would be no theology.

In the previous chapter, we made frequent use of the rather vague phrase that no matter what difficulties are involved in continuing to do theology, we do continue because we feel that we are 'on to something'. Part of what we are on to involves this infinite qualitative distinction. What is here at stake is the appropriate way in which we might give expression to this necessary element. The method which

2. Herbert Braun, 'The Problem of a New Testament Theology', *The Bultmann School of Biblical Interpretation: New Directions? Journal for Theology and the Church*, Vol. 1, 1965, p. 183.

3. Helmut Gollwitzer, *The Existence of God: as Confessed by Faith*, trans. James W. Leitch, S.C.M. Press, London, 1965, especially pp. 94–7.

springs most readily to mind is the device of the supernatural and the natural. Indeed, as Barth, in the quotation dealing with this idea, elucidates what is implied in the infinite qualitative distinction, he makes use of this framework by referring to 'heaven' and 'earth'. Distance, especially upwards, gives expression to the distinction which we feel to be necessary in theology. Of course if we were to take this literally it would only yield a quantitative distinction. But literalism is the mark of 'enlightened' men, and men in the Old Testament period, for example, were not quite so naïve. Distance was used only to evoke part of the sense of the infinite qualitative distinction. I think originally another element in the distinction would be sheer power, and by human standards sheer, often irrational, power. In either case attention is focused on the autonomy of God, and the inability of man to get control of God. For Israel, God represented a reality presenting an insurmountable obstacle to man in so far as he pursued his own ends, but equally, a never-failing source of power to pursue quite different ends. I believe that this is basically what theology is on to, and our task involves the reconceiving and redescribing of this understanding of reality.

In the debate concerning demythologizing, a good deal has been made of the three-storey universe, of heaven–earth–hell. This was the primitive conceptual structure within which men attempted to give an adequate account of their experience of reality. As a conceptual structure it is no longer a live option for secular men. (The fact that many people who are alive today manage to maintain essentially pre-scientific views of the world does not alter this fact.) In the history of dogma, reality was split into two realms, the natural and the supernatural. This was congenial to some aspects of Hellenistic philosophy, but in our own time has become a complete disaster for Christianity. With the split in reality, God on one side and the world on the other, the supernatural has been gradually rejected – for many good reasons – and this has led inevitably to atheism and often to positivism.

The terminology of the natural and the supernatural cannot serve theology today. It carries with it too many problems, so that the disadvantages of adopting it outweigh any possible advantages of retaining it. But before leaving this way of speaking we should note that its perversion was not inevitable. Andronicus of Rhodes classified the treatises of Aristotle into Physics and Metaphysics (*meta ta physika*). In this original division the treatises did not deal with what might be called 'geographical' areas, but with areas of concern. The first ones dealt with questions about the natural world. In the later treatises Aristotle went 'beyond' these questions. The prefix *meta* has no spatial reference in this context. There are certain questions appropriate to our concerns with the natural world, but if our concerns go beyond such scientific concerns, then our inquiries become metaphysical. In this strict sense, most of our concerns, apart from our activities as natural scientists, are metaphysical. But the word metaphysical has connotations now which make it difficult, if not impossible, to use. Those who are critical of metaphysics regard it not as the area of concerns which go beyond the concerns appropriate to the study of nature, but as somehow dealing with supposed issues which have no empirical content at all.[4] In a similar manner, however, I think it could be shown that the biblical view of reality, while involving the three-storey structure, was nevertheless a unified view. The idea of the supernatural need not have involved the spatial connotations which it now has, and certainly need

4. 'Metaphysics is the philosophy which goes beyond nature [*die über die Natur hinausgeht*].' W. Schulz 'Metaphysik', *Die Religion in Geschichte und Gegenwart*, ed. Kurt Galling, (Vol. IV (1960), p. 908.) It is such ambiguous and unguarded definitions which lead to hostility towards metaphysics.

not have involved a split view of reality. But all that is in the past. Words and concepts *have* developed in specific ways with unfortunate connotations. Men have allowed their concepts to distort as well as clarify reality, so that, if only for this reason, we must be grateful that Wittgenstein has come to our aid in the 'battle against the bewitchment of our intelligence by means of language'.[5]

Theology is on to something when it affirms the infinite qualitative distinction, but we cannot express it today in terms of the supernatural, nor, I fear, the metaphysical. It would be rather pedantic to use these words in the entirely unfamiliar sense in which they would have to be used if they were to be serviceable to us and at the same time escape the valid criticisms levelled against their traditional use. It is for this reason that I think the terminology of transcendence more helpful. It has not been used quite so much as the other terms, either in the history of philosophy or in common speech. For this reason, even if for no other, it is less likely to be misunderstood. Of course it does have a tendency to be assimilated with the language of the supernatural, and we shall have to define it at least negatively in relation to this way of speaking. But before we turn to transcendence, it must be admitted that the phrase 'infinite qualitative distinction' is not completely satisfactory. The word 'infinite' has connotations from its long history that could be misunderstood, for example a spatial reference, 'finite/infinite', might also suggest the supernatural realm once again, but now at unimaginable distance. Again, 'infinite' has a temporal reference, so that 'time/eternity' suggests that once again we are dealing with a split reality, one which is short, the other endlessly extended in both directions. These metaphysical (pejorative use) connotations are unfortunate. Yet such is the burden of theology that it chooses limited concepts and pushes them beyond their limits. If we did not

5. Wittgenstein, *Philosophical Investigations*, section 109.

choose the word 'infinite' we should have to choose 'absolute', or 'ultimate', or some other term already used by theology at some time. Yet we need some superlative to indicate the nature of the qualitative distinction. 'Infinite' will do, so long as it is not taken to indicate the furtive re-entry of the old spatial and substantial (i.e. mythological) categories of the supernatural/natural terminology.

In discussing the possibility of a secular understanding of transcendence, we might begin by referring to the point we reached in considering the biblical, especially the early Hebrew, view of God. There we concluded that God represented reality experienced in two ways: first as an insurmountable obstacle to men pursuing their own ends, and second, as a never-failing source of power to pursue quite different ends. In view of what was said in the previous chapter, we could restate this by saying that 'God' is the name they gave to this experience of reality. The doctrine of God developed in a very erratic manner over the centuries, but always through an empirical process, almost a pragmatic learning experience. It would not be difficult to go through the Old Testament and show how this reinterpretation could be sustained. Indeed, it might be claimed that it gives a better account of the history of Old Testament religion than the theistic interpretation given by the Jews themselves! The cult, to put it crudely, represents the typical attempt of man at that stage to discover how to manipulate reality (God) by ritual words and actions. The Law represents the required framework within which a man might expect to live without being overtaken by disaster. And the prophetic movement provides us with a very interesting series of men who appeared in troubled times, when neither cult nor law actually did their work well, pointing to a more radical view of the cult (often its rejection as a tempting but false way), and calling for a readjustment of the law in the light of current experience.

I do not wish to pursue this rough and ready reinterpretation of the Old Testament. A section like this has almost become obligatory in any work on contemporary theology. The point I am making, however, is simply that it is not difficult to see a secular meaning of transcendence in the Old Testament. In fact there is a positive and a negative side to the concept. The Old Testament cannot be understood apart from the decision of a people, exemplified in the Joshua narrative – not a sentimental or romantic decision, but one of which the consequences were borne in on them in every generation. In their terminology it involved Election and Covenant, but in its simplest terms it involved living one life and not another. It was not the most obvious life to live. It certainly distinguished them from their neighbours. Indeed they failed to keep faith with that life precisely when they were tempted to conform to the norms of the other nations. The implications of that decision involved them in a pilgrimage which did not end when they crossed the Jordan, and perhaps it has not ended even yet. The pilgrimage should have been marked by a continual advance in sensitivity to the requirements of this peculiar life. But the advance was uneven, and perhaps in the sixth and fifth centuries B.C. they were little different, except in racial terms, from their neighbours.

In the Introduction we spoke briefly of two lives, one immanent, the other transcendent. To come to the point, the immanent life is the one represented by the neighbours of Israel: the transcendent the one to which Israel was covenanted. Of course *historically* this is an oversimplification. Israel slowly and very painfully discovered some elements in the 'way of transcendence', but more often than not fell back to the 'way of immanence'. I have said that in some respects the non-theistic account of the period of the Old Testament gives a better interpretation than the one offered in the biblical narratives. There is, for example, the problem of the other nations. In what sense were they rejected by not being elect? Had they no knowledge of God? Had he no dealings with them? 'Did I not bring up Israel from the land of Egypt, and the Philistines from Caphtor and the Syrians from Kir?'[6] There is no problem about admitting that given their progress in identifying the way of transcendence, the people of Israel were much more blameworthy than those still blind to it or largely indifferent to it. Nor is there any doubt that these nations faced the same reality, if they had had eyes to see.

Historically it might well be said that the people of Israel did not live up to what they knew to be 'their' way, but Israel was created and maintained as a people by the knowledge of the way, even if they failed in practice to keep it. They knew about the choice, the division, even when they inconsistently went back on it. Their acknowledgement of condemnation by the Law was a sign of their real acceptance of the validity of the Law. The way of transcendence was never exemplified by Israel, but they did identify it and this is their lasting contribution to mankind.

I do not wish to avoid the fact that throughout this cursory discussion I have not mentioned Yahweh. I am not denying that they believed Yahweh to be a god, the supreme God, and finally the only God. But then, they believed many other things that we find problematic today. For example, the whole sectarian movement of the inter-testamental period believed fervently in the imminent end of the age (world). Jesus himself may well have been more influenced by this tradition than by any of the more orthodox schools within Judaism. Certainly his proclamation is almost identical with that of John the Baptist, and reminiscent of the apocalyptic themes of the *eschaton*. 'The time is fulfilled, and the kingdom of God is at hand; repent, and believe in the gospel.'[7] If it is objected that my appropriation of the Old Testament is inadequate because I try to deal with it without affirming the

6. Amos ix, 7b.   7. Mark i, 15.

existence of God, then no doubt the same point will be made about the New Testament. How could Jesus be wrong about such a matter? But then the other issue must be faced. How could Jesus be so wrong about the matter of the Kingdom? The early Church expected the world to come to an end at any moment. This, together with the words of Jesus in the parables of urgency,[8] confirms that Jesus believed that the world would come to an end very soon. It is only in this century that biblical scholars have finally come to admit that the message of Jesus is *primarily* eschatological. He is not to be understood as a miracle worker or a teacher of morality. Indeed, it is only by viewing him as an eschatological prophet that many of his parables can be understood at all. It is now two centuries since Reimarus pointed out that the non-occurrence of the *eschaton* surely invalidates the whole position of Jesus. We have had various attempts at interpreting what Jesus actually did mean with regard to the Kingdom. Did he think it already present, or to come in the near future?[9] The point still remains that no matter how he ex-

8. In our discussion of Braithwaite, we had occasion to refer to the eschatological rather than purely moral intention of the parables of Jesus. Dodd and Jeremias have shown the extent to which even the apparently 'moral' parables must be understood eschatologically. Their work has not been exhaustive, however, and even yet some parables are misread in exegesis and preaching. Cf. my articles 'The Question about Fasting', *Novum Testamentum*, Vol. 11, No. 3, 1969, pp. 161–73, and 'The Old Coat and the New Wine', *Novum Testamentum*, Vol. 12, No. 1, 1970, pp. 13–21.

9. The debate over eschatology in the preaching of Jesus led from Reimarus to the 'thorough-going eschatology' of Johannes Weiss (*Die Predigt Jesu vom Reiche Gottes*, 1892) and Albert Schweitzer (*Von Reimarus zu Wrede*, 1906). The debate then moved to C. H. Dodd's theory of 'realized eschatology' (*The Parables of the Kingdom*, (1st edition 1935), Nisbet, 1950, p. 51), and the rejoinder by W. G. Kümmel that the Kingdom for Jesus was not yet, but was tokened in 'premonitory signs' (*Promise and Fulfilment*, trans. D. M. Barton, S.C.M. Press, London, 1957, p. 21). In all this debate the basic point of Reimarus has been lost sight of: it was not whether Jesus

pected the Kingdom to come, it did not come. In view of this, other scholars have tried to show that 'in a sense' the *eschaton* has come.[10] But a moment's thought surely convinces us that the world has not come to an end, or we should have noticed !

Orthodoxy has no answer to Reimarus. If we hold to the orthodox, largely mythological, way of speaking of Jesus, then his views of God and the Kingdom go together. In such terms, and they are exposed to be rather crude, Jesus as the Son of God could not be wrong about God, but neither could he be wrong about the coming of the Kingdom of God. The 'higher' the Christology, the more impaled it becomes on Reimarus's insistent challenge. The more Jesus is exalted as Messiah, Son of God, the Second Person of the Blessed Trinity, the more it is impossible to conceive of his being mistaken about something which was absolutely fundamental to his message.

How is it possible that this conclusion has been avoided throughout the history of the Church? There are three obvious reasons. The first is that very early, the death of Jesus became his most important work, more important than any of his works during his lifetime. Interest in his human life, for the purposes of atonement doctrine, was reduced to the dogmatic view of his sinlessness. But this only poses the problem in another way. Quite apart from the problems inherent in any theory of atonement, why should Jesus become involved in this absurd preaching about the end of the world, if all that mattered was that he should live a perfect life and die

---

thought the Kingdom had arrived, or was breaking in, or was coming very soon; it was rather that the awaited Kingdom has not come.

10. According to A. L. Moore, both Jesus and the early Church had the same view on this question: 'The conviction that the End has – *in a hidden manner* – come ...'. (*The Parousia in the New Testament* (Supplement to *Novum Testamentum*, Vol.13), E. J. Brill, Leiden, 1966, p. 207.)

a terrible death? The second reason is that at various times in the history of the Church (but I suspect not always, and not in the earliest days) the words of Jesus on moral issues have been taken as the basis for personal conduct. This led to an ignoring of those words of Jesus which could not be applied directly to moral situations. The third reason is very significant: it is that, after all, Jesus was a real man. We must not ignore his humanity. Of course he spoke in the terms of the day. Now this is said in two ways. The first way in which it is said suggests that Jesus knew better, but spoke *ad hominem*. These were the only terms the people could understand. But by this approach the problem is only compounded. Did Jesus not only know that the world was not going to come to an end, but did he encourage people to think it was? And to what result? But the second way in which the humanity of Jesus is brought in is even more intriguing. It is a typical liberal move, and like other liberal moves, pulls the rug out from under the orthodox position, without being able to establish a stable alternative. This liberal position is to say that Jesus was at least a man of his time. Galilee (it is said) was a centre of the sectarian, apocalyptic movement. To suppose that he would not share the views of his fellows is somehow to deny his true humanity. But with this concession the game is up. If Jesus was really a Jew of his own time and place, using the category of the eschatological Kingdom to interpret reality, then of course the way is open to say that he also used the familiar category 'God'. If indeed Jesus was a man, then he did not have 'independent' knowledge of the nature of reality. What he knew, like anyone else, was a function of his own experience, peculiar insights and sensitivity, always in the context of what he inherited from the history of his people.

What Jesus inherited was the ancient covenant choice, which we have interpreted in terms of transcendence. He sharpened the necessity for choice to its limit. The choice must be made now, and lived with utmost consistency. It is after all quite justifiable to say that Jesus was right 'in a sense'. Eschatology can be given a secular interpretation, as Bultmann did in his Gifford Lectures. 'Eschatology is the doctrine of the "last things" or, more accurately, of the occurrences with which our known world comes to its end.'[11] If we commit ourselves without reserve to the way of transcendence, then indeed our little world, the world which we construct to suit our own (immanent) purposes, does come to an end. Although orthodoxy has no answer to Reimarus, there is an answer. Jesus was a man who inherited not only an understanding of reality, but, inevitably, an understanding shaped by the conceptual form in which it was transmitted. When he sharpened this understanding to its limit he confirmed the understanding, but in doing so destroyed the conceptual form. The way of transcendence was set out with final clarity, but the imagery of the end of the world was exposed as wholly inappropriate. As in the titles of Jesus, history corrected mythology, confirming the reality but radically revising the forms in which the understanding was hitherto expressed. Once this is said – and refusal to say it returns us to Reimarus's challenge – we are in a position to ask whether or not the same point cannot be made about Jesus' belief in God.

As we have seen, the reluctance to discuss this derives traditionally from the belief that Jesus is the Son of God. How could a Son be mistaken about his Father in any important respect? But we really cannot fall into the mistake of thinking that the dogma of Sonship was revealed. What happened to Jesus, and his significance for his contemporaries, was interpreted likewise in the conceptual categories of the day. Thus quite contradictory titles such as 'Messiah' and 'Son of Man' were ascribed to him. Neither was completely

11. Rudolf Bultmann, *History and Eschatology* (American edition, *The Presence of Eternity*, Harper, New York, 1957, p. 23).

apt, but if the question of whether to bestow a title or not were raised, then inevitably the title was bestowed. As previously noted, the end result was that the historical events corrected the apocalyptic speculation embodied in the titles. 'Messiah' came to mean 'Jesus', indeed 'Christ' became his surname, and any elements in it not compatible with Jesus were simply dropped. 'Son of God' was a possible title, and it was also used, but it has a special place. Though the meanings of the titles of 'Messiah', and more especially 'Son of Man', are far from clear,[12] they do not normally entail divine kinship. The doctrine of Sonship is intimately related to the doctrine of the Incarnation. Yet this cannot be said without qualification. Although the idea of Jesus as the Son of God might seem more congenial to Hellenistic than Jewish religious thinking, it is not inconceivable that he should receive this title as a consequence of the title 'Messiah'. The ancient Hebrew understanding of the place of the king included the metaphorical application of the title 'son'. The chosen/ anointed one has a special place: 'You are my son, today I have begotten you.'[13] Thus it was thought appropriate to add these very words at the account of the baptism of Jesus, transforming the occasion into the choosing or identification of the Messiah.[14] The Messiah, because of the regal associations

12. cf. H. E. Tödt, *The Son of Man in the Synoptic Tradition*, trans. D. M. Barton, S.C.M. Press, London, 1965; F. H. Borsch, *The Son of Man in Myth and History*, S.C.M. Press, London, 1967; F. Hahn, *Christologische Hoheitstitel: Ihre Geschichte im frühen Christentum*, Vandenhoeck & Ruprecht, 1963, (English translation *The Titles of Jesus in Christology*, trans. Harold Knight and George Ogg, Lutterworth, London, 1969). See also R. Leivestad, 'Der apokalyptische Menschensohn ein theologische Phantom', *Annual of the Swedish Theological Institute*, Vol. 6, 1967-8, pp. 49-105.

13. Psalm ii, 7b.

14. The baptismal address combines the reference from the Psalm with words from Isaiah xlii, 1: 'Behold my servant, whom I uphold, my chosen, in whom my soul delights; I have put my spirit upon him, he will bring forth justice to the nations.' cf. Mark i, 11.

of the title, might easily be called God's son. But the doctrine of the Incarnation demands a less metaphorical understanding of sonship, and *this* may well have been possible only in the Hellenistic culture.

In discussing the contribution of Thomas Altizer we noted that he clarified the concept of Incarnation. Traditionally the Incarnation has been reckoned as a way of speaking about Jesus. This presupposes that before Jesus we knew precisely the nature of God; then, when the time was fulfilled, this nature became incarnate in a chosen man. But this is far from being the case. The doctrine of the Incarnation really tells us nothing about Jesus that we did not already know. At most it provides us with the conceptual apparatus for speaking of his ultimate significance. But speaking of his significance, *pro nobis*, does not tell us anything more about Jesus. This kind of approach has led, in the history of dogma, to some exceedingly tedious explanations. The importance of the doctrine of the Incarnation is what it tells us about God. In this doctrine we do not point to God (as if he were 'given') and say 'Jesus is like that.' No, we point to Jesus and say 'God is like that.' Or in the terminology we have been developing, we might say 'Jesus is the very incarnation of the way of transcendence.'

We have looked briefly at the way in which the experience of Israel could be interpreted not in terms of a relationship to a supernatural being, but with respect to secular transcendence. This would not be a difficult exercise in the context of the faith of the early Church. In the previous chapter we defined Christian faith as 'commitment with ultimate concern to that which came to expression in Jesus Christ'.[15] Familiarity with dogmatic formulations often disguises from us the problematic nature of these statements for us today. This stems largely from their dependence on the categories appropriate to the ancient world-view, and often therefore

15. See above, p. 193.

quite inappropriate on the basis of our secular modern world-view. Thus, to pursue our previous example, we know that we are on to something when we speak of the Incarnation, and we are right to insist that its witness be maintained. Let this be the test. The doctrine of the Incarnation has never been satisfactorily stated. We are familiar with the course of its development, but the name of Chalcedon has become almost synonymous with failure. After almost four centuries, the best minds of the Church (some of them the ablest in the Roman Empire) could only agree to say that Jesus Christ was of two natures, a human nature and a divine nature. But that is no solution to the problem. It is simply the problem stated. Nor has any advance towards a solution been made in the remaining fifteen hundred years since then. The central doctrine of Christianity, and it cannot even be stated. 'The assertion that "God has become man" is not a paradoxical but a non-sensical statement. It is a combination of words which make sense only if it is not meant to mean what the words say.'[16] We know that we are on to something, but just as clearly, the traditional doctrine of Incarnation does not express it. However, there is no difficulty at all in seeing how we can express it in our terms. Jesus Christ is the incarnation of transcendence. He is the veritable embodiment of the way of transcendence. Not only can this be said in a straightforward and meaningful way, it is to be understood quite literally. When 'God' is what theology is about, then Jesus Christ is quite literally the incarnation of God.

Or take the example of the Atonement, Jesus considered as Saviour. Here again, we know that we are on to something which should not be lost sight of. But how well does the traditional doctrine give expression to what it is we are on to? The difficulty, once again, is not that all solutions to the problem have been abject failures: that is even clearer if anything than in the case of the Incarnation. The issue is

16. Tillich, *Systematic Theology*, Vol. 2, p. 109.

that the problem should never have been stated in its traditional form, or rather, we must not make ourselves responsible for solving a problem which makes no sense in the terms
in which we think today. But the language of Atonement
has permeated the whole of our theology. Paul speaks about
Jesus appearing 'when the time had fully come'.[17] The Old
Testament has been forced into the exegetical straitjacket of
Heilsgeschichte. Thus the history of Israel is seen as the history of God's plan of salvation, culminating in the appearance of Jesus. This sounds very grand until we ask what it
amounts to. In what sense was the time fulfilled when Jesus
appeared? Certainly not in a theological sense, some five
hundred years after Deutero–Isaiah, when Judaism was in
disarray. Certainly not in a covenantal sense, for Israel was
no more obedient in the first century A.D. than it had been
on many occasions before. Some historians of the Church
have even suggested in all seriousness that the time was fulfilled because communications under the auspices of the *pax
Romana* gave unprecedented facilities for the spread of the
gospel. If that is all that 'the time had fully come' meant,
we might surely be forgiven for wondering why the
Almighty did not wait till Baird invented television.

The Old Testament is better understood as *Offenbarungs-
geschichte*, but I should prefer to put it another way altogether, coining the term *Bewusstseinsgeschichte*. It is not
the history of something done to them or shown to them, but
rather the course of their growing awareness of the true
nature of the world, and of social and individual existence.
It is the history of Israel's understanding of transcendence.
Why was the time fulfilled? Of course we do not know. Rather, we should not ask this question, because we need not
be committed to the view that there was some cosmical significance in the appearance of Jesus at precisely that moment.
To say that Jesus appeared when the time was fulfilled is

17. Galatians iv, 4a.

the typical view of the traditional atonement theology. But this gets things the wrong way round. It was not because the time was cosmically fulfilled that Jesus appeared. On the contrary, it was because of what came to expression when he appeared that the whole history of the revelation of transcendence came to fulfilment. This is a truly historical understanding of Christianity, but it is also a secular way of confessing faith in Jesus Christ. Indeed he is Saviour, to those who see what he brought to fulfilment.

It would not be difficult to go through the elements of Christian faith to show the secular meaning of judgement and grace; faith, hope and love; Kingdom and eschatology; the cross and resurrection; all in terms of transcendence. It is tempting to do this, to demonstrate that nothing of the Christian tradition is left out. More than that, to show that, understood in terms of transcendence rather that traditional theism, the reinterpretation would be not only more comprehensible, but more appropriate to our time. It would overcome many of the difficulties which we should not accept as valid representations of Christian experience. And yet, where does all this get us? Those who still believe in God will never accept anything as a valid statement of Christianity if it omits reference to him. What remains to be done is to show that what they believe about God is already contained within this new position.

CHAPTER 10

Reality in Dispute

CHRISTIANS feel that they are on to something, yet it is clear that fewer and fewer people in society are concerned with religion. Is it possible that Christians are on one side of a line, and that everyone else is on the other side? No doubt some very conservative Christians might try to maintain this position, but it does not fit the facts. There are many lines drawn through society, and many more through the world. They may be relatively unimportant, though very well defined, as in the support of a football club. They may be of vital importance, even if less clearly defined, as in the general division between the Developing World and the Third (Under-developed, relatively non-developing) World. News programmes and coverage of current affairs bring divisions which are new every morning. Religion is a divisive issue, or has been in the past, but at least in the West, religion cannot be taken as a decisive dividing line in society.

It may be quite simple to determine those who believe in God and those who do not, those who go to Church and those who do not. But we find that in practice the religious division does not make the distinctions that we feel are important. As Christians we approve of the work of Oxfam, Shelter, Care, Link and many other organizations aimed at tackling human problems. But whereas, perhaps a century ago, these would have been seen to be clearly Christian movements, today they are quite secular. The fact that some of their founders or office-bearers may be Christians only confuses the issue still further. The fact that these organizations are not religious seems to be quite irrelevant. The fact that their active workers are not religious – or are religious –

seems quite irrelevant. The same could be said of political activists and those promoting conservation of natural amenities, or opposing pollution of land or sea. The religious line does not seem to be a significant line. Worse than that, it has negative implications. Some political activists will not work with Christians on any basis. Christian bodies are often slow to enlist the services of non-religious experts.

The point I wish to make is that there are important lines drawn through society, and throughout the world, but whether a man is religious or not does not seem to be an important line.[1] In the West we have clearly reached a post-religious cultural stage, but it is my intention in this book to show that this need not mean that modern men must turn away from Christianity. In the previous two chapters we have been developing an understanding of Christianity as ultimate concern for the way of transcendence, specifically the way identified by Jesus Christ. This is a secular concern, and I want now to say that while the religious line is of no importance, the line drawn by transcendence is important. The division within society is precisely between those who are committed to transcendence and those committed to immanence. To be realistic, of course, we must see that the line not only runs through society, but runs through our individual lives. We none of us stand completely on one side or the other. But it is this line which has become the decisive one for us. Belief in God does not, as a matter of fact, tell us that a man is ultimately committed to the way of transcendence. The fact that another man does not affirm

1. I make this as a general point, although I know that in specific areas, notably Ireland in the West and the Indian sub-continent in the East, there are 'religious' problems. It could be argued, however, that such disputes are rarely about theology, i.e. the content of belief. They are more likely to reflect hostility between racial or factional groupings, who identify themselves by adherence to a particular religion. 'Religious' troubles, ironically, rarely seem to have anything to do with religion.

belief in God tells us nothing about his ultimate concern.

This way of putting the matter – in view of the argument of the book so far – has the advantage of overcoming the anomalies already noted. We no longer have to say of a good man, who gives his life for others, that he is 'really' a Christian, although he does not believe in God. Nor do we have to say that he 'really' believes in God. Of course under our reinterpretation he could very well be a Christian without believing in a supernatural being called God. He would be a Christian if he took as his ultimate concern what came to expression in Jesus Christ. What could it add if he believed also in God? Two answers might be offered to this question, neither of which, I think, is acceptable.

The first answer would be to say that if such a man believed in God he would be more sensitive to what he must do. On empirical grounds this will not do. It is one of the embarrassing features of our contemporary situation that non-believers are often seen to be as sensitive, possibly more sensitive, than believers. But the answer might be intended in a theological sense, that each particular man would gain insight beyond what he might otherwise have had. But if he had already taken Jesus Christ to be the definitive revelation of the way of transcendence, what could be added? The only possible meaning to the answer is then that there is direct communication between God and man, for example a specific answer to prayer. We have already dealt with this in our discussion of religious experience. It is not possible to demonstrate that the 'answer' to prayer is different from the conclusion reached after considerable and serious thought.

A second answer might be that belief in God would strengthen the good man's motivation to pursue his way of transcendence. This is to propose a very dangerous line of argument.[2] If a man will not do something although he

2. Stephen Toulmin appears to argue in this way. 'Where there is a good moral reason for choosing one course of action rather than

believes it to be right, there is little likelihood that he will do it if told it is also the will of God. Indeed such heteronomous ethics may well be regarded as less moral than autonomous ethics. It has sometimes been argued that theonomous ethics do not fall under the category of heteronomy. God's law, it is claimed, is not like any other authority. Yet in so far as God is conceived of as a supernatural being, then his will is simply a special case of heteronomy. By contrast, if Jesus does indeed embody the way of transcendence, then the ethics of *this* theology are not alien to man.

In short, I do not think that a case can be made out for saying that a man who takes the way of transcendence as his ultimate concern lacks anything because he does not believe in God.

We have been making the point that there is a division among (and within) men, as to whether to pursue the way of transcendence, or the way of immanence. Christian faith, in this context, is a secular faith that Jesus Christ is the norm of what is entailed in the way of transcendence. The biblical tradition, by which he must be understood, also has a great deal to say about the alternative. The division is clearly drawn by Paul in his analysis of man in sin and man in (Christian) faith.[3] It is common throughout many forms of

---

another, morality is not to be contradicted by religion. Ethics provides the *reasons* for choosing the "right" course: religion helps us to put our *hearts* into it.' (*An Examination of the Place of Reason in Ethics*, Cambridge University Press, 1969, p. 219.) Both statements represent a very restricted view of religion, and perhaps a degree of naïve liberal optimism about how the content of 'right' gets defined in practice. But if Christianity is defined in relation to the way of transcendence, then we should have to reject Toulmin's position altogether at this point. Since morality may very often reflect the common, immanent, standards of society, the way of transcendence might well lead to a higher form of moral sensitivity.

3. cf J. Macquarrie, *An Existentialist Theology* (*a comparison of Heidegger and Bultmann*), S.C.M. Press, London, 1955.

existentialism and is not completely absent even in the views of Freud. The ills of life cannot all be attributed to external factors, and 'the suspicion dawns upon us that a bit of un-conquerable nature lurks concealed behind this difficulty as well – in the shape of our own mental constitution'.[4] It is significant that just at a time when Churchmen are deplor-ing the lack of interest in religion, this concern for the way of transcendence is breaking out in a bewildering number of directions. A brief mention of some might indicate the scope.

As noted already, it is to be found in the growth of secular 'caring' organizations. Is it not more natural to spend one's time and talents in having a good time, guarding against any encroachment on one's standard of living from within the country or from abroad, more natural to do all this than to go to the trouble of helping others, fighting for their rights, affecting one's own position and even career? Of course it is more 'natural', and that is the way of immanence. But it is a fact today that a very significant number of people are rejecting this way, and turning to something higher. This, at a time when religion is in decline.

The same striving for something else is to be seen in the New Left. We are no longer dealing with a form of Marxism which can be rejected as sheer materialism. On the contrary, materialism is now the characteristic of the affluent society, while the New Left is asking under what conditions human life may reach fulfilment. It is as often as not the religious establishment which conceives of solutions to human prob-lems in purely economic terms.[5]

4. *Civilization and its Discontents*, trans. Joan Riviere, Hogarth Press, London, 1949, p. 44.

5. This leads us into an area which may yet occupy another book, but two examples will indicate what is involved. While we in the West thought of the end of the Empire in terms of the economic effects it would have, Frantz Fanon was saying: 'Decolonization is the veritable creation of new men.' (*The Wretched of the Earth*, Allen Lane The Penguin Press, 1967, p. 28.) Daniel Cohn-Bendit

Perhaps the strangest example of all is the current interest in religion. This may at first sight appear to contradict the main thesis of this book. What is this new interest in religion at a time when radical theology has been pointing to the rapid and dramatic decline in religion? It takes many forms. For example some Westerners are becoming interested in eastern religions, particularly Zen Buddhism. Others are investigating the Western mystical traditions. Still others are exploring techniques of 'transcendental [sic] meditatation'.[6] Elsewhere the sacramental aspects of Christianity are being re-examined, and 'sacred' meals celebrated. In all this I think it is possible to see some common themes. It is very often part of a general disillusionment with secular Western culture, especially when it exhibits precisely those materialistic characteristics previously referred to. Those who are disillusioned reject or at least question the view of man projected in the affluent society, for the most part a getting-and-spending image. This is another very wide topic, but the point is that they have turned to Western religion, or to the East, for help. And this of course is the final irony. Throughout this book the complaint has been that Christianity has been reduced in the Church to religious belief and religious practices. And yet apparently the Church is not even very good at this level! These people are looking for a broader view of man, and yet the Church seems to present no particular view of man except the image of the average 'decent' middle-class citizen. Those who are disillusioned by the common image of man projected in our society are

---

protested against those who viewed the situation in Paris in May 1968 merely as the opportunity to gain higher wage rates. 'While most of man's problems are admittedly economic, man also demands the right to find fulfilment on every other possible level.' (*Obsolete Communism*, Penguin Books, Harmondsworth, 1969, p. 104.)

6. I am not referring to the medical interest in Buddhist meditation techniques, for possible use in auto-psychotherapy.

attempting to discover a richer way of life. They use the techniques that religion has developed, but they use them in exploring the unknown depths in their own natures. The new interest in religion is not a revival in theistic belief. It can be of no comfort to traditional Christians. But it is trying to extend the individuals' sensitivity to his own potentialities and those of his fellows. For this reason the new interest in religion has affinities with the seeking of the way of transcendence. The further irony is that the figure of Jesus is also of interest to this group, not because they have any religious beliefs, but because, almost in spite of the Church's dogmatic tradition, they seem to have stumbled across a primitive view of Jesus. While many of the attempts to appropriate aspects of religion will be objectionable to believers, it would be a good thing if it caused a re-examination of religion by those who practise it. Perhaps there is something about it that even they, the experts in it, have not realized. But this too would lead in the direction of transcendence, not religious belief.

To lead into even deeper waters, we might also have considered the modern 'spirit' phenomenon which is sweeping the world. It is to be found in the astonishing expansion of the pentecostalist churches in Africa, and the sects of the west coast of the United States. Is it related to the possibly demonic revival of voodoo in Haiti, Brazil and Argentina – not merely among the peasants, but among the highly educated? How is all this to be tied in with the fascination for the occult so prevalent in England, both at the theoretical level of *Man, Myth and Magic* and in the practical activities of the 'Beast 666' and the Witches? I suspect that this could all be connected with our theme of transcendence, though the analysis would have to take account of the different ends served in the different cultural settings. If this line were developed it might lead towards the doctrine of the Holy Spirit. At regular intervals the complaint is made within the Church that we have no doctrine of the Spirit. Little wonder, since the origin of the conception is a pre-scientific world-view which involves myriads of spirits both good and evil. We do not need a revival of a doctrine which stems from this background. Yet it may be that a truly secular understanding of the Holy Spirit could be derived from our exposition of transcendence. Indeed, strange though it may seem, the Spirit may be the only element of the Trinity compatible with a radical theology.

It is tempting to pursue this investigation of the signs of a seeking after transcendence in our contemporary culture. We should have to mention the whole hippie scene and of course the theme of celebration of life expressed in pop music. But we must not be carried away. Although the theory of the Underground is liberation and re-creation, life before death, its practice is sometimes reminiscent of the old immanent way.[7]

In a bewildering range of activities in our world it seems to me the line is drawn not between religious and non-religious, but between two ways of understanding life and living it. Throughout the world reality is in dispute. In all sorts of places, in new ways inconceivable a few years ago, man is in dispute, human fulfilment is discussed and investigated, even the destiny of the world is at stake. What is so frustrating is that somehow or other Christians are inhibited from entering the fray. We above all should have a vital interest in this dispute. And we above all – we pride ourselves – should have something to contribute to it. Yet so long as we must wait till belief in God is established as a presupposition, we shall never be able to get in there and get

7. For a lively critique, see 'Letter to a Dying Underground' by Angelo Quattrocchi. 'You have danced to the Beatles, stoned yourselves to the Rolling Stones, copulated to the Zeppelins, and accomplished nothing. Expanded nothing. Certainly not your consciousness, as you claim.' (*New Statesman*, 13 February 1970.)

on with the job to which we are called. The word 'Church' actually means 'those who are called', and yet somehow we have got ourselves into the position where we cannot get on with our vocation. Yet if our ultimate concern is the way of transcendence, as revealed supremely in Jesus Christ, we are surely ready to enter this dispute about reality, for they are playing our tune, discussing our very theme, perhaps even struggling in the darkness that could be enlightened by our gospel.

CHAPTER 11

The Continuing Problem of Theology

THE position we have been developing is not a positivist one. Since transcendence is a secular category, the whole of Christian theology can be reinterpreted in a secular way. But no area of concern in traditional theology has been ruled out in advance. Everything that has been said about God can be interpreted in terms of transcendence. Nor is it a reductionist approach to theology, and it is this point which must be further elucidated in this section. There has been a good deal of reductionism in contemporary theology, but it might be worth turning the question around, and asking to what extent traditional theism has actually represented a reduction. The deciding factor has normally been the existence of God. A position is represented as reductionist if it eliminates God, and conversely a system including God has been taken as the fullest position possible. But if what we have outlined briefly in the previous chapter has any validity, it will be seen that as a matter of fact, religion, based on traditional theism, is not covering the field. Religion, focused on worship of a supernatural being, is not a decisive issue in the modern world, but not because the modern world is dead to the vital issue of transcendence – rather because religion represents an inadequate method of raising the vital issue. A generation ago the slogan was that 'your God is too small'. In this generation it may be that any God is too small. I do not wish to labour this point, except to make it clear that whether a position is reductionist or not cannot be decided simply on whether it includes the existence of a supernatural being or not, and also that we may now have reached the stage where a system *including* a supernatural being would inevitably itself be, if not reductionist, at least inadequate. In the chapter on reductionist solutions the criticism was that such solutions were either more problematic (Feuerbach) than traditional theism, or positivist (Braithwaite/van Buren). The position represented in this book does not include a supernatural being, but it deals with the dimensions of reality previously 'answered' by the God-solution. It is not a positivist position, nor is it a reduction. But if what has just been said is correct, it is not enough to claim that a reinterpretation misses out nothing previously included in theology. If traditional theology is inevitably inadequate today, then a new approach to theology must be capable of enlarging the scope of theology. Reduction is unacceptable, but so also is the maintenance of theology at its present level. It is for this reason that we have already indicated that a reinterpretation must be in some sense not reduction but escalation.

Theology must not simply concern itself with man : it must not be reduced to ethics, not even a Jesus-ethic. It is inevitable that a secular interpretation of theology will be largely taken up with what it says about man, but if it warrants the name of theology it will involve larger issues too. It is in this direction that the escalation must take place, and to begin to sharpen the issue I wish to refer briefly once again to Nietzsche, who understood the implications of all this perhaps better than anyone in the whole history of Western culture.

As we noted in dealing with Nietzsche, the significance of the death of God was that a new basis had to be found for human judgements. The sanction enabling men to make ultimate judgements, whether aesthetic or moral, was removed, and the comforting view that the world was involved in a controlled and fore-ordained process, natural or historical, had to be given up. Nietzsche saw – and felt at an existential level – more clearly than the other atheists of the nineteenth century, that a world without God was at once liberating and terrifying. 'Alas, if you should be seized by homesickness for land, as if there had been more freedom there – and there is no "land" any more.' But although there might be no familiar basis for judgement, Nietzsche knew that judgements must be made, and therefore a new basis must be found. No doubt this new basis would entail new standards of judgement. Hence his *magnum opus* was to be the *Revaluation of All Values*.

I do not wish to repeat all that has been said earlier about Nietzsche, but because of his radical honesty he does bring out very clearly the issues with which we must deal. We have seen that his attempts to give a purely natural basis for judgements failed. He failed in dealing with a natural account of man, when he introduced the qualitative terms 'super' and 'higher' without any justification. But he also failed to maintain his psychological monism when he was forced to distinguish between two approaches to the will to power. What emerges in *The Antichrist* is a way of life and valuation completely opposed to the way of Christ. I wish to adapt this to throw light on the issues which face us. Nietzsche saw the matter very clearly. He focused attention on what might be called the natural life for man, and the natural basis for judgement. This is what I have been calling 'the way of immanence'. It is indeed the more obvious and apparently natural way for man to live. Nietzsche argues with some force that it is the way by which man has evolved to his present level. He also saw very clearly the contrast between that way and the Christian way (the way of transcendence). He even anticipated that Christianity would lead to a reversal of evolution. 'Wherever the will to power declines, no matter in what form, then there is always a physiological retrogression, decadence.' And so to the revaluation. 'What is good? All that augments the feeling of power, the will to power and power itself in man. What is bad? All that stems from weakness.' In this contrast Nietzsche is actually confirming and developing what Paul says about the natural man. He unconsciously agrees with the New Testament view that man does not automatically choose the way of Christ. The Christian man does not emerge from the gradual refinement of the natural man, as Tillich pointed out in a sermon on the text 'Behold, all things are become new'. 'The new is created not out of the old, not out of the best of the old, but out of the death of the old.'[1] It is salutary to realize that Nietzsche at this point has a much more realistic view of the issues than most Christians. The Christian view of man has too often been simply the image of the average decent citizen who does not beat his wife and who certainly does not maltreat his dog. I have no doubt that the lack of interest in Christianity among our contemporaries derives in large part from the fact that it is difficult to see in Christianity an alternative view of man to the common (rather materialistic) one prevalent in the affluent society. But Nietzsche saw the complete incompatibility of Christianity and the 'natural' view of man: a veritable 'infinite qualitative distinction'. He would have understood only too well the continual theme of the early Church, that becoming a Christian was the most traumatic experience a man could undergo, appropriately described as dying and rising. From this it follows that the way of Christ is not likely to be a popular or attractive way. The contemporary condemnation of Christianity, at least as presented in the Church, is that it does not demand a radical and costly decision. Those who see what commitment to transcendence involves, e.g. in the 'caring' organizations, regard the demands of the Church as irrelevant to this choice, or worse, quite trivial. In the work of Nietzsche we are presented with the incompatibility of the way of immanence and the way of transcendence, the

1. P. Tillich, *The Shaking of the Foundations*, S.C.M. Press, London, 1957, pp. 180–82.

logical extension of the life that seems so natural to men and the life which requires that they be born anew. It is for this reason that I have questioned Kaufmann's attempt to drive a wedge between Nietzsche and the Nazis. The Nazis understood Nietzsche only too well, and they pursued his way of immanence to its logical and therefore demonic and destructive conclusion. The fact that the Deutsche Christen, the Dutch Reformed Church of South Africa, and many other Christian bodies have all believed in God while being committed to demonic immanent paths, should remind us that the religious division is neither relevant nor very enlightening.

It has already been noted that the line drawn between immanence and transcendence runs through each of us, for no one is wholly committed to one way or the other. But even on the side of transcendence there is a dispute about what is actually involved. This is why the religious division is not decisive. Christians are not distinguished from all other men as the only ones committed to transcendence. Rather they are distinguished by the fact that they claim that Jesus Christ is the very embodiment and final revelation of the way of transcendence. At a certain stage in the evolution of man the natural way was not the only option. The way of immanence is a real way, but no longer the only way. The discovery of this other way marks the course of the history of Israel, culminating in what came to expression in Jesus Christ. Being a Christian means being committed with ultimate concern to that which came to expression in Jesus Christ. But, and this is of the utmost importance, the choice of the way of transcendence is based on a value judgement. We do not choose the way of the cross because it is the natural way. Far from it. Our 'natural' way of approaching life must be negated before we can accept this new way. Nietzsche is probably right in suggesting that the Christian way is against nature. It is certainly against the way of the old Adam. But in choosing the way of transcendence, we

make a value judgement that things are not as they seem. We
are disputing reality. We are disputing what the nature of
man really is. In choosing the way of transcendence we make
an act of faith. We test out our suspicion that the 'real' nature of man is (to put it in summary fashion) embodied in
Jesus Christ, and not a Nazi Führer. 'Man is something that
must be surpassed,' said Nietzsche. Yes, but surpassed, we
must insist, not by becoming an outstanding example of immanence, but by overcoming the immanent way altogether.

In the Introduction we deplored the fact that today more
men cannot be challenged by the call to have faith. This has
been further clarified. I do not believe that men were ever
called upon to have faith that God exists. Faith involves commitment to a decision. It is confirmed if the decision is the
right one. Secular faith in Christ involves asking men to risk
themselves on the way of transcendence. Is it in fact the right
way, against all superficial appearances? In spite of what
seems to be the natural way for man and for society, is there
another way which is the right way? They may not in fact
choose this way of transcendence, but there is no problem
about making the decision. It is the decision to live this way
or not. The decision about whether there is or is not a supernatural being called God is a decision of quite a different order. As we discussed earlier, it seems impossible for modern
secular men to act in faith on this question. But what it
would mean in practice would be precisely the same as having secular faith in Jesus Christ. According to our reinterpretation, faith in 'God' would mean faith that what came
to expression in Jesus Christ is to be made our ultimate concern.

We are now at the point of indicating how our reinterpretation of theology in terms of transcendence rather than
of a supernatural being is not only still theology, but is actually an escalating theology. So far we have been discussing
what distinguishes the Christian view of transcendence from

other views of transcendence, and of course how the way of transcendence in any terms is different from the way of immanence. These are the practical areas of concern, and inevitably they take up most of our time. But we should not lose sight of the awesome question which we have been begging throughout this discussion. Not *which* value judgement is the mystery, but why *any*.[2] A purely natural theory of value would be concerned entirely with immanence. It may not be impossible to construct such a natural basis. Nietzsche attempted to do just this. But he failed because he recognized that there are other possible value judgements. He rejected them (in particular those identified with Christianity), but note that when he chose immanence rather than transcendence he made this choice on a *non-natural* basis.

As matter of fact we all make value judgements on a nonnatural basis, so that a purely natural theory of value is ruled out. But that does not tell us anything about such value judgements. The fact that we make them may simply mean that we are misguided. Perhaps we should only make value judgements connected with immanence. Earlier we said that faith involves commitment to a decision, and that the risk of faith is justified (or invalidated) by subsequent experience.[3] The mystery is that secular faith in the way of transcen-

2. In making this point I am reminded of that strange statement in the *Tractatus Logico-Philosophicus* (Routledge & Kegan Paul, 1961, section 6.44), where Wittgenstein says, 'Not *how* the world is, is the mystical, but *that* it is.' (Revised translation.)

3. This terminology comes to us from Kierkegaard and Tillich. 'Without risk there is no faith . . . . If I wish to preserve myself in faith I must constantly be intent upon holding fast the objective uncertainty so as to remain out upon the deep, over seventy thousand fathoms of water, still preserving my Faith.' (S. Kierkegaard, *Concluding Unscientific Postscript*, trans. S. F. Swenson and Walter Lowrie, Princeton University Press, 1944, p. 182.) Tillich applies this terminology not only to the life of faith, but to the language of faith when he says that all theological assertions are made 'with passion and risk . . .'. (*Systematic Theology*, Vol. 1, p. 8.)

dence *is* confirmed by subsequent experience. That this is so is not only the experience of those who confess Jesus Christ as the embodiment of transcendence, but also the experience of all those mentioned in the previous chapter. Contrary to all appearances it transpires that transcendence and not immanence is the 'right' way for man. Christians should welcome this affirmation among non-Christians. They can then go on meaningfully to present Jesus Christ as the final revelation of transcendence.

It should now be clear why our study is not only still theology, but an escalating theology. The question beyond the discussion about immanence or transcendence, or about which transcendence, is this: Why is faith in transcendence confirmed? The mysterious and awesome question breaks through upon us: what kind of reality is it which invites faith in transcendence and then confirms that faith? This may seem to some a very modern question, but in the light of what has already been said about the history of Israel, I believe it is simply our version of their question. As we outlined it, their pilgrimage was in response to reality as they experienced it, and it was marked by an uneven sensibility to the transcendent. God was their answer to the question: What kind of a reality is it? That 'answer' had a superficial continuity for almost three thousand years. 'Superficial' because the name in fact disguised radical changes in the content of the answer. But increasingly in the last two hundred years this answer has been less and less satisfactory. It is not wrong, but simply inadequate. It is astonishing that essentially the same answer could have been flexible enough to survive for that period. But with the advent of modern scientific knowledge and philosophical skills the God-answer is no longer serviceable. This conclusion is widely recognized by theologians, such as Ogden, Macquarrie and Robinson, who regard the God of supernaturalism to be no answer at all to the basic theological problem.

The critical juncture we have reached in Christianity is that the concept of God cannot be further expanded, if there is to be any recognizable continuity between the meaning of the word in the Bible and our use of it. It was for this reason (and others) that the redefinitions offered by Macquarrie and Ogden were rejected. With regard to Tillich,[4] although his criteria of theology were useful in developing our position, his phrase 'ultimate concern' tends to cut off theology at its human level. That is to say theology is always a function of what concerns us. But the position represented now in an escalating theology leads towards a mystery beyond our ultimate concerns, beyond precisely because it is raised by our *having* an ultimate concern. The terminology of transcendence seems more flexible and serviceable.

The main danger to the conclusion to which we have come is not that it will be shown to be wrong, but that an attempt will be made to use it as a way of reintroducing God again, further up the ontological ladder. What is the mystery of a reality which confirms faith in transcendence? I fear the temptation is to say that the answer is once again God. Anyone who was tempted to give this answer should first of all consider whether he has not failed to grasp the arguments

4. I hesitate to 'deal with' Tillich in a few sentences, but the terminology of transcendence seems prefable to his onto-theology. Transcendence is mentioned in several places throughout Vol. 3 of *Systematic Theology*, but it does not extend the system already mapped out in the first two volumes. Apart from the general critique of all onto-theologies, Tillich's has the peculiar problem connected with calling for faith in the New Being. Without developing this point, it could be shown that *this* use of the word 'Being' is not consistent with his general ontology. A new being, meaning a unique variation of possible modes of existence open to man, would not strictly qualify for the title New Being. Alternatively, if Being is used in a basically Heideggerean sense it is difficult to see what New Being could actually mean apart from the complete annihilation of what is and its replacement with some quite different ontological structure.

proposed throughout the whole book. It would involve interpreting the whole of this mysterious reality not only as
God, but as somehow personal. This would bring us back to
square one, or rather page one. We should then have to point
out that many people today just do not experience reality as
personal, and yet are committed to the way of transcendence.
We should also have to make the point again that the question 'Why Jesus?' is just as difficult to answer for those who
say he is the Incarnation of God the Father, as for those who
say he is the incarnation of the way of transcendence. And
so the whole book would be presented again. I anticipate
this temptation because of the work of John Robinson. Contrary to the opinion of some, it is clear that Robinson is a
good Anglican, in the great Both–And tradition. Thus Ved
Mehta concludes, 'Dr Robinson seems to want both to refuse
his cake and have it.'[5] And Gerald Downing uses another
metaphor in presenting Schillebeeckx's advice to the author of
Honest to God. 'Dr Robinson is invited gently, persuasively,
to put his hesitant heretical left foot back into the Catholic
orthodoxy in which his right is obviously most firmly plan-
ted.'[6] We have already noted that in *The New Reformation?*
Robinson wished to speak of experiencing reality in personal
terms. This is still his position in a later book. 'In spirituality
as in theology, I find myself returning to the utterly personal
panentheism of the God dwelling incognito at the heart of
all things.'[7] No matter how firmly he denies the God of traditional theism, he maintains the personal element in the experience of a 'relational reality',[8] which keeps the door open
to some form of theism. My concern is that many people
today are prevented from coming to faith in Christ because

5. Mehta, *The New Theologian*, p. 27.

6. Gerald Downing, Review of *God and Man*, in *New Christian*,
No. 113, 22 January 1970.

7. J. A. T. Robinson, *Exploration into God*, S.C.M. Press, London,
1967, p. 129.   8. ibid., p. 132.

culturally it is impossible for them to believe in God. There is nothing in their experience of reality which would justify their use of this word in any sense remotely in continuity with its meaning in the past. What I have sought is a viable way of reinterpreting Christianity so that a secular faith in Christ is possible. But I have not pursued this end at all costs. I have rejected any suggestion of reductionism or positivism. The solution I propose is not less, but perhaps more inclusive than traditional Christianity.[9] The attempt to reintroduce God (using the word in some recognizable continuity with traditional theism) would actually destroy the intention of this book. It would once again make God the presupposition of faith in Christ, i.e. would make Christianity impossible for contemporary men.

9. Much of contemporary theology has not taken this dimension seriously. I therefore agree with John Macquarrie that 'The question is not whether you are going to have an ontology or not, but whether you are going to have an examined ontology or an unexamined one.' (*God and Secularity*. p. 33.) I have indicated that I am aware of the ontological implications of being able to choose the way of transcendence. But I do not feel that at the present moment we are in a position to formulate a satisfactory ontology which would take account of this fact. I have not been able to accept Macquarrie's own position on onto-theology.

Index of Names

Index of Subjects

BIBLICAL REFERENCES